COMMITTEES AND COMMISSIONS

ELEMENTARY EDUCATION

Select Documents

M.K. Jain
Former Director,
Planning Commission Library,
Government of India, New Delhi

SHIPRA

(First Published 2007)

Rs. 1250; US$ 42.50

ISBN: 978-81-7541-379-5

2014 Impression

Committees and Commissions: Elementary Education

Published by:
SHIPRA PUBLICATIONS
LG 18-19, Pankaj Central Market,
I.P. Ext., Patparganj, Delhi 110092, India
Ph.: +91 11 22235152/6152
Email: info@shiprapublication.com
Website: www.shiprapublication.com

Preface

Acts and Minutes, Dispatches and Commissions but nothing under the banner of policies were landmarks of British education in India resulting the crawled literacy rate of less than 20 percent in 1947 . After Independence, Government of India articulated the educational policies and in framing these policies various committees and commissions played the advisory role to the government, to achieve the goal of universalisation of elementary education also. More than half of the battle is already won, and now the next target is 'Scheme for Universalisation of Secondary Education'.

This volume is a compilation of such reports from British period to till date. It is divided into five parts—Colonial period, From Independence to 1967, 1968 to 1985, 1986 to 1997-98 and 1998 onwards. The book may be useful to students of education, interested in development of elementary education system, but are unable to approach these documents due to one reason or the other.

Utmost care has been taken in compiling these select documents from various sources tapped including Ministry of Human Resource Development, NCERT archives mainly and are acknowledged with due thanks. Efforts are made to maintain the serial numbers given in the respective document/report, however for any omission/authenticity original document should be referred.

It is hoped that relevance of this book will be find by all those with a stake in teaching and growth of children. Suggestion for further improving the book will be thankfully received.

M.K. Jain

Contents

Preface

1. Development of Education During the British Rule: Policy Documents 1

- The Charter Act of 1813 1
- Macaulay's Minute on Education, 1835 1
- Indian Education Commission (Hunter Commission), 1882-83 4
- Resolution of Government on Educational Policy, 1904 5
- Gopal Krishna Gokhale's Resolution, 1910 and Elementary Education Bill, 1911 6
- Government Resolution on Education Policy, 1913 8
- Lala Lajpat Rai's Exposition, 1918 10
- Hartog Committee, 1928 11
- Government of India Act, 1935 13
- Abbot and Woods Report, 1937 13
- First Congress of National Education (Wardha), 1937 14
- Post-war Educational Development in India (Sargent Report), 1944 20
- CABE Report—the Post-war Educational Development in India, 1944 21

2. Development of Elementary Education: Independence to 1967 26

- Fourteenth CABE Meeting, 13-15 January, 1948 26
- Committee on the Ways and Means of Financing Educational Development, 1948-50 28
- Committee on the Relationship between State Governments and Local Bodies in the Administration of Primary Education, 1951 29
- Assessment Committee on Basic Education, 1955 31
- Basic Education Standing Committee of Cenral Advisory Board of Education, 1957 34
- First All India Educational Survey, 1957 35
- National Seminar on Orientation of Elementary Schools Towards the Basic Pattern, 1959 35
- Twenty-eight CABE Meeting—16-17 January, 1961, New Delhi 36
- Committee on the Pre-Primary Education in Mysore State, 1961 37

- Thirty-first CABE Meeting—11-12 October, 1964, Bangalore 40
- Education Commission, 1964-66 (Kothari Commission) 41
- Second All India Educational Survey, 1965 67
- Committee of Members of Parliament to Prepare Draft of Statement on National Policy on Education, 1967 67

3. 1968 to 1985: Select Documents 70

- National Policy on Education, 1968 70
- National Seminar on Primary and Work-Oriented Education, (International Education Year) 1970 75
- Study Group to Prepare Programme of Action for Development of the Pre-School Child, 1972 77
- Third All India Educational Survey, 1973 81
- National Policy for Children, 1974 91
- Ishwarbhai Patel Review Committee, 1977 93
- Draft National Policy on Education, 1979 94
- National Plan of Action for International Year of The Child, 1979 95
- Revised 20-Point Programme, 1982 98
- Conference of Education Secretaries, January, 1983 99
- Central Advisory Board of Education, 39th Session, June 6-7, 1983 101
- National Commission on Teachers-I Chattopadhaya Commission, 1983-85 102
- NCERT on Curriculum Load, 1983-85 103
- Status Report on Challenge of Education, 1985 106
- Challenge of Action: A Policy Perspective 1985 108

4. Commissions and Documents on Elementary Education: 1986-1996 116

- National Policy on Education, 1986 116
- Programme of Action for Implementation of NPE, 1986 121
- Innovations in Education, 1986 122
- Fifth All India Educational Survey, 1986-89 123
- National Curriculum for Elementary and Secondary Education: A Framework, 1988 125
- Education for All by 2000, 1990 129
- Committee to Review the National Policy on Education (1986), 1990-91 138
- Central Advisory Board of Education, 46th Session, 1991 145
- Central Advisory Board of Education Working Group on Elementary Education, 1991 146

- Committee on Minimum Levels of Learning (MLL) at Primary Stage, 1991 150
- Committee to Review NPE (1986) and Report of the Committee to Review the NPE (1990-91), 1991 157
- National Plan of Action, 1992 159
- National Plan of Action for the SAARC Decade of Girl Child, 1991-2000 AD, 1992 163
- Revised National Policy on Education, 1992 166
- Programme of Action on National Policy on Education, 1992 169
- National Advisory Committee on Learning without Burden, 1992-93 177
- CABE Committee on Decentralised Management of Education, 1993 197
- Group to Examine the Recommendations of the National Advisory Committee on Learning without Burden, 1993 211
- Sixth All India Educational Survey, 1995 222
- Synergy Sub-Group on Primary Education and Literacy, 1995 223
- Committee of Education Ministers on Making Elementary Education a Fundamental Right, 1997 230
- Education Commission, 1964-66 (Kothari Commission), Government of India, 1966 231

5. Elementary Education: 1997 Onwards 238

- Ninth Five Year Plan, 1997-2001 238
- Tenth Five Year Plan, 2002-2007 243
- National Curriculum Framework for School Education (2000), NCERT 251
- The Constitution (Eighty-Sixth Amendment) Act, 2002 255
- "National Curriculum Framework 2005" NCERT (2005) 255
- CABE Committee on "Free and Compulsory Education Bill and other Issues Related to Elementary Education (2004-05)" 257
- National Knowledge Commission, June 8, 2005 262
- Sachar Committee Report, 2006 262
- Conference of State Education Ministers, April 11, 2007 264

1

Development of Education During the British Rule: Policy Documents

THE CHARTER ACT OF 1813

The period was marked by policy decisions. Several Committees and Commissions on education were also appointed to make recommendations on the improvement of Education in India.

The Charter Act of 1813: For the first time during the East India Company made an annual provision for a sum of not less than one lakh of rupees for the promotion of learning. It was admitted by the British Parliament that 'education in India had a claim on public revenues'. Clause 43 of the Act reads, "It shall be lawful for the Governor-General-in-Council to direct that out of any surplus which may remain of the rents, revenues, and profits arising from the said territorial acquisitions, after defraying the expense of the military, civil, and commercial establishment and paying the interest of the debt in manner hereinafter provided, a sum of not less than one lakh of rupees in each year shall be set apart and applied to the revival and improvement of literature and the encouragement of the learned natives of India and for the introduction and promotion of a knowledge of the sciences among the inhabitants of the British territories in India."

MACAULAY'S MINUTE ON EDUCATION, 1835

Macaulay's Minute on Education, 1835: The famous minute of Lord Macaulay, the first Law Member of the Governor-General's Executive Council, submitted in 1835, opened a new chapter in the educational history of India. He advocated the education of the upper classes and through them the education of others—'Theory of Downward Filtration' and made a vigorous plea for spreading western learning through the medium of English.

At that time, a major Oriental (classical) and Occidental controversy between the Orientalists (classists) and the Anglicists (Occidentalists) was going on in respect of the following issues:

1. *Aim of Education of the British Policy*: Whether it should be to educate the classes in higher branches of learning or the masses in elementary education.

2. *Type of Knowledge*: Whether to preserve and promote oriental learning (learning of the East) or to introduce Western knowledge, culture and science.

3. *Medium of Instruction*: Whether English or Persian and Sanskrit in Bengal, English or Indian languages in Bombay and Madras should become the medium of instruction. It may be recalled that at that time the Presidencies/Provinces of Bengal, Bombay and Madras contained numerous areas which now form new states like Orissa, Bihar, Tamil Nadu etc.

4. *Agency of Education*: Whether the Government should assume direct responsibility of educating the Indians or the indigenous system of the country to continue.

5. *Missionaries*: Whether the shores of India to be thrown open to missionaries of all parts of the world to promote education or to a few missionaries or not at all.

There were important English Officers of the East India Company who were the supporters of the Oriental point of view. H.T. Princep, who was the Education Secretary in Bengal was the leader of the Orientalist Group. On the contrary some prominent Indians like Raja Rammohan Roy supported the Anglicists who were in favour of English and Western learning.

Macaulay's Views on Indian and European Literature: Macaulay in his Minute made the following observations.

(i) "A single shelf of a good European literature was worth the whole native literature of India and Arabia."

(ii) Regarding imparting instruction through the media of Arabic, Persian and Sanskrit, he wrote, "We are to teach false history, false astronomy, false medicine, because we find them in the company of false religion."

(iii) About the claim of English language, he stated, "It stands pre-eminent even among the languages of the West… . It is likely to become language of commerce throughout the seas of the East."

Main Aim of Introducing English System of Education in India: "We must at present do our best to form a class of persons, Indian in blood and colour, but English in taste, in opinions, in morals and in intellect."

Macaulay's Arguments in Favour of English: 1. It is the key to modern knowledge and is, therefore, more useful than Arabic or Sanskrit.

2. It stand pre-eminent even among the language of the West. In India, English is the language sponsored by the ruling class. It is likely to become the language of commerce throughout the seas of the East.

3. It would bring about renaissance in India, just as Greek or Latin did in England or just as the languages of Western Europe in civilized Russia.

4. The natives are desirous of being taught English and are not eager to learn Sanskrit or Arabic, and that demand of the latter was maintained artificially through, "bounty money".

5. It is possible to make the native of this country good English scholars, and to that end our efforts ought to be directed.

6. It was impossible to educate the body of people, but is was possible through English education to bring about "a class of persons, Indian in blood and colour, but English in tastes, in opinions, in morals and in intellect" and that education was to filter down from them to the masses.

Acceptance of Minute by Lord William Bentinck: Lord William Bentinck endorsed the Minute by writing one line beneath it, "I give my entire concurrence to the sentiments expressed in the Minute". He passed the Resolution of March, 1835 which determined the aim, content and medium of instruction in India.

Downward Filtration Theory of Education

Meaning of Filtration Theory: The British rulers in India though that in order to run the administration peacefully and smoothly it was essential to make the higher classes blind followers of the Britishers. This they wanted to achieve through educating the classes. This theory meant "Education is to be filtered to the common people. Drop by drop, the education would go to the common public so that at due time it may take the form of vast stream which remained water desert of the society for starved a long time and high class of people would be educated and common people would gain influence from them."

"Education was to permeate from above. Drop by drop from the Himalayas of Indian life useful information was to trickle downwards forming in a time a broad and steady stream to irrigate the thirsty plains."

WOOD'S DESPATH, 1854

After Macaulay's Minute (1835), the Court of Directors of the East India Company in England appointed a Select Committee of the House of Commons to hold a thorough enquiry into educational developments in India. On the basis of this enquiry, Wood's Despatch—an important document on education was prepared for the functioning of education system in India. The document written at the instance of Charles Wood, the President of the Board of Control, came to be known as Wood's Despatch. It is a long document of a hundred paragraphs and deals with a number of important questions of educational importance in India.

Some historians and thinkers have described the Wood's Despatch as "The Magna Charta of Indian Education". They argue that Macaulay's Minute was by and large, translated into action in several matters on the basis of this report. It, once for all, decided that Western Arts, Philosophy and Science were to be the areas of knowledge to be imparted to the people of India. It led to the creation of Departments of Education, establishment of universities, a graded school system, grant-in-aid rules, setting of training colleges and educational institutions—all elements that led to the development of modern system of education in India. The Despatch not only strengthened the foundations lay down by Macaulay but also built up a durable structure of the system of education.

Major Directions, Observations and Recommendations

1. *Object of Education in India*: The declared object was "not only to produce a higher degree of intellectual fitness but to raise the moral character and to supply with servants."

2. *Spread of European Knowledge*: It was also declared that the function of education was to diffuse European knowledge—arts, science, philosophy and literature.

3. *Languages*: English language and vernacular languages of India would be the media for the diffusion of European knowledge.

4. ......in each of the five provinces under Company's rule—Bengal (Bengal at that time consisted of Bengal, Bihar, Orissa), Madras, Bombay, North-Western Province—NWP and the Punjab.

5. *Establishment of Universities*: The Despatch directed to establish Universities at Calcutta, Bombay and Madras or in any part of India, on the model of the London University, which was then an examining body.

6. *Establishment of a Network of Graded Schools all over India*: The Despatch provided for the establishment of High and Middle Schools and below them the indigenous elementary schools.

7. *Grant-in-Aid*: Principles for grant-in-aid were laid down.

8. *Training of Teachers*: The scheme of training of teacher as prevalent in Great Britain was put forward.

9. *Women Education*: Some suggestions for the education of women were offered.

INDIAN EDUCATION COMMISSION (HUNTER COMMISSION), 1882-83

The first Indian Education Commission under the Chairmanship of Sir William Hunter was appointed by Lord Ripon in 1882. It is also known as 'Hunter Commission'. There were two important reasons for the appointment of the Commission. One, it was necessary to enquire into the manner in which effect had been given to the principles of the Charles Wood's Education Despatch of 1854 and to pay special attention to primary education; two, agitation conducted by the missionaries.

Relevant Recommendations

Primary Education

While every branch of education can justly claim the fostering care of the State, it is desirable, in the present circumstances of the country, to declare the elementary education of the masses, its provision, extension and improvement to be that part of the educational system to which the strenuous efforts of the State should now be directed in a still larger measure than heretofore.

That primary education be declared to be that part of the whole system of public instruction, which possesses an almost exclusive claim on local funds set apart for education, and a large claim on provincial revenues.

We recommend that supply of normal schools whether government or aided, be so localized as to provide for the local requirements of all primary schools whether government or aided, within the division under each Inspector...We recommend that the first charge on provincial funds assigned for primary education be the cost of its direction and inspection, and the provision of an adequate supply of normal schools.

RESOLUTION OF GOVERNMENT ON EDUCATIONAL POLICY, 1904

Lord Curzon emphasized 'expansion' side by side with 'improvement'. For expansion large grants were sanctioned and for improvement, he emphasized the training of teachers and revision and enrichment of the curriculum. Regarding recognition of secondary schools it stated, "Whether these schools are managed by public authority or by private persons, and whether they received aid from public funds or not, the Government is bound in the interests of the community to see that the education provided in them is sound. It must, for example, satisfy itself in each case that a secondary school is usually wanted, that its financial stability is assured, that its managing body where there is one, is properly constituted, that it teaches the proper subjects up to a proper standard, that due provision has been made for the instruction, health, recreation, and discipline of the pupils, that the teachers are suitable as regards character, number and qualifications, and that the fees to be paid will not involve such competition with any existing schools as will be unfair and injurious to the interests of education. Such are the conditions upon which alone schools should be eligible to receive grant-in-aid or to send up pupils to compete for, or receive pupils in enjoyment of Government scholarships, and schools complying with them will be ranked as recognised schools. These conditions were soon incorporated in the provincial code of grant-in-aid.

GOPAL KRISHNA GOKHALE'S RESOLUTION, 1910 AND ELEMENTARY EDUCATION BILL, 1911

The concept of national education strengthened with the resolution of Calcutta Congress (1906) that the time arrived "for the people of the country to earnestly take up the national education for both boys and girls." Curzon believed what Indian education needed most i.e. "qualitative reforms" under British control, while Gokhale believed that the need of India was 'quantitative advance', so that education could reach to the masses. The nationalist opinion began to press British government for the introduction of compulsory education at the primary level. This demand was strengthened as State of Baroda had already introduced compulsory education in 1906. Gokhale made heroic efforts in the Imperial Legislative Council for the acceptance of the principle of free and compulsory education for the whole country. In 1910, he moved a resolution in the Council but later withdrawn on an assurance from the government that it would be examined most carefully. But he introduced the bill incorporating most of his resolution of 1910. In 1912, in spite of the memorable eloquent pleading of Gokhale the bill was thrown out by a majority vote. Gokhale had already indicated the fate of such an unofficial bill at the hands of the British masters in his speech; but the failure strengthened the movement in favour of mass education.

Extracts (Gokhale's Resolution, 1910)

"I beg to place the following resolution before the Council for its consideration: That this Council recommends that a beginning should be made in the direction of making elementary education free and compulsory throughout the country, and that a mixed Commission of officials and non-officials be appointed at an early date to frame definite proposals.

My Lord, there is much truth in the homely adage that where there is a will there is a way. I think that this question of compulsory and free primary education is now in this country the question of questions. The well-being of millions upon millions of children who are waiting to be brought under the humanizing influence of education depends upon it. The increased efficiency of the individual, the higher general level of intelligence, the stiffening of the moral backbone of large sections of the community, none of these things can come without such education. In fact, the whole of our future as nation is inextricably bound up with it. My Lord, however, this resolution may be disposed of here today, I feel that in this matter we are bound to win."

Extracts—The Statement of Objects and Reasons of The Bill

"The object of this Bill is to provide for the gradual introduction of the principle of compulsion into the elementary education system of the country. The experience of other countries has established beyond dispute the fact that the only effective way to ensure a wide diffusion of elementary education among the mass of the people is by a resort to compulsion in some form or the other. And the time has come when a beginning at least should be made in this direction in India. The Bill is of a purely permissive character and its provisions will apply to areas notified by municipalities or district boards which will be necessitated, as may be laid down by the Government of India, by rules. Moreover, no area can be notified without the previous sanction of the Provincial Government and further it must fulfill the test which the Government of India may, by rules, lay down as regards the percentage of children already at school within its limits. Finally the provisions are intended to apply in the first instance only to boys, though later on a local body may extend them to girls; and age limits proposed are only six and ten years. It is hoped that these are sufficient safeguards against any rash or injudicious action on the part of local bodies. This measure is essentially a cautious one, indeed to some it may appear to err too much on the side of caution."

Extracts (Gokhale's Elementary Education Bill, 1911

"This, my Lord, is briefly the whole of my Bill. It is a small and humble attempt to suggest the first steps of a journey, which is bound to prove long and tedious, but which must be performed, if the mass of our people are to emerge from their present conditon. My Lord, this question of a universal diffusion of education in India depends, almost more than any other question, on the heartly and sympathetic co-operation of the government and the leaders of the people. The government must, in the first instance, adopt definitely the policy of such diffusion as its own, and it must, secondly, not grudge to find the bulk of the money, which will be required for it, as governments in most other civilized countries are doing. And this is what we are entitled to ask at the hands of the government in the name of justice, for the honour of the government itself, and in the highest interests of popular well-being. The leaders of the people, on their side, must bring to this task high enthusiasm, which will not be chilled by difficulties, courage,which will not shrink from encountering unpopularity if need be, and readiness to make sacrifices, whether of money or time or energy, which the cause may require.

If a beginning is made without further delay, if both the government and the people persevere with the task in the right spirit, the whole problem may be solved before another generation rises to take our place. If this happens the next generation will enter upon it own security of success. As for us, it will be enough to have laboured for such an end—laboured with not only profound humility but also profound wisdom in the faith which says:

"I do not ask to see the distant scene; One step enough for me."

Extracts (Gokhale's Speech in the Council)

"My Lord, I know that my Bill will be thrown out before the day closes, I make no complaint. I shall not even feel depressed. I know too well the story of the preliminary efforts that were required even in England, before the Act of 1870 was passed. Moreover, I have always felt and have often said that we, of the present generation in India, can only hope to serve our country by our failures. The men and women who will be privileged to serve her by their successes will come later. We must be content to accept cheerfully the place that has been allotted to us in our onward march. The Bill thrown out today, will come back again and again, till on the stepping-stones of its dead selves, a measure ultimately rises which will spread the light of knowledge throughout the land... . But, my Lord whatever fate awaits our labours, one thing is clear. We shall be entitled to feel that we have done our duty, and, where the call of duty is clear, it is better even to labour and fail than not to labour at all."

GOVERNMENT RESOLUTION ON EDUCATION POLICY, 1913

British Government rejected Gopal Krishan Gokhale's bill and refused to recognise the principle of compulsory education for paucity of funds, they promised to extend grants for the widest possible extension of primary education on a voluntary basis and passed the Resolution on Education Policy in 1913.

Extracts

"The proposition that illiteracy must be broken down and that primary education has, in the present circumstances of India, a predominant claim upon the public funds, represents accepted policy no longer open to discussion. For financial and administrative reasons of decisive weight the Government of India have refused to recognize the principle of compulsory education; but they desire the widest possible extension of primary education on a voluntary basis. As regards free elementary education, the time has not yet arrived when it is practicable to dispense wholly with fees without injustice to the many villages which are waiting for the provision of schools. The fees derived from those pupils who can pay them are now devoted to the maintenance and expansion of primary education, and a total remission of fees would involve to a certain extent a more prolonged postponement of a provision of schools in villages without them. In some provinces elementary education is already free and in the majority of provinces liberal provision is already made for giving free elementary instruction to those boys whose parents cannot afford to pay fees. Local Governments have been requested to extend the application of the principle of free elementary education amongst the poorer and more backward sections of the population. Further than this, it is not possible at present to go...

It is the desire and hope of the Government of India to see in the not distant future some 91,000 primary public schools added to the 100,000 which already exist for boys and to double the 4½ millions of the pupils who now receive instruction in them."

The Resolution advocated three cardinal principles of educational policy:

1. The curricula of primary and secondary schools should be made more practical and useful;
2. Facilities of higher education should be provided in India so that Indian students may not have to go abroad;
3. Instead of increasing the number of existing institutions their standard should be raised.

Relevant Recommendations of the Government Resolution

1. The inspection and management of private schools should be made more efficient;
2. In the urban schools teaching of geography and school excursions, should form part of the curricula;
3. Teachers of primary education should have refresher courses during vacations;
4. The number of students under one teacher should range between 30 and 40;
5. For the education of women, there should be special curriculum of practical utility for girls and too much importance should not be attached to their examinations.

The First World War which broke out the next year delayed the implementation of many recommendations set out in the Resolution.

Resolution of the Government of India on Education (1913): The Resolution advocated three cardinal principles of educational policy—(1) Instead of increasing the number of existing institutions their standard should be raised; (2) The curricula of primary and secondary schools should be made more practical and useful; (3) Facilities of higher studies and research should be provided in India so that Indian students may not have to go abroad.

Calcutta University Commission (1917-1919): The Commission was appointed by the Government of India in 1917 under the Chairmanship of Dr. Michael Sadler, the Vice-Chancellor of the University of Calcutta and to consider the question of a constructive policy in relation to the question it represents'. Among the Indian Members of the Commission were Sir Asutosh Mukerji and Dr. Zia-Uddin Ahmed. The major recommendations were (i) introduction of three-years degree course, (ii) Establishment of a Board of Secondary and Intermediate Examination in each province, (ii) Less rigit control over universities, (iv) Appointment of staff by special Selection Committees, (v) Safeguard of interest of Muslim students.

The Report of the Commission became a constant source of suggestion and information. It greatly influenced the subsequent course of secondary and higher education in the country.

LALA LAJPAT RAI'S EXPOSITION, 1918

The Nagpur Congress (1920) advised in a resolution the gradual withdrawal of children from schools and colleges, and the establishment of national schools and colleges in the various provinces. It was supported by Mahatma Gandhi. In a couple of months a large number of national schools were started all over the country. In Bengal a society for the Promotion of National Education was formed under the Chairmanship of Guru Das Banerji. Rabindranath Tagore, Rashbehari Ghosh and Aurobindo Ghosh also took up the cause of national education. Swami Shradhanand established a Gurukul at Haridwar. The main emphasis of the educational movement was on (1) Indian control of education; (2) Indian ideals of education; (3) Reverence for the motherland; (4) Growth of Indian languages; and (5) Development of technical and national education.

The idea of national education had matured. In his book The Problems of National Education in India, Lala Lajpat Rai gave elaborate and comprehensive exposition of "National Education".

Extracts

(1) Love of India as a whole.

I am sure Indian Nationalists do not want to set up an aggressive nationalism of the kind which will breed contempt or hatred of other nations. The idea that love of one's country necessarily involves hatred of others, or even indifference to the welfare of the rest of mankind, is absolutely fallacious and mischievous, and should be combated through and through. We love our country because that alone, can enable us to ascend to the heights of humanity... .

Text books for the primary schools should be free from discussions of Nationalism and Internationalism. They should inculcate the love of India, of Indian rivers, Indian hills, Indian landscape, Indian scenes, in choice, simple language. Is there any place on earth which is more beautiful and more sublime than our Himalaya? Is there any river which is more majestic and inspiring than Ganga or Brahmaputra or Narbada or even Sindh?

Patriotism, however, does not include only the material and the physical aspects of a country. It includes all that Renan has called J'aime d'une nation, the more delicate shadings of feelings such as piety for the past, admiration and love of the heroic figures in the history of the nation, and its great achievements; love of language, community of tradition, laws and customs, and all that gives individual character to the civilization of each nation.

The love of the nation as a whole, regardless of the various religious creeds and castes into which it is internally divided.

Every Indian child should be taught in so many words that every human being who is born in India, or of Indian parents, or who has made India his or her home, is a compatriot, a brother or a sister, regardless of colour, creed, caste or vocation. The diversity of race, religion and language is often exploited by the foreigner as a pretext to deny us the status and the privileges of a nation. Now it should be made absolutely clear to every Indian youth that in India there is no such thing as the conflict of races. No Indian, Hindu or Mohammedan, ever attaches any importance to his racial origin or to the rest of his countrymen. There is no country on the face of the globe which has a pure race... .

To be Indians, first, last, and all the time, in all political and economic matters and in our relations with non-Indians, must be taught to our boys and girls by written and printed lessons as well as by word of mouth. It is a necessary and a vital article of faith in the religion of patriotism that we must teach to our boys and girls.

HARTOG COMMITTEE, 1928

Education was treated as a transferred subject under a dyarchical system of government in the provinces of India, introduced in 1921 as a result of the Government of India Act, 1919 passed by the British Parliament. Subjects of administration were divided into two categories i.e., Reserved and Transferred Subjects. Education was made transferred subject and the development of education was the responsibility of the Minister for Education. Finance was a reserved subject with the result that the Education Minister had to face many difficulties to obtain the funds essential for a large-scale expansion, qualitative improvement and reorganisation of education. The most important thing that happened under dyarchy was the rapid development of mass education and the passing of Compulsory Education Acts in most of the provinces. However, the expansion of education that took place brought into sharp focus some of its existing defects. In May 1928, a royal commission was appointed under the Chairmanship of Sir John Simon. This Commission appointed an auxiliary Committee presided over by Sir Philip Hartog to report on the growth of education in British India. The Hartog Committee submitted its report in 1929.

Extracts

General Observation

Our review of the growth of education reveals many points of fundamental interest for the political future of India. The largely increased enrolment in primary schools indicates that the old time apathy of the masses is breaking down... On all sides there has been a desire on the part of understand and to grapple with the complex and difficult problems of education; and large additional expenditure has been proposed by Education Ministers, and willingly voted by the legislative councils. That is one side of the picture, but there is another.

Primary Education

Throughout the whole educational system there is waste and ineffectiveness. In the primary system, which from our point of view should be designed to produce literacy and the capacity to exercise an intelligent vote, the waste is appalling. So far as we can judge, the vast increase in numbers in primary schools produces no commensurate increase in literacy, for only a small proportion of those who are at the primary stage reach Class IV, in which the attainment of literacy may be expected. The wastage in the case of girls is even more serious than in case of boys.

Need for a Well-directed Policy

We have no doubt that more and more money will be gladly voted for education by the legislatures of India but, as we have shown, the improvement and expansion of education do not depend merely on money. Money is no doubt essential, but even more essential is a well directed policy carried out by effective and competent agencies, determined to eliminate waste of all kinds. We were asked to report on the organization of education. At almost every point that organization needs reconsideration and strengthening; and the relations of the bodies responsible for the organization of education need readjustment.

Provincial Governments and Local Bodies in Education

We have not suggested, nor do we suggest, that the responsibilities of Ministers in the provinces should be reduced. On the contrary, we are of opinion that they have been reduced by a devolution on local bodies who have taken the control of primary education to a large extent from them with unfortunate results. The relations between Provincial Governments and local bodies need further consideration and adjustment. Under the legislation, powers have been devolved on local bodies in such a way that the Ministers have no effective control on the expenditure voted for mass education; and in some cases. It is clear that the new factor of ministerial responsibility has not been taken sufficiently into account."

The main conclusion of the report was that quantity had been gained at the cost of quality and therefore there should be more diversified curricula in schools.

GOVERNMENT OF INDIA ACT, 1935

The system of governance, known as Provincial Autonomy, abolished the distinction between reserved and transferred departments and placed the whole field of provincial administration under a ministry. The Government of India Act, 1935, divided all educational activities into two categories—Federal (or Central) and State (or Provincial):

(a) *Federal (or Central) Subjects*

(i) The Imperial Library, Calcutta; the Indian Museum, Calcutta; the Imperial War Museum; the Victoria Memorial, Calcutta; and any similar institution controlled or financed by the Federation;
(ii) Education in the Defence forces;
(iii) The Banaras Hindu University and the Aligarh Muslim University;
(iv) Preservation of ancient and historical monuments;
(v) Archaeology; and
(vi) Education in Centrally Administered Areas.

(b) *State (or Provincial) Subjects*

All matters regarding education of all other categories other than those included in the Federal list given above were regarded as State or Provincial subjects.

And thereby, education of children became the direct responsibility of State/Provincial Government.

ABBOT AND WOODS REPORT, 1937

In 1936, on the recommendation of the Central Advisory Board of Education, the government invited two experts—A. Abbot, Ex-chief Inspector of Technical Schools, and S.H. Wood, Director of Intelligence, Board of Education, England—to advise 'whether any vocational or practical training should be imparted in primary, secondary and higher secondary schools, and if so, what should be its nature and extent'. The report submitted in 1937 had two parts: (i) Vocational, and (ii) General. It stressed that vocational education was as important as general education. "Neither of them can claim to be more useful and necessary. If general education brings about the development of the non-material culture of a country, vocational education does the same thing for material culture. Hence, both are necessary for the progress of a country".

Major Recommendations

General Education

1. The education in the primary school should be based upon the

national interests and activities of young children and less upon book learning.

2. The curriculum of the rural middle school should be closely related to the children's environment.
3. English taught in the middle school should not result in an excessive amount of linguistic load.
4. The mother-tongue should, as far as possible, be the medium of instruction throughout the high school but English should form a compulsory language.
5. Systematic attention should be paid to the teaching of fine arts.

FIRST CONGRESS OF NATIONAL EDUCATION (WARDHA), 1937

In 1937, while assuming office in seven provinces Congress was irrevocably committed to the introduction of universal, free and compulsory primary education in the shortest time possible and but find it difficult to raise huge sums for its implementation by fresh taxation. Mahatma Gandhi came forward and asked if schooling could be made self-supporting through a useful and productive work.

Mahatma Gandhi's articles in the *Harijan* created a storm, but controversies also arose. It was the thought desirable to get the scheme thoroughly examined by expert educationists. Accordingly, the First Congress of National Education was called at Wardha on 22-23 October, 1937 to discuss the proposed educational system. As a result of discussions the following four resolutions were passed.

1. that in the opinion of this Conference 'free and compulsory education' be provided for seven years on a nation-wide scale;
2. that the medium of instruction be the 'mother tongue';
3. that the Conference endorses the proposal, made by Mahatma Gandhi, that the process of education throughout this period should centre round some productive form of manual work, and that all other abilities to be developed or training to be given should, as far as possible, be integrally related to the central handicraft chosen with due regard to the environment of the child;
4. that the Conference expects that the system of education will be gradually able to cover the remuneration of the teachers.

The Zakir Hussain Committee soon submitted a report known as the Wardha Scheme of Basic Education. It was approved by Mahatma Gandhi and the Congress (Haripura Session 1938) passed a resolution incorporating the first three points of the resolution, the last point of the resolution concerning the self-supporting aspect was left out. An all-India Board (Hindustani Talimi Sangh) was formed 'to work out in a consolidated manner a programme of Basic National Education'.

Wardha Scheme of Education

Craft Work in Schools

Modern educational thought is practically unanimous in commending the idea of educating children through some suitable form of productive work. This method is considered to be the most effective approach to the problem of providing an integral all-sided education.

Psychologically, it is desirable, because it relieves the child from the tyranny of a purely academic and theoretical instruction against which its active nature is always making a healthy protest. It balances the intellectual and practical elements of experience, and may be made an instrument of educating the body and the mind in co-ordination. The child acquires not the superficial literacy which implies, often without warrant, a capacity to read the printed page, but the far more important capacity of using hand and intelligence for some constructive purpose. This, if we may be permitted to use the expression, is the literacy of the whole personality.

Socially considered, the introduction of such practical productive work in education, to be participated in by all the children of the nation, will tend to break down the existing barriers of prejudice between manual and intellectual workers, harmful alike for both. It will also cultivate in the only possible way a true sense of the dignity of labour and of human solidarity—an ethical and moral gain of incalculable significance.

Economically considered, carried out intelligently and efficiently, the scheme will increase the productive capacity of our workers and will also enable them to utilize their leisure advantageously.

From the strictly educational point of view greater concreteness and reality can be given to the knowledge acquired by children by making some significant craft the basis of education. Knowledge will thus become related to life, and its various aspects will be correlated with one another.

Curriculum

In order to work out an effective and natural co-ordination of the various subjects and to make the syllabus a means of adjusting the child intelligently and actively to his environment we have chosen three centres, intrinsically inter-connected, as the foci for the curriculum i.e., the physical environment, the social environment, and craft work, which is their natural meeting point since it utilizes the resources of the former for the purpose of the latter.

It is essential for all teachers and educational workers to note that we have really attempted to draft an 'activity curriculum', which implies that our schools must be places of work, experimentation and discovery, not of passive absorption of information imparted at second hand. So far as the curriculum is concerned, we have stressed this principle by advocating that all teaching should be carried on through concrete life situation relating to craft or to social and physical environment, so that whatever he learns becomes assimilated into his growing activity.

It should be noted in this connection that in the preparation of this syllabus, we have attempted to organize the subject-matter into significant and comprehensive units of experience which will, when mastered, enable the child to understand his environment better and to react to it more intelligently because they throw helpful light on the problems and conditions of life around him. We are conscious of the fact that there is much scope for environment in the actual units selected, but we are confident that it is the right approach to the syllabus, rather than the current practice of making it a collection of unrelated and miscellaneous facts having no direct bearing on children's experiences or on social life. The syllabus in social studies and general science will illustrate this principle. When, for instance, work in social or general science is related to drawing, and the knowledge of history and geography enriches the child's understanding and appreciation of his craft, when gardening and agriculture are an integral part of his education the school should become an active centre of experience and of abundant life.

But the working of this curriculum is in itself a problem of great importance, and demands intelligent alertness and responsiveness on the part of the teachers, for even the best of curricula can be made a mere dead letter, if the method of teaching and discipline adopted are not inspired by the spirit of activity. In order to indicate, therefore, how the full possibilities of this curriculum can be exploited, it seems necessary to point out by way of illustration, the method to be adopted in the approach to some of the subjects included in the curriculum. For if subjects such as social studies and general science are presented by the teachers as catalogues of facts to be passively accepted and learnt up by the children, the whole object of the syllabus will be defeated, and they will entirely fail to appreciate the real nature of the correlation amongst the various subjects. This can only be realized when they are acquired through real learning situations involving self-activity on the children's part.

The teaching of these subjects should not only be closely co-ordinated, but it should spring from actual social situations—the child's home, his village, its occupations and crafts—and then be extended and enriched by stories of primitive life and ancient civilizations, and by showing how different ways of life and work have developed under different social and geographical conditions. The teaching of geography and nature study in the lower classes should, for example, be gathered round the different seasons which provide a starting point for observing natural phenomena, and the intelligent teacher will take care that the children make their early acquaintance with all these phenomena through active personal observations, excursions, gardening, tending of pets and survey of the locality. But it is necessary, throughout the course, to ensure that the child acquires his knowledge actively and utilizes it for the understanding and better control of his social environment. Hence, the need for correlating the school with the activities of the environing community life which we have duly stressed in the Report.

Main Outlines of the Seven Years' Course of Basic Education

1. *The Basic Craft*: Such reasonable skill should be attained in the handicrafts chosen, as would enable the pupil to pursue it as an occupation after finishing his full course.

The following may be chosen as basic crafts in various schools:

(a) Spinning and weaving.
(b) Carpentry
(c) Agriculture
(d) Fruit and Vegetable gardening.
(e) Leather work
(f) Any other craft for which local and geographical conditions are favourable and which satisfies the conditions mentioned above.

Even where an industry other than spinning and weaving or agriculture is the basic craft, the pupils will be expected to attain a minimum knowledge of carding and spinning with the takli, and a practical acquaintance of elementary agricultural work in the local area.

2. *Mother Tongue*: The proper teaching of the mother tongue is the foundation of all education. Without the capacity to speak effectively and to read and write correctly and lucidly, no one can develop precision of thought or clarity of ideas. Moreover, it is a means of introducing the child to the rich heritage of his people's ideas, emotions and aspirations, and can therefore be made a valuable means of social education whilst also instilling right ethical and moral values. Also, it is a natural outlet for the expression of the child's aesthetic sense and appreciation, and if the proper approach is adopted, the study of literature becomes a source of joy and creative appreciation.

3. *Mathematics*: The objective is to develop in the pupil the capacity to solve speedily the ordinary numerical and geometrical problems arising in connection with his craft and with his home and community life. Pupils should also gain a knowledge of business practice and book keeping.

4. *Social Studies*: The objectives are:

(1) To develop a broad human interest in the progress of mankind in general and of India in particular.
(2) To develop in the pupil a proper understanding of his social and geographical environment, and to awaken the urge to improve it.

(3) To inculcate the love of the motherland, reverence for its past, and a belief in its future destiny as the home of a united co-operative society based on love, truth and justice.
(4) To develop a sense of the rights, and responsibilities of citizenship.
(5) To develop the individual and social virtues which make a man a reliable associate and trusted neighbour.
(6) To develop mutual respect for the world religions.

A course in history, in geography, in civics and in current events, combined with a reverential study of the different religions of the world showing how in essentials they meet in perfect harmony, will help to achieve these objectives. The study should begin with the child's own environment and its problems. His interest should be awakened in the manifold ways in which men supply their different wants. This should be made a starting point to arouse their curiosity about the life and work of men and women.

5. *General Science*: The objectives are:

(1) To give pupils an intelligent and appreciative outlook on nature.
(2) To form in the pupils habits of accurate observation and of testing experience by experiment.
(3) To enable them to understand the important scientific principles exemplified in:
   (a) The natural phenomena around, and
   (b) The application of science to the service of man.
(4) To introduce them to the more important incidents in the lives of the great scientists whose sacrifices in the cause of truth make a powerful appeal to the growing mind.

6. *Drawing*: The objectives are:

(1) To train the eye in the observation and discrimination of forms and colours.
(2) To develop the memory for forms.
(3) To cultivate a knowledge of and appreciation for the beautiful things in nature and in art.
(4) To draw out the capacity for tasteful design and decoration.
(5) To develop the capacity to make working drawings of objects to be constructed.

These objectives can be obtained by:

(a) Drawings made by children to illustrate, read or observe material.
(b) Object and memory drawings, e.g., drawings of plants and of animal and human form (correlated with work in general science, handicraft, etc.)

(6) Designing.

(7) Scale drawing, graphs and pictorial graphs.

The work in drawing during the first four years should be correlated chiefly with work in reading and pictorial representation in nature study and the craft. During the last three years emphasis may be laid on design and decoration and mechanical drawing, so as to enable pupils to make correct working drawings.

7. *Music*: The objective is to teach the pupils a number of beautiful songs and to cultivate in them a love for beautiful music. The child's natural sense for rhythm should be developed by teaching him to keep his own time by beating with the hand. Walking in time to a fixed rhythm can be a great aid in achieving this.

Care should be taken to select only the best and most inspiring songs, the artistic interpretation of some healthy and elevating theme. Special emphasis should be placed on group or choral singing.

8. *Hindustani*: The object of including Hindustani as a compulsory subject in the school curriculum is to ensure that all the children educated in these national schools may have a reasonable acquaintance with a common lingua franca. As adult citizens they should be able to co-operate with their fellow-countrymen belonging to any part of the country. In teaching the language the teacher should in various ways quicken in the students the realization that this language is the most important product of the cultural contact of the Hindus and Muslims in India. It is the repository—in its more advanced forms—of their best thoughts and aspirations. They should learn to take pride in its richness and vitality and should feel the desire to serve it devotedly.

In Hindustani speaking areas this language will be the mother-tongue, but the students as well as the teachers will be required to learn both the scripts, so that they may read books written in Urdu as well as in Hindi. In non-Hindustani speaking areas, where the provincial language will be the mother-tongue, the study of Hindustani will be compulsory during the 5th and 6th years of school life, but the children will have the choice of learning either one or the other script. However, in the case of teachers who have to deal with children of both kinds, knowledge of both the scripts is desirable.

At any rate, every public school must make adequate provision for the teaching of both scripts.

In general outlines, the syllabus of studies will be the same for boys and girls up to the 5th grade of the school. In grades 4 and 5 the syllabus in general science should be so modified as to include domestic science for girls. In grades 6 and 7, the girls will be allowed to take an advanced course in domestic science in place of the basic craft.

Distribution of Work

The Basic Craft	3 hours 20 minutes
Music, Drawing and Arithmetic	40 minutes
The Mother Tongue	40 minutes
Social Studies and General Science	30 minutes
Physical Training	10 minutes
Recess	10 minutes
Total Time Allotted	5 hours 30 minutes

In making this estimate, we have kept spinning and weaving as the basic craft. The distribution might vary from craft to craft, but in no case should the time allotted to the basic craft exceed the above estimate. The school is expected to work for 288 days in a year, average of 24 days in a month. In view of the diversity of pupils' interests we recommend that as far as possible a variety of crafts should be provided for, at least during the last two years of the school course. We are of the opinion that every school should have attached to it a plot of land big enough for a school garden and a playground.

POST-WAR EDUCATIONAL DEVELOPMENT IN INDIA (SARGENT REPORT), 1944

This was a first systematic and national level attempt at tackling the problems of education as a whole. In fact, work on the problems of education had started in 1938 when a National Planning Committee had taken up the assessment of educational reconstruction at national level. The World War interrupted the effort. The CABE had also started that work in 1938 but the piecing together of the report of various Committee could be done only in 1943-44.

The report reveals that the pre-war Britain was spending Rs. 33.20 per head on education, whereas India's comparable expenditure was only Re. 0.89 per head. The merits of this report are—concise, comprehensive and workable. It unfolds that a national system of education would take 30 to 40 years to be evolved.

The report was drafted when the research available on planning was meager, nor were the national goals precisely known. The projections of population, the rate of economic growth, the likely price levels were not there. Then, the plan could be acceptable neither to the aspiring State Governments who could ill afford to have a four-year period of preparation and 30 to 35 years of implementation nor to the Centre because per capita cost was to be Rs. 11 in 30 years, exclusive of the cost of building.

CABE REPORT—THE POST-WAR EDUCATIONAL DEVELOPMENT IN INDIA, 1944

Basic Education/Primary Education

Basic (Primary and Middle) education as envisaged by the Central Advisory Board, embodies many of the educational ideas contained in the original Wardha Scheme, though it differs from it in certain important particulars. The main principle of learning through activity has been endorsed by educationists. At the lower stages the activity will take many forms, leading gradually up to a basic craft or crafts suited to local conditions. So far as possible the whole of the curriculum will be harmonised with this general conception. The three R's by themselves can no longer be regarded as an adequate equipment for efficient citizenship. The Board, however, are unable to endorse the view that education at any stage and particularly in the lowest stages can or should be expected to pay for itself through the sale of articles produced by the pupils. The most, which can be expected in this respect, is that sales should cover the cost of the additional materials and equipment required for practical work.

Basic education, while preserving its essential unity, will consist of two stages- the junior (or Primary) stage covering a period of five years and the senior (or Middle) stage covering three years. Those, who find the term "Basic" unattractive and prefer the existing nomenclature of "Primary" and "Middle" for these two stages, are of course at liberty to retain these, provided they accept the essential unity of the two stages and the necessity of so planning the Primary course that it leads up naturally to the Middle. The reason for this division is that at about the age of eleven to twelve, with the onset of adolescence, certain mental and physical changes occur in boys and girls which necessitate a corresponding adjustment both in the content of the curriculum and in the methods of instruction. "Hence", as the second Basic Committee says, "arises the need for treating the instruction given before and after this psychological break as forming two well defined stages, each with its own scope, aim and technique though inspired by the same fundamental aim.

The Sargent Report endorsed the recommendations of the two Committees of the Central Advisory on Basic Education.

Two Committees of C.A.B.E. made the following recommendations:

(a) *First Committee*

(1) The scheme of 'basic' education should first be introduced in rural areas.

(2) The age range for compulsion should be six to fourteen years, but children can be admitted to the 'basic' school at the age of five.

(3) Diversion of students from the 'basic' school to other kinds of schools should be allowed after the 5th class or about the age of eleven plus.

(4) The medium of instruction should be the mother tongue of the pupils.

(5) A common language for India is desirable. This should be Hindustani with both the Urdu and Hindi scripts. Option should be given to children to choose the script and provision should be made for teaching them in that script. Every teacher should know both scripts, viz, Urdu and Hindi. Some members of the Committee suggest that the adoption of Roman script might prove a solution to the language difficulty and greatly minimise the work of both scholar and teacher.

(6) The Wardha Scheme of basic education is in full agreement with the recommendations made in the Wood-Abbott Report so far as the principle of learning by doing is concerned. This activity should be of many kinds in the lower classes and later should lead to a basic craft, the produce from which should be saleable and the proceeds applied to the upkeep of the school.

(7) Certain elements of cultural subjects, which cannot be correlated with the basic craft, must be taught independently.

(8) The training of teachers should be reorganized and their status raised.

(9) No teacher should receive less than Rs. 20 per mensum.

(10) Efforts should be made to recruit more women teachers and to persuade girls of good education to take up teaching.

(11) Basic schools should be started only when suitable trained teachers are available.

(12) The curriculum will need revision in the light of experience.

(13) English should not be introduced as an optional subject in basic schools.

(14) The State should provide facilities as at present for every community to give religious teaching, when so desired but not at the cost of the State.

(15) No external examinations need be held. At the end of the basic school course a leaving certificate based on the internal examination should be given.

(16) Pupils wishing to join other schools at the end of the 5th class (age eleven plus) should also be granted a leaving certificate.

(17) Promotion from class to class will be determined by the school, though the results of the internal examinations should be subject to the supervisor's inspections.

(b) *Second Committee*

(1) While the provision of 'pre-basic' education in Nursery and infants schools and classes is highly desirable, it is not practicable at this stage, in view of the lack, both of money and of trained women teachers, to advocate

its introduction on a compulsory basis. Provincial Governments should aim in the first place (a) at providing model infants and Nursery Schools in suitable centres, (b) at increasing the supply of properly trained infants' teachers, who should be women, (c) at encouraging the enrolment in 'basic' schools of children below the minimum age for compulsory attendance, and (d) at stimulating the provision by voluntary agencies of efficient pre-basic schools.

(2) 'Basic' education should comprise a course of eight years from the age of six to fourteen years and that this course while preserving its essential unity should consist of two stages—the first stage, the 'Junior' stage, covering a period of five years and the second stage, the 'Senior', three years.

(3) The transfer of children from the 'basic' school to other forms of post-primary education should be allowed after the 5th grade, i.e., at the conclusion of the 'Junior basic' stage.

(4) The various types of post-primary school (other than the 'senior basic' school) to which suitable children may be transferred at the end of the 'junior basic' stage should provide a variety of courses extending over a period of at least five years after the age of eleven. These courses, while preserving an essential cultural character, should be designed to prepare pupils for entry to industrial and commercial occupations as well as to Universities.

(5) Special arrangements should be made in these schools for assimilating pupils who decide to continue their education after completing the full course in the 'basic' school, i.e., after reaching the 8th class.

(6) Suitable courses should be framed for girls attending 'senior basic' schools which should include such subjects as cookery, laundry work, needle work, homecrafts, the care of children and first aid, the remainder of the institutions to be correlated with this course of domestic science in accordance with the general principles of the 'basic education' scheme.

(7) A standing committee of the Central Advisory Board of Education should be appointed to watch new educational experiments carried on in the provinces as well as the progress of educational developments generally, with special reference to 'basic' education, and to make recommendations to the Board for necessary action. There should be a representative of the Hindustani Talimi Sangh on this committee.

(8) Subject to such conditions as are set out in the report, the Central Government should contribute not less than half the amount of the approved net recurring expenditure on 'basic' education in each province, the balance to be found by the Provincial Government and the local bodies entrusted by it with the administration of compulsory education. For capital expenditure on buildings, equipment, etc., a loan system should be adopted.

(9) A Central agency should be established in each province for the disposal of marketable articles produced in schools.

Relevant Conclusions

Basic (Primary and Middle) Education

(a) A system of universal, compulsory and free education for all boys and girls between the ages of six and fourteen should be introduced as speedily as possible though in view of the practical difficulty of recruiting the requisite supply of trained teachers it may not be possible to complete it in less than forty years.

(b) The character of the instruction to be provided should follow the general lines laid down in the reports of the Central Advisory Board's two Committees on Basic Education.

(c) The Senior Basic (Middle) School, being the finishing school for the great majority of future citizens, is of fundamental importance and should be generously staffed and equipped.

(d) All education depends on the teacher. The present status and remuneration of teachers and especially those in Primary Schools, are deplorable. The standards in regard to the training, recruitment and conditions of service of teachers prescribed in the report of the Committee approved by the Central Advisory Board in 1943 represent the minimum compatible with the success of a national system, these should be adopted and enforced everywhere.

(e) A vast increase in the number of trained women teachers will be required.

Nursery Education (Pre-primary Education)

(a) An adequate provision of pre-primary instruction in the form of Nursery Schools or classes is an essential adjunct to any national system of education. The provision in this respect at present is negligible.

(b) In urban areas, where sufficient children are available within a reasonable radius, separate Nursery Schools or departments may be provided; elsewhere Nursery classes should be attached to Junior Basic (Primary) Schools.

(c) Nursery Schools and classes should invariably be staffed with women teachers who have received special training for this work.

(d) Pre-primary education should in all cases be free. While it may not be feasible to make attendance compulsory, no efforts should be spared to persuade parents to send their children to school voluntarily, particularly in areas where housing conditions are unsatisfactory and/or mothers are accustomed to go out to work.

(e) The main object of education at this stage is to give young children social experience rather than formal instruction.

(f) On the basis of normal age-range of three to six years provision has been made for 1,000,000 places in Nursery Schools and classes.

Education of the Handicapped

Provision for the mentally or physically handicapped should form an essential part of a national system of education and should be administered by the Education Department... Whoever possible, handicapped children should not be segregated from normal children. Only when the nature and extent of their defect make it necessary, should they be sent to special schools or institutions.

Recreative and Social Activities

The provision of recreative and social activities on an adequate scale is an essential feature of any modern educational system... Apart from the needs of boys and girls in schools and colleges, special attention should be paid to those in the 14-20 age group who are no longer attending school.

2

Development of Elementary Education: Independence to 1967

FOURTEENTH CABE MEETING, 13-15 JANUARY, 1948

The meeting was held in New Delhi on 13 to 15 January. Maulana Abul Kalam Azad, Education Minister of India was the Chairman.

Pandit Jawaharlal Nehru—Inaugural Address—Extracts

Great changes had taken place in the country and the education system must also be in keeping with them. The entire basis of education must be revolutionized. The present system might have been suited to the past situation, but maintaining the status quo in the field of education under present circumstances would do nothing but harm to the country… .

The younger generation is our future hope. The way their faculties were developed and minds moulded would make or mar Indian destiny and their proper education must be given top priority... There are so many tasks that lie undone because we feel we do not have the men for them, and yet there are men in the country who have the necessary qualifications and are not employed... .

Our system of education must not be formed in isolation from our social and economic life of tomorrow. Different sides of our life and activities must be correlated. The primary aim of any system is to create balanced minds, which cannot be misled. We must be strong mentally before we can think of building a nation.

Extracts from Maulana Azad, Chairman's Address

Historically speaking it is the fourteenth session as thirteen have already been held. But to be more accurate. I think we should call it the Inaugural Session of the Board, since the first thirteen took place in the Indian Empire which on 15th August 1947 came to an end and with it a long chapter of Indian History. Today, we are assembled in a new India which has yet to make its history… . The scales in which the educational problems were weighed by this Board up till now have grown out of date. New scales with new weights will have to be substituted... .

With whatever depth of vision and sympathetic imagination the Board might have tackled the educational problems in the past, it could not escape the fact that there was no free national government to support it. In spite of its desire to have the fullest scope it had to keep itself somewhat in restraint. Now things have changed… .

At first it was considered that religions would stand in the way of the free intellectual development of a child but now it has been admitted that religious education cannot be altogether dispensed with. If national education was devoid of this element, there would be no appreciation of moral values or moulding of character on human lines… .

It is obvious that millions of Indians are not prepared to see that their children are brought up in an irreligious atmosphere and, I am sure, you, too, will agree with them. What will be the consequence if the government undertake to impart purely secular education? Naturally, people will try to provide religious education to their children through private sources. How these private sources are working today or are likely to work in future is already known to you... . To them religion means nothing but bigotry. The method of education, too, is such in which there is no scope or broad and liberal outlook... . If we want to safeguard the intellectual life of our country against this danger it becomes all the more necessary for us not to leave the imparting of early religious education to private sources. We should take it rather under our direct care and supervision. No doubt, a foreign government had to keep itself away from religious education. But *a* national government cannot divest itself of undertaking this responsibility. To mould the growing mind of the nation on right lines is its primary duty. In India, we cannot have an intellectual mould without religion.

There is another problem on which you have to take a final decision now. What is to be the medium of instruction in our educational institutions? I am sure there are two things with which you will agree. First that in future English cannot remain the medium of instruction. Secondly, whatever the change may be in this direction, it should not be sudden but gradual… .

I put it to you if only till recently a Madrasi or a Punjabi or a Bengali felt no difficulty in receiving education through a foreign language, why should he be handicapped if he were to be educated through one of the Indian languages. We shall certainly be able to retain the same intellectual unity which was created for us by the English language. But if we fail to substitute an Indian language for English, our intellectual unity will certainly be affected.

The alternative course before us is to have regional languages for university teaching and one common compulsory language for Central Government and for inter-provincial communication… .

Some Significant Resolutions/Recommendations

Item XX. To consider (a) whether English should be retained in high schools from Class. III to Class VI; (b) the appointment of a committee to investigate the state of secondary education in India and to report on its aims and scope in the light of the present conditions and future requirements.

The Board in agreement with the standing committee, noted; that they had already agreed that no provision for English should be made in the junior basic schools, i.e., up to Class V.

The Board considered the state of secondary education in the country, and in view of its importance in the whole structure of the educational system, decided to recommend that a commission may be appointed by the Government of India to review the present position of secondary education in India and to make commendations.

COMMITTEE ON THE WAYS AND MEANS OF FINANCING EDUCATIONAL DEVELOPMENT, 1948-50

In the 14th meeting of CABE and the All-India Educational Conference held in 1948, the issue of future development and planning was discussed and the Government of India accordingly appointed a Committee consisting of the following members:

B.G. Kher, Premier, Bombay Province (Chairman); B.P. Adarkar, Ministry of External Affairs & Commonwealth Relations; Tara Chand, Educational Adviser to the Government of India; Acharya Narendra Deo, Vice-Chancellor, Lucknow University; Humayun Kabir, Joint Educational Adviser to the Government of India; Shri Rustom P.Masani; V. Narahari Rao, formerly Secretary to the Government of India, Ministry of Finance; N.R. Sarkar, Finance Minister, Government of West Bengal; K.T. Shah, Member, Constituent Assembly.

The Committee held its first meeting in May, 1948.

Basic Education: It was hoped that compulsion for the 6-11 age group would be introduced throughout the country within a period of 10 years by 2 five-year plans.

Summary of Relevant Recommendations

1. The State must undertake the responsibility of providing at least Junior Basic Education for everybody...
2. The Provinces should aim at introducing universal compulsory education for the children of 6-11 age-group within a period of ten years but if financial conditions compel, the programme may be extended over a larger period but in no circumstances should it be given up.

3. The basic minimum salary of trained Basic school teachers should be Rs. 40 per mensem and should on no account be reduced.
4. In view of the present emergency, the Committee, with great reluctance, agrees that only for five years, the teacher-pupil ratio may be 1: 40 instead of 1: 30, though from the educational point of view, this change would be most undesirable. The ratio of 1: 30 should be restored earlier, if possible, but in any case the position must be reviewed at the end of five years.
5. In urban areas, where conditions justify, the same school buildings should be used for two shifts provided different teachers are employed in each shift.

COMMITTEE ON THE RELATIONSHIP BETWEEN STATE GOVERNMENTS AND LOCAL BODIES IN THE ADMINISTRATION OF PRIMARY EDUCATION, 1951*

The Government of Bihar in the 18th meeting of the CABE held in 1951, raised the question of the relationship between the state governments and the local bodies in respect of the administration of elementary education, as it was found that in practice even the partial withdrawal of the powers from the district boards had led to considerable opposition from local bodies. To examine the question thoroughly the Minister for Education appointed a Committee with B.G. Kher, as Chairman. The Committee held its first meeting on 23rd October, 1951.

Terms of Reference: To examine, in detail the present set-up of local administration of education in the different states, the experiments carried out in some of the states in the assumption of more powers by the state governments, the requirements of different state governments in this regard and to recommend a more uniform pattern which may, with a few variations, be adopted in all the states of India.

Major Recommendations

1. *Association of local bodies with the administration of primary education*

It would be an advantage to associate local bodies with the administration of primary education in some form or the other.

2. *Creation of educational bodies*

(a) In all village panchayats and smaller municipalities which have been given only a limited control over primary education, the local body should be required to elect a school committee and to delegate to it the task of supervising the local school or schools.

---

* Ministry of Education, Commission of India, New Delhi, 1954.

(b) In district local boards and in bigger municipalities which exercise wider powers over primary education, a school board be constituted and charged with the responsibility of looking after its educational powers as well as an administrative officer having adequate authority to carry on the day-to-day administration of its primary schools.

3. *Division of authority on a functional basis*

(a) Inspection should be regarded as a duty of the government and should be carried out by government officers. All inspecting officers should be directly under the government and the local bodies should have no control over them.

(b) State Governments should be solely responsible for maintaining or aiding the requisite number of training institutions for primary teachers.

(c) The authority to define curricula or courses of study at the primary level should continue to vest in the State Governments.

(d) In every major municipality authorised to administer primary school within its area and in every district school board, the authority to recruit and control the teaching staff should vest in the Staff Selection Committee, the Administrative Officer, and the Appellate Tribunal constituted on lines similar to those adopted in Bombay.

(e) The service conditions of primary teachers should be determined by the local bodies concerned with the sanction of State Governments and as far as possible these should be uniform throughout the state.

(f) The primary teachers should continue to be treated as servants of local bodies as at present.

(g) Regarding textbooks, it is suggested that State Governments should prescribe, on the advice of official and non-official experts in the subject, the books to be used in primary schools.

4. *Division of authority on the basis of the local body associated*

(a) *City corporations*: The general policy should be to devolve as large an authority upon city corporations as possible.

(b) *Authorised municipalities*: The larger municipalities may be designated as "authorised municipalities". They will differ from corporations in three ways. Firstly, the government will actually conduct inspections instead of merely reserving the right to do so. Secondly, the general control of the government will be a little more detailed, and thirdly, the administrative officers should preferably remain the servants of State Governments.

(c) *District School Boards*: The powers and duties of these bodies should be similar to those of the municipal school boards with two main differences: firstly, the administrative officers of district school boards should necessarily be government servants, and secondly, there would be a greater indirect control by the government through its financial sanctions that will be more frequently required here than in the case of Municipal School Boards.

5. *Finance*

(a) The Union Government should assign specific grants for universal and compulsory primary education in the states.
(b) A sum not less than sixty per cent of the total educational expenditure of the state should be spent on primary education.
(c) The Municipal Acts should be amended so as to make the levy of all education cess obligatory on all municipalities.
(d) In village panchayats a portion of the total revenue should be earmarked for primary education.

6. *Approved schools*

(a) Local bodies associated with the administration of primary education should ordinarily be in charge of all primary schools in their area.
(b) The authority to control and guide the private primary schools in their areas should generally vest in the local bodies themselves.

ASSESSMENT COMMITTEE ON BASIC EDUCATION, 1955

The Ministry of Education appointed a Committee on Basic Education in 1955 with G. Ramachandran as Convener.

Terms of Reference: To survey the existing situation regarding basic education in the various states and to suggest ways and means of bringing about effective improvements.

Some Significant Resolutions/Recommendations

I. *The Government of India*: (1) The Government of India should take appropriate steps to make it clear to all those concerned that the elucidation of basic education given by the Basic Education Standing Committee of the Central Advisory Board of Education has their concurrence.

(2) All India and regional conferences of the basic education should be arranged periodically.

(3) A Central Research Institute of Basic Education should be established.

(4) A small Special Committee of educational experts should be set up to lay down the criteria to evaluate the achievements and progress of pupils in basic institutions.

(5) The establishment of full-fledged Post-Graduate Basic Training Colleges can no longer be delayed.

(6) Post-basic education should get due recognition and place in the present schemes for the reorganisation of secondary education.

(7) The Union Government should insist that any financial aid given by it directly or indirectly to improve or spread elementary education is strictly earmarked by the states for basic education.

II. *The Government of the States*: (1) State Governments should no longer delay to make a clear and unambiguous declaration of policy that all elementary schools will be converted into basic schools and that all teacher training at this level will become basic teacher training within reasonable time limits.

(2) The compact area method of developing basic education should yield place to the whole of elementary education becoming basic.

(3) State Governments should take effective steps for the supply of raw materials, equipment, for repairs and for marketing of surplus produce.

(4) Steps should be taken to effect economy in basic education. Craft equipment whose cost is to be met by the pupils themselves must essentially belong to them. Whatever is produced should, as far as possible, be consumed by the teachers and pupils at reasonable rates and only the surplus need be taken over by the state for marketing.

III. *The Universities*: It will presently become necessary for Universities to recognise post-basic education for purposes of admitting pupils passing out of post-basic schools into colleges.

IV. *Administration*: (1) Inspecting staff connected with basic education should be fully trained in basic education.

(2) English should be offered as an optional subject from the 6th grade onward, wherever knowledge of English is considered necessary for entrance into high schools and other similar institutions.

(3) It is of the utmost importance to guarantee proper dovetailing of basic education with secondary education in such a manner that equal years of study in different types of institutions will be considered as of equal value for purposes of admission into institutions of higher education.

V. *Basic Teachers' Training*: (1) It is urgently necessary to make teachers' training more efficient and real. Improvement is called for in craft training in handling the technique of correlated teaching and in a new and dynamic approach to the study of psychology. Any craft for basic education must be a whole craft and not split into pieces, nor learned in isolated parts.

(2) The staff of basic training schools and the pupil-teachers should prepare manuscripts of reading books for basic school children.

(3) Every basic training school should plan and execute appropriate extension programmes.

(4) Basic training schools should be residential for the purpose, among other things, of giving day-to-day training in actual living and practising of the principles of a cooperative democratic community work and learning together and producing much of what is necessary for daily life.

(5) Sanitation, common kitchen and cultural and recreational activities based on community self-government will be the vital centres of such cooperative community and, therefore, of basic education.

VI. *Basic Schools*: (1) No school may be considered as basic school or assessed as such, unless the following requisites at least are fulfilled:

(a) It provides for an integrated course of 8 years of basic education and where there are only the junior 5 grades, such a school should necessarily be the feeder for a senior basic school.
(b) Adequate quantities of needed raw materials are supplied in time.
(c) Adequate craft equipment and repair material is provided.
(d) There is minimum land available, and in no case less than three acres for a senior basic school of 8 grades.
(e) The majority of teachers at least are basic trained, with the untrained teachers getting training under them all the time.
(f) There is community living and work based on democratic student self-government under the guidance of teachers.
(g) Craft work is systematic and not truncated.
(h) There is the correlated method of teaching, with correlation not restricted to productive work only, but also extending to the natural environment and the social environment.
(i) There is commensurate extension work linking the school with the community and vice versa.
(j) Congregational prayers are organised.
(k) A library with suitable books is available.
(l) Cultural and recreational activities are organised.
(m) Examinations in basic schools will be wholly internal and based on assessment of continuous progress of students and cumulative records.
(n) Basic education should apply equally to urban and rural areas.

VII. *The Public*: The Central and State Governments must, therefore, consider ways and means of convincing the public about basic education and securing their cooperation for its rapid development. The peaceful and constructive evolution of a socialistic pattern of society depends so largely on the development of basic education, that the education of the public in regard to all the relevant issues in and for basic education should be undertaken in all seriousness without delay.

BASIC EDUCATION STANDING COMMITTEE OF CENRAL ADVISORY BOARD OF EDUCATION, 1957

Extracts (Statement on the Concept of Basic Education)

Broadly speaking, it may be stated that the concept of basic education is the same as defined in the Report of the Basic National Education Committee (Zakir Hussain Committee) and elucidated by the Central Advisory Board of Education.... So far as the provision of eight years of compulsory universal schooling and the use of mother tongue as the medium of instruction are concerned there is now no difference of opinion about them...The other implications and features of basic education that need to be clarified and stressed are the following:

1. Basic education, as conceived and explained by Mahatma Gandhi, is essentially an education for life and, what is more, an education through life… . That is why productive, creative and socially useful work in which all boys and girls may participate, irrespective of any distinction of caste or creed or class, is placed at the very centre of basic education.

2. The effective teaching of a basic craft, thus, becomes an essential part of education at this stage… . It is also to be clearly understood that the sale of products of craft work may be expected to contribute towards part of the expenditure on running the school or that the products will be used by the school children for getting a mid-day meal or a school uniform or help to provide some of the school furniture and equipment.

3. As there has been controversy and difference of opinion regarding the position of craft work in basic schools, it is necessary to state clearly that the fundamental objective of basic education is nothing less than the development of the child's total personality which will include productive efficiency as well.… We must insist that the articles made should be of good quality, as good as children at that stage of their development can make them, socially useful and, if necessary, saleable.… This productive aspect should in no case be relegated to the background.… But on the other hand, never should the productive aspect be allowed to take precedence over the educational aspect.

4. In the choice of basic crafts which are to be integrated into school work, we should adopt a liberal approach and make use of such crafts as have significance from the point of view of intellectual content, provide scope for progressive development of knowledge and practical efficiency. The basic craft must be such as will fit into the natural and social environment of the school and hold within it the maximum of educational possibilities.

5. In basic education as, indeed, in any good scheme of education, knowledge must be related to activity, practical experience and observation. To ensure this, basic education rightly postulates that the study of the curricular content should be intelligently related to three main centres of

correlation, viz., craft work, the natural environment and the social environment.... It should also be realised, however, that there may be certain items in the syllabus which cannot be easily correlated directly with any of the three above centres. In such cases there should be no objection to these being taught according to the methods of teaching adopted in any good school.... In any case, forced and mechanical 'associations' which pass for correlation in many schools should be carefully avoided.

6. The emphasis on productive work and crafts in basic schools should not be taken to mean that the study of books can be ignored.... The value of the book, both as a source of additional systematised knowledge and of pleasure cannot be denied and a good library is as essential in a basic school as in any other type of good school.

7. The basic scheme envisages a close integration between the schools and the community so as to make education as well as the children more social-minded and co-operative.

8. Basic education should no longer be regarded as meant exclusively for the rural areas. It should be introduced in urban areas as well, both because of its intrinsic suitability and also to remove the impression that it is some inferior kind of education designed only for the village children.

FIRST ALL INDIA EDUCATIONAL SURVEY, 1957

Findings

59.7 per cent of the rural population in the country was served by primary schools or primary sections within habitations of residence. Again, 83.09 per cent of the population was served by primary sections either in the habitation of residence or nearby. The word 'nearby' had a specific connotation which meant a convenient walking distance of one mile except in some areas where the limit had been fixed at 1.5 miles. It was proposed that after the implementation of the recommendations of that survey, 99.03 per cent of the rural population would be served by primary sections either in the habitations of residence or in nearby habitations.

NATIONAL SEMINAR ON ORIENTATION OF ELEMENTARY SCHOOLS TOWARDS THE BASIC PATTERN, 1959

The Assessment Committee on Basic Education, 1955 observed that the Compact Area Method of developing basic education was no longer satisfactory and the need was to turn the elementary education towards basic education. This recommendation was accepted and the National Programme for the orientation of elementary schools towards the basic pattern was initiated. The need for this National Seminar held from May 11 to 13, 1959 at New Delhi was to take stock of the programme of basic education in the light of the Government's decision.

Major Resolutions/Recommendations

1. The following broad activities should form the content of the orientation programme in the schools:

(a) Activities leading to healthy living;

(b) Activities leading to citizenship training and social living;

(c) Activities leading to a better knowledge of the environment;

(d) Recreational and cultural activities;

(e) Social service activities linking the school with home and community; and

(f) Purposive activities connected with simple crafts.

2. It is necessary to arrange suitable orientation training courses for the inspectors at different levels and the head-teachers in addition to the school teachers.

3. It is necessary to produce suitable literature for this programme intended to give necessary guidance to teachers, head-teachers, inspectors and others connected with the programme.

4. 1960-61 is the accepted target date for the completion of this programme.

5. The funds and other resources available for education under Community Development Programme should be availed of and fully utilised. The voluntary contributions from the local community represent a vast potential source in the matter of equipping the schools, and should be tapped to the maximum advantage so as to supplement the orthodox ways of finding funds for such purposes.

6. It is necessary to provide for adequate follow-up and evaluation of the programmes simultaneously with its implementation by the state government through appropriate agencies.

TWENTY-EIGHT CABE MEETING—16-17 JANUARY, 1961, NEW DELHI

The Twenty Eighth CABE meeting held at New Delhi on 16-17 January, 1961, Minister of Education said;

This meeting has a special significance for us. It marks the Silver Anniversary of the Board.

A Central Advisory Board of Education was originally set up in 1921, but was wound up two years later for reasons of financial stringency, providing an apt illustration of the apathy and indifference of the then Government towards education. The present Board was established in 1935.

The activities of the Board may be roughly divided into three periods, the first of which culminated in 1944 with the adoption of the Post-War Plan of Educational Development, otherwise known as the Sargent Report.

This was the first landmark in educational planning on a national scale. The second period, covering the years 1945 to 1950, was an era of transition both in the political and the educational spheres.... The third phase which began with 1951, and coeval with the two five-year plans has been the formulation of a new pattern of national education accompanied by far-reaching reforms at the secondary and the university level.

In the field of primary education, while our emphasis at present has necessarily to be on expansion, it is quite obvious that the claims of quality cannot be ignored for long.... It has been decided to set up pilot projects for intensive development of primary education in 30 selected community development blocks at the rate of two projects for each State.

Some Significant Resolutions/Recommendations

Item No. 4: Central and Centrally sponsored schemes of the Ministry of Education.

Greater attention should be given to the provision of schemes in the Third Five-Year Plan for pre-primary education designed to promote the total development of the child. Special programme for women's education should be promoted as a centrally sponsored scheme and accordingly funds should be allocated for the purpose.

Adequate measures should be taken to ensure that during the course of the Third Plan all training institutions for primary -teachers should become basic training institutions, an integrated syllabus covering the entire field of primary education is introduced In all primary schools and that all teachers and primary schools are oriented to the basic pattern.

The Central and State Governments should arrange the supply text-books of and writing material free or at low cost to the primary school children.

Item No. 7: Metric system in the education syllabi.

The Board recommended the introduction of the metric system to the text-books at all stages of education.

COMMITTEE ON THE PRE-PRIMARY EDUCATION IN MYSORE STATE, 1961

Major Resolutions/Recommendations

1. *Objective of pre-primary education*: The objective of pre-primary education may be broadly defined as the provision of experiences and the proper environmental conditions which will promote the physical, mental, emotional and social growth of children between the ages of three and six.

2. *Curriculum*: The following forms of activity should be provided:

(1) Developing muscular coordination and health: Outdoor activities such as running and skipping round the field; climbing and sliding; jumping; balancing;

swinging; imitative activities involving large-muscle movement; rhythmic activities as part of musical experience in physical education.

(2) Personal health activities and activities for developing health habits : Activities with the object of training children to look after their personal hygiene and to develop permanent health habits such as, cleaning hands, legs, nose and mouth; combing the hair; taking care of clothes.

(3) *Keeping surroundings Clean*: Activities such as sweeping, dusting, wiping, etc.

(4) *Sensory training with special apparatus*: Activities for creative expression such as, drawing and painting; clay work; paper cutting, cutting pictures and pasting; block building; stringing beads and flowers.

(5) *Observation of nature*: Observing plants, animals, birds and natural phenomena; collecting natural objects.

(6) *Language and number work*: The object is not to introduce the children to formal reading, writing and arithmetic but to provide experiences psychologically suited to the needs of children at this age, which will make them more fit, and 'ready' for the systematic and formal training in the primary school. The activities should include: conversation, story telling and dramatization for developing expression; building up experiences about letters by means of their shapes, and sounds associated with them; obtaining first experiences about number, shape, size and position by means of concrete objects and pictures.

(7) *The School Meal*: This should form an essential service not only from the point of view of nutrition but also from the point of view of social training through this activity. The simplest form of this is to make provision for a cup of milk during the session.

3. *Equipment*: Much of the equipment could be made locally, using locally available materials. 'Toy Banks' may be organised for the purpose of collecting useful toys for children in the pre-primary schools.

4. *The two sessions*: Pre-primary schools should work in two sessions of three hours each per day. The children should be divided into two batches, each batch attending one session.

5. *Number of children*: There should be not more than 20 children in a group per teacher. The teacher should also have the assistance of a helper. The staffing will be on the basis of one teacher and helper for 40 children.

6. *Buildings*: The items of non-recurring expenditure will have to be provided by the public, the government grant covering the pay of the teacher and helper. Simple structures will be adequate.

7. *Teachers and their training*: (1) The minimum general educational qualification for a pre-primary school teacher should be S.S.L.C. Before employment as a teacher in the pre-primary school, the teacher should be trained.

(2) Three types of training courses should be provided:

(i) Nursery training should be made a part of the regular teacher-training course for primary school teachers; (ii) The special course of training for pre-primary school teachers should be of one year's duration; and (iii) Short-term training courses of six months' duration should be provided for training teachers in primary schools who possess the requisite educational qualification and who desire to change over to pre-primary schools.

(3) There should be a public examination at the end of the course. A diploma should be awarded by the Board of Pre-Primary Education on the results of the examination.

8. *Agency for pre-primary education*: The pre-primary school is an educational as well as a social welfare agency. The agency for the organization of the pre-primary education should be the Social Welfare Board.

9. *Board of pre-primary education*: A Board of pre-primary education should be set up. It should be an expert advisory body.

10. *Grant-in-aid*: The underlying principle of grant-in-aid is the sharing up of the responsibility between the private agencies and the government. Considering practical conditions now obtaining, government should give financial aid to the extent of the full pay of the staff. A non-recurring expenditure for buildings, equipments, etc., should be met by the private agency.

11. *Establishment of pre-primary schools by the government*: While the establishment of pre-primary schools by local bodies and other private agencies should be general pattern of expansion in this grade of education, the government should also establish schools on its own.

12. *Books*: Government should aid the publication of good books for children by means of subventions.

13. *Statistics*: A survey should be made, covering the whole country, so as to collect full information about the pre-primary education and about the several agencies working in the field.

14. *Spread of pre-primary education in rural areas*: (1) A definite and positive policy of initiative and effort for the spread of pre-primary education to the rural areas should be under-taken by government.

(2) It is essential to undertake an extensive scheme for school meals to serve the basic needs of children between the ages of 3 and 6.

(3) The appointment of teachers for the pre-primary schools in the villages should be made by the village panchayats with the assistance of the education department for selecting the right type of teachers. Other things being equal, woman teachers should be appointed.

(4) A regular programme of visits to homes should form part of the work of the pre-primary school teacher. Efforts should be made to set up Mothers' Association in every village.

THIRTY-FIRST CABE MEETING—11-12 OCTOBER, 1964, BANGALORE

The Twenty-first CABE meeting held at Bangalore on 11-12 October, 1964.

Some Significant Resolutions/Recommendations

Item No. 3: Special steps required to step up the enrolment of girls in the 6-11 age group.

The Board recommended that special measures (such as those mentioned below) to encourage girls' education should be included in the centrally sponsored sector of the Fourth Plan, with 100% Government of India assistance:

(i) Construction of teachers' quarters;
(ii) Rural allowance for teachers;
(iii) Provision of school mothers;
(iv) Construction of sanitary blocks in schools;
(v) Hostels;
(vi) Creches;
(vi) School meals; and
(viii) School uniform.

Item No. 4: Measures for improving standards of education at the elementary stage.

The Board observed that practically all elementary schools were at present working at sub-standard level in so far as their qualitative standards were concerned. To effect improvement it recommended that the following measures be provided for:

(i) Better paid, better qualified and better trained teachers; (training including initial as well as in-service training)
(ii) Suitable text-books and other reading material; |
(iii) Suitable buildings, equipment and teaching aids;
(iv) Improvement in teacher-pupil ratio;
(v) Provision of improved syllabi;
(vi) Development of school health programme;
(vii) More effective inspection; and
(viii) Full development of State Institutes of Education and expansion of Extension Service Centres.

Simultaneously selected schools should be developed a model institutions, adequate safeguards being provided in the location, admissions, etc. to ensure that socially, economically an educationally backward sectors of children particularly from rural areas are also enabled to derive full benefit from these schools.

The Board reiterated that the minimum qualification for new teachers of primary schools should be matriculation (or equivalent qualification) with professional training and it recommended that no relaxation should be made in this direction.

EDUCATION COMMISSION, 1964-66*
(KOTHARI COMMISSION)

A Commission was set in 1964 under the Chairmanship of Prof. D.S. Kothari. The report was submitted in 1966.

Extracts—School Education: Problems of Expansion

An Integrated Approach to School Education

7.01 We have divided the entire period of formal education into two main stages—school and higher—and we have so far treated school education as one continuous unit. Some explanation for this procedure is necessary. The traditional practice has been to divide the period of school education into three stages—pre-primary, primary and secondary—and to discuss the problems of each separately. This is based on several considerations. In the first place, the three stages of education are regarded as corresponding to the three stages in the development of a child—infancy, childhood and adolescence. Again, from the social point of view, primary education has long been considered as education meant for the masses and secondary education for the select few. In our own country, distinctions have been made sometimes even on cultural grounds: primary education was defined as education through the modern Indian languages while secondary education was regarded as education in English. In recent years, however, these distinctions have either become blurred or have vanished altogether. For instance, it is increasingly realized that the dividing lines between pre-primary and primary or primary and secondary are arbitrary and variable. Similarly, the traditional view that primary education should provide undifferentiated general education while secondary education should be diversified to meet the varying aptitudes, interests and abilities of children is no longer universally held; and in some countries, such as the USSR, the entire course of school education—primary and secondary—has been designed on one set of principles. With the phenomenal expansion of secondary education in India, the social distinction between primary and secondary education as meeting respectively the needs of the masses and the classes has already ceased to be valid; and so has the justification for classifying primary as 'vernacular' education and secondary as 'English' education. We have found it, therefore, more convenient and appropriate to

---

* Education and National Development: Report of the Education Commission, 1964-66, National Council of Educational Research and Training, New Delhi, 1971.

Note: 1. Para numbers refer to para number of the document.
2. Original Table number have been changed to conform to this chapter.

treat the entire pre-university period of education as one stage and have structured our Report accordingly. Such a treatment is almost inescapable for a proper planning and development of the school curriculum. It is true that in this chapter, which deals largely with problems of enrolment, the need to divide the school period into several sub-stages—pre-primary, primary (lower and higher) and secondary (lower and higher) has been recognized. But our general approach in the Report has been to regard the similarities between the problems of the different stages as being far more significant than the differences and to treat school education as a single whole.

Pre-Primary Education

7.03 The objectives of pre-primary education may be stated as follows:

- to develop in the child good health habits and to build up basic skills necessary for personal adjustment, such as dressing, toilet habits, eating, washing, cleaning, etc.;
- to develop desirable social attitudes and manners, and to encourage healthy group participation, making the child sensitive to the rights and privileges of others;
- to develop emotional maturity by guiding the child to express, understand, accept and control his feelings and emotions;
- to encourage aesthetic appreciation;
- to stimulate the beginnings of intellectual curiosity concerning the environment and to help him understand the world in which he lives, and to foster new interest through opportunities to explore, investigate and experiment;
- to encourage independence and creativity by providing the child with sufficient opportunities for self-expression;
- to develop the child's ability to express his thoughts and feelings in fluent, correct and clear speech; and
- to develop in the child a good physique, adequate muscular coordination and basic motor skills.

7.04 *Importance of Pre-primary Education*: Pre-primary schools were first established to meet social needs such as looking after the children of working mothers or providing a suitable environment to little boys and girls from urban families whose small tenements or flats were hardly appropriate for the children's proper growth. These schools also attempted to compensate for the unsatisfactory home environment of children from slum areas or poor families. Recently, however, the educational significance of this stage is being increasingly realized. Modern researches have shown that the years between three and ten are of the greatest importance in the child's physical, emotional and intellectual development. It has also been found that children who have been to a pre-primary school show better progress at the primary stage and help in reducing wastage and stagnation. The modern trend in educational policy, therefore, is to emphasize pre-primary education, especially for children with unsatisfactory home backgrounds. This is the direction in which we also should move.

7.05 *Recent Developments in Pre-primary Education*: Prior to 1947, little attention was paid to pre-primary education and it was not even regarded as a State responsibility. For the first time in our educational history, the Report of the Central Advisory Board of Education on *Post-War Educational Development in India* (1944) emphasized its significance and recommended that an adequate provision of pre-primary education should be an essential adjunct of a national system of education. We are happy to note that pre-primary education has been rapidly gaining in popularity in the post-Independence period. In 1950-51, the number of pre-primary schools was only 303 with 866 teachers and an enrolment of about 28,000. The total direct expenditure on pre-primary education was about Rs. 1.2 million or 0.1 per cent of the total educational expenditure. In 1965-66, the number of pre-primary schools increased to 3,500 with 6,500 teachers and a total enrolment of about 250,000. The total direct expenditure also rose up to Rs. 11 million or 0.2 per cent of the total educational expenditure*. These are mainly urban institutions. In rural areas excellent pioneering work has been done by the Central Social Welfare Board (CSWB) and the Community Development Administration which, taken together, run about 20,000 balwadis having a total enrolment of about 600,000. The progress is no doubt small in relation to our goals, but it marks a tremendous advance over earlier achievements.

7.06 *Recommendations*: While we recognize the need to develop pre-primary education as extensively as possible, our advice in this sector will necessarily be restricted on account of the inadequacy of the resources available, and especially because primary education must be accorded a higher priority. It is also necessary to reconcile the competing claims of quality and quantity. Some educationists are of the view that the pre-primary education to be provided must be of the proper quality, and they insist on maintaining standards which increase the cost per pupil to a level where any large-scale expansion becomes impossible. Others deliberately advocate the adoption of less costly techniques so that the benefit of pre-primary education may be extended to a larger proportion of children. There are also differences of opinion regarding the agency of development: some would prefer the responsibility for pre-primary education to be largely assumed by the State while others would leave it mainly to private enterprise. In these circumstances, we shall have to take a pragmatic view and adopt a policy which promotes experimentation and the best utilization and combination of existing resources and agencies.

7.07 We make the following recommendations for the development of pre-primary education during the next 20 years:

(1) There should be a State-level centre for the development of pre-primary education located in the State Institute of Education. In addition, a pre-primary education development centre should be established in each district in a phased programme spread over the next 20 years. The main functions of these centres would be to train pre-primary teachers to provide supervision and guidance to pre-primary teachers working in the area, to hold refresher courses and in-service training programmes for them, to undertake the preparation of teaching aids out of the locally available materials, to conduct experimental pre-primary schools and to provide education to parents regarding child care. They can also advantageously undertake programmes of initial training of pre-primary teachers.

(2) The establishment and conduct of pre-primary schools may be left, as at present, mainly to private enterprise. The State should assist through grants-in-aid on a basis of equalization. Accordingly, pre-primary schools catering to the needs of children from the under-privileged groups will have a higher claim on State funds.

(3) Every encouragement should be given to experimentation, particularly in devising less costly methods of expanding pre-primary education. We strongly commend the scheme recently adopted by the State of Madras. Under this programme, a local woman is selected as a teacher on a small honorarium, is given a short course of training, and is assisted in her work by the local Mahila Mandal. The outstanding features of the scheme are its low costs (the cost per child per year is less than Rs. 20) and its adaptability and suitability to rural areas. It works well and, unde. active teachers, children show better health, more mental alertness and a lively interest in the environment.

(4) Another important experiment of this type, which has been tried with success in some parts of the country, is the establishment of children's play centres in close association with the primary schools. These are conducted by a specially trained teacher in the primary school, who is given an allowance for the purpose, or by a separate teacher. The programme, which lasts for about two hours a day, is simple and consists of group singing, story-telling and games, with considerable attention being given to personal hygiene and health. These centres serve as pre-school classes and smoothen the transition of the child from its play-dominated world of infancy to the formal atmosphere of the primary school. They are comparatively less costly to run and serve a very useful purpose in reducing wastage and stagnation, particularly in class I. Such centres should be attached to as many primary schools as possible.

(5) The role of the State should be to maintain such centres at the State and district levels, train pre-primary teachers, conduct research, assist in the preparation of materials and literature needed for pre-primary education and provide supervision and guidance to pre-primary schools and training institutions. As suggested above, it should assist private institutions. At this stage through grants-in-aid; and in exceptional cases, it may also conduct some pre-primary schools to serve the needs of urban slums or rural areas or to serve as model institutions.

(6) We can hardly talk about a curriculum for pre-primary schools; it is more appropriate to think of it as a programme of activities. We agree with the suggestion of the Committee on Child Care (1961-62), appointed by the CSWB, that the programme should consist of the following activities:

- (a) Play activities:
  - (i) Free play including educational and constructional toys, indoor games, and outdoor activities in association with other children;
  - (ii) Physical activities involving muscular and limb movement;
  - (iii) Play involving contact, acquaintance, imitation and experience of physical, family and social environment;
  - (iv) Organized play, group activities and directional play;
  - (v) Playground activities using playground apparatus.
- (b) Physical training including simple exercise, dance and eurhythmics.
- (c) Manual activities and play like gardening, simple chores and participation in simple community efforts.
- (d) Sensorial education using natural objects and specially constructed apparatus.
- (e) Handwork and artistic activities involving the use of finger skills and tools; and activities like drawing, painting, singing, music and dancing.
- (f) Learning activities including language; personal hygiene and health rules; elementary nature study involving contact with the physical, plant and animal world; counting and arithmetic, etc.
- (g) Self-service in school eliminating as far as possible the use of servants and adult helpers.

We have often found that the programmes tend to be rigid and authoritarian, that adequate opportunities are not given to children to know their environment, that group work tends to be emphasized at the cost of the children's needs, and that the educational possibilities of the provision of mid-day meals and snacks are not utilized fully. To overcome these, it is necessary to improve the training of teachers and to give them greater freedom in planning their programmes.

(7) There is need for more coordination among the different agencies that work for child-care and pre-primary education, both at the national and at the State levels. In particular, it is necessary for the State Education Departments to develop close relations with the CSWB, the Indian Council of Child Welfare and the Community Development Administration.

(8) With regard to enrolment, we consider that a feasible target would be to enrol five per cent of the children in the age-group 3 to 5 by 1986. This will mean an enrolment of about 2.5 million. If the inexpensive techniques we have recommended above are adopted, this enrolment could be higher. We have also recommended the addition, on as wide a scale as possible, of a pre-school class to which children of the age 5-6 will be admitted. We anticipate that it may be possible to cover about 50 per cent of the children in this age-group by 1986. This will mean an enrolment of about 7.5 million. The total enrolment at this stage would thus be about 10 million.

Primary Education: Fulfillment of the Constitutional Directive

7.08 *Targets*: We shall now proceed to discuss another highly significant programme of educational reconstruction, namely, the fulfillment of the directive principle contained in Article 45 of the Constitution: that the State should strive to provide free and compulsory education for all children up to the age of 14 years. This was to have been achieved by 1960. But in view of the immense difficulties involved, such as lack of adequate resources, tremendous increase in population, resistance to the education of girls, large number of children of the backward classes, general poverty of the people and the illiteracy and apathy of parents, it was not possible to make adequate progress in primary education, and the Constitutional Directive has remained unfulfilled. There has, therefore, been an insistent demand that Government should fix an early deadline for its fulfillment and prepare a concrete programme of action for the purpose. We are in sympathy with this demand and we believe that the provision of free and universal education for every child is an educational objective of the highest priority, not only on grounds of social justice and democracy, but also for raising the competence of the average worker and for increasing national productivity. In view, however, of the magnitude of the problem, the uneven development of primary education in the different parts of the country and the large financial resources needed for the programme, we think that the best strategy for fulfilling the Constitutional Directive would be as follows:

(1) Each State, and even each district, should prepare a perspective plan for the development of primary education taking into account the

stage of development already reached and the local conditions and problems. The objective of the plan should be to fulfill the Constitutional Directive as early as possible;

(2) Each State and district should be assisted to go ahead at the best pace it can, and the progress in no area should be allowed to be held up merely for want of essential facilities or financial allocations; and

(3) While the Constitutional Directive may be fulfilled in some places such as urban areas or advanced States as early as in 1975-76, *all* the areas in the country should be able to provide five years of good and effective education to *all* the children by 1975-76 and seven years of such education by 1985-86.

7.09 The targets proposed above may appear to be rather modest. But a closer examination will show that they are really formidable, and that the nation will have to strive its utmost to realize them. For instance, they involve a large increase in enrolments at this level—from 50 million in 1965-66 to 125 million in 1985-86. The enrolment at the lower primary stage or in classes I-IV will rise from 37 million in 1965-66 to 72 million in 1975-76 and 76 million in 1985-86 and thus, be doubled in a period of about 20 years. At the higher primary stage `or in classes V-VII, the enrolment will increase from 13 million in 1965-66 to 32 million in 1975-76 and 49 million in 1985-86, which is an increase of about four times in the same period.

7.10 But we would like to emphasize, not the increase in enrolment, but two other more significant and difficult aspects of these proposals. The first is the reduction of wastage and stagnation. At present, out of every 100 children who enter class I, only about half complete class IV and only 34 complete class VII. The extent of stagnation is extremely large, particularly in class I. We shall have to rectify this position and ensure that every child who enters class I will progress regularly from year to year and reach class V, and that not less than 80 per cent reach class VII. Secondly, we must emphasize quality. It is generally agreed that the standard of education given in the primary schools is unsatisfactory and that it imparts little beyond literacy and some elementary knowledge in a few academic subjects. What is expected is that primary education should lay the foundation for a child to grow into a responsible and useful citizen of the country. The magnitude of the targets proposed above would be realized in its proper perspective if due weight is given to both these considerations.

7.11 *A further point needs clarification*: our proposal for making a seven-year course of primary education compulsory does not conflict with the Constitutional Directive of providing education to all children till they reach the age of 14 years. For various reasons, a large number of children reach the age of 14 even before they come to the end of class VII. There is also no problem about those children who will complete class VII earlier but proceed to secondary education. This leaves only those children (estimated to be about 10 per cent of the age group) who are not yet 14 at the end of class VII and who wish to enter working life as early as possible. We consider that the needs of these children will be better served, not by lengthening the primary course by one year, but by the provision of short vocational courses of their choice. Such provision has been included in our estimates.

7.12 *The Programmes*: We have now to consider certain practical measures for the implementation of this programme of providing good general education of seven years' duration to every child. A careful study of the development of compulsory primary education in the advanced countries of the world shows that this programme is divided into three stages requiring:

- the provision of a school within easy distance from the home of every child;
- the enrolment of every child of the prescribed age into class I of a school through propaganda, persuasion and even penal action, if necessary; and
- the retention of every enrolled child in school till he reaches the prescribed age or completes the prescribed course.

These are the three stages of universal provision,universal enrolment, and universal retention. They are not mutually exclusive and genrally overlap and run into one another. Moreover, they presume the simultaneous implementation of a programme of qualitative improvement of education, because universal enrolment or retention depends very largely on the attracting and holding power of the schools. The progress of universal education in India can also be expected to follow this broad general pattern.

7.13 *Universal Provision of School Facilities*: The objective of universal provision of school facilities at the lower primary stage has almost been reached at the end of the Third Plan. In almost all States, villages with a population of 300 or over are provided with schools and, in several areas, even smaller villages have been given the facility. At the higher primary stage, however, the position is still far from satisfactory. Taking the country as a whole, there are about 78,000 such schools or about one higher primary school to about five lower primary schools, as against a desirable target of one to three. The situation varies greatly from State to State: while the target has already been reached in some States, the ratio of higher primary schools to lower primary schools is one to ten in several others.

7.14 The problems connected with planning and location of schools—primary, secondary and vocational—will be discussed in a later section of this chapter. Briefly, it may be said that steps will have to be taken to bring a primary school within easy reach of every child. Lower primary schools including single-teacher schools, which are attended by younger children, will have to be set up within about a mile from the home of every child. A higher primary school needs at least three teachers and cannot therefore be set up on financial grounds in every small village. Such schools have to be shared by groups of small villages which, taken together, can provide a reasonable attendance. Moreover, as they are attended by older children it is possible to plan them in such a way that every child will have a middle school within one to three miles of his residence. The first educational survey (1957) helped greatly in the planning of primary schools. It is now being revised, and we hope that the results of the revision will take this planning a step further.

7.15 *Universal Enrolment of Pupils*: A programme of increasing enrolment should be organized side by side with attempts to provide primary schools in the remotest parts of the country. Obviously, there are two main points at which fresh enrolments are made at this stage—class I and class V. The problems that arise at each of these points are very different and have to be examined separately.

7.16 *Enrolment in Class I*: The problem of enrolment in class I (which may be called the initial cohort of the educational system) is of great significance. In all progressive countries, this initial cohort is homogeneous and consists mostly of children of the prescribed age for admission. In India, on the other hand, the initial cohort in class I has always been extremely heterogeneous and its heterogeneity is being reduced only slowly.

In a good system, the children of the age 6-7, the prescribed age for admission, who are enrolled in school, should form the bulk of the total enrolment in class I and should be about 95 to 97 per cent of the total population of children in that age-group.

7.17 In advanced countries, parents are required to pre-register at least one year in advance the names of children who are to be admitted to school for the first time and only those children are enrolled in class I who are within the prescribed age range. There is no system of pre-registration in India. A large number of parents, especially in rural areas, cannot even give the ages of their children correctly, and in many cases the teachers are required to guess them. Moreover, when enrolment drives are organized, the general trend is to enrol children of all ages into class I. This heterogeneous character of the enrolment creates difficult pedagogic problems in the class besides increasing stagnation and wastage. We, therefore, recommend as follows:

(1) A system of pre-registration should be developed for all fresh admissions. The school teachers should take an annual census of all the children whose age is less than the prescribed admission age by one year and who would be seeking admission to the schools in the following year. Except in some big cities where the migratory

population may be large, such census-taking and pre-registration will be very useful and will not present any insuperable administrative problems. During the pre-registration year, an attempt should be made to provide children's play centres described earlier in paragraph 7.07 (4), in as many schools as possible.

(2) Fresh enrolments to class I should, as far as possible, be restricted to children within the single year prescribed for admission. In the beginning, older children who have not yet been to school will have to be admitted to the class; but if intensive efforts are made every year to enrol all the children of the prescribed admission age, the number of over-age children seeking entry into class I will diminish year by year and will disappear almost completely in a period of about 5-10 years.

7.18 *Enrolment in Class V*: At present, the rate of transfer of pupils from class IV, which is the end of the lower primary stage, to class V is about 85 per cent. This transfer rate should be raised to 90 per cent by the end of the Fourth Plan and to 100 per cent by the end of the Fifth Plan. It is necessary for this purpose to conduct surveys and investigations to find suitable measures to deal with the problem. From the evidence available at present, it appears that the drop-out at this stage is mainly due to the non-availability of a higher primary school in the neighbourhood; inadequate facilities for free education; economic need for the child to work in or for the family (especially in the case of girls); and reluctance of parents either to educate their daughters further or to send them to mixed higher primary schools. The establishment of higher primary schools in villages of a certain size, as suggested earlier, and the provision of free primary education and also of part-time education at the higher primary stage will meet the first three of these difficulties. It will be possible to meet the last difficulty in some areas by opening separate schools for girls. In most cases, however, it can only be met by parental education and by persuading the parents to accept the inevitability of mixed schools for boys and girls.

7.19 *Universal Retention of Pupils*: Having enrolled every child in a school, it is essential to see that he progresses regularly from year to year (i.e., there is no stagnation) and that he does not leave the school till he completes the prescribed age or class (i.e., there is no wastage). As is well known, the extent of wastage and stagnation in our system is very large. The evil was first highlighted about forty years ago by the Hartog Committee; and although the issue has been discussed almost continuously since, very little effective action has been taken to reduce it. Precise studies of the problem spread over a time-series are not available.

In a good system of school education, the distribution of pupils over the different classes should be fairly uniform, but it is not so in our country.

7.20 *Stagnation*: In order to have some idea of the extent of stagnation at the primary stage, from class to class, the Commission collected data regarding enrolments in classes I-VIII in 29 districts out of 312. For each class, information was gathered on two points: total enrolment and number of repeaters, classified according to the total period they had spent in the class. From this information, the average period spent by the pupils in the class was calculated and its excess over one year—which is the normal period—was described as the 'stagnation index' for the class in that year.

7.21 *Wastage*: It will be seen that:

- stagnation is highest in Class I;
- it is reduced considerably in Class II and then remains fairly constant in Classes III and IV;
- at the higher primary stage, stagnation decreases still further;
- on the whole, stagnation among girls is greater than among boys; and
- the extent of stagnation shows considerable variations from area to area.

7.22 Wastage is very large at the lower primary stage—about 56 per cent for boys and 62 per cent for girls. About two—thirds of this wastage occurs in Class I. Moreover, it has remained fairly constant in the case of boys while showing a slight improvement in the case of girls. At the higher primary stage, wastage is much less about 24 per cent for boys and 34 per cent for girls; and what is more important, it is decreasing consistently, although at a slow rate.

7.23 The foregoing discussion shows that the most important programme to be implemented at the primary stage during the next ten years is to improve the quality of education and to reduce stagnation and wastage to the minimum. In fact, the task of universal education begins when children are enrolled in class I. It is completed only when they are successfully retained till they complete class VII. In this overall programme, the reduction of wastage and stagnation in class I is obviously the most important element.

7.25 The remedy for some of these defects is self-evident; and most of them could be eliminated through the development of qualitative programmes which are being discussed separately. In this connection, however, we would like to emphasize the following programmes:

(1) The examination at the end of class I should be abolished and the first two classes (and wherever possible, even the first three or four) should be regarded as one teaching unit, within which each child can progress according to his own pace.

(2) The introduction, as recommended earlier, of a year of pre-school education of an economical type.

(3) The adoption-of play-way techniques in class I for introducing the child to school life in a pleasant way. For this purpose, methods of instruction in class I should be patterned in the light of the techniques utilized at the pre-primary stage and the teachers in charge of this class should be trained or oriented accordingly.

7.26 *Stagnation and Wastage in Other Classes*: The extent of stagnation and wastage in other classes of the primary stage is comparatively small. Its causes may be broadly divided into three categories—economic, educational and social. A closer analysis of these causes will also show the remedies.

7.27 *Economic Causes*: The few studies conducted on the subject have shown that about 65 per cent of the wastage is due to poverty. A child is willingly sent to school between the ages of 6 and 9 because at this stage he is more a nuisance at home than a help. After the age of 9 or 10, the child becomes an economic asset because he can work at home or earn something outside. This is especially true of girls who have to assist the over-worked mother at home. The child is, therefore, withdrawn from the school and thus, becomes a 'wastage' case. The long-term solution to this problem of wastage can only come through general economic improvement. But in the immediate situation, the only way to overcome this difficulty is to provide part-time education so that children can work as well as learn.

7.28 *Literacy Classes*: From this point of view, we suggest two programmes. The object of the first is to prevent additions to the ranks of non-literacy. At present, such additions are being continuously made on a large scale for several reasons. A number of children do not get enrolled in schools. Even among those who are enrolled, a large number drop out before completing class IV or V and attaining permanent functional literacy; and some even relapse into illiteracy a little later. To prevent such additions and to help in reducing illiteracy, we recommend that all children in the age-group 11-14, who are not attending schools and who have not completed the primary stage of education and have become functionally literate, should be required to attend 'literacy classes' for a period of one year at least.

7.29 Experiments conducted by some institutions in the country have shown that if we begin with grown-up children of this age-group and provide them with part-time education (of about one and a half to two hours per day for about three days a week), it is possible to make them functionally literate in the course of one year. Such classes can be conveniently organized by teachers in primary schools outside the regular school hours, utilizing the buildings and equipment of the same schools. The timings of the classes would have to be elastic; they should be determined by local conditions and the needs of the children attending, in the sense that attendance in such classes should not interfere with the work they do for the families. In most cases, they will be organized on a part-time basis for about one and a half hours per day, either in the morning or in the evening. For girls, some time in the afternoon is always more convenient. The teachers should be adequately remunerated for the purpose. There need be no separate curricula; but as the size of the average class will be small, it may be possible for teachers to give individual attention to each child and to make them functionally literate during this period. The cost of running these classes will be comparatively small, not more than about Rs. 40 per child per year, but its results will be very substantial.

7.30 There is hardly any reason to doubt the success of the programme, and it can even be adopted on a nation-wide scale forthwith. But if it is considered necessary, a few pilot projects may be tried in each district for a short time in order to gain experience before the scheme is launched on a nation-wide basis. In any given area, it may be desirable to begin these classes on a voluntary basis in the first instance. Attendance at such classes should be made obligatory only after the local community becomes familiar with the concept and begins to appreciate it.

7.31 It is important to realize that the total size of this problem is comparatively small and that it is of a vanishing character. At present, the population of children in the age-group 11-13 is about 34 million. Of these, 11 million are attending schools in classes VI-VII; and about 3 million are expected to have completed the primary stage although they are not attending at present. This leaves 20 million children in the age-group 11-13 who will come under this compulsory programme in 1966.

7.32 *Part-time Education at the Higher Primary Stage*: (1) The second programme to offset wastage is to provide part-time education to children who have completed the lower primary stage, and who desire to study further but cannot, for economic reasons, afford to do so on a full-time basis. The number of such children is large even at present; and it will increase as education reaches the still poorer sections of society. The only way in which these children can receive education is by getting it on a part-time basis; and it should be a deliberate object of policy to provide such education on as large a scale as possible.

(2) The content of this part-time education would have to be elastic and should be determined according to the needs and aptitudes of the children receiving it. For some children who desire to complete this stage of education and prepare themselves for the next, it should be patterned on the lines of the full-time courses. But for those who do not wish to do so-and these would be the large majority—the content of education should have a large vocational element and should be so developed as to serve their immediate needs.

(3) To begin with, attendance at these classes should be voluntary. But obligatory attendance may be introduced in an area as soon as the ground is

ready. This may be done in some areas almost immediately, and all parts of the country should be covered in the Fifth and Sixth Plans.

(4) It is not possible to determine precisely the proportion of students who will be in part-time education at this stage. The policy adopted should be to provide a place in full-time education for every student who desires to receive such education and to make available part-time education for all those who cannot, for some reason, follow a full-time course. The proportion of students in part-time and full-time education would thus vary, depending upon economic factors, from area to area, and even in the same area, from one class of society to another. For purposes of financial estimates, however, we have assumed that, for the country as a whole, enrolment in part-time education would be about 10 per cent of the total enrolment at this stage in 1975-76 and about 20 per cent in 1985-86.

7.34 *General Observations*: An effective way to reduce the evils of wastage and stagnation is for the State Education Department to treat every school as an individual entity and for every school to give individual attention to every child. The Department should use the techniques which have been developed to measure the extent of wastage and stagnation from year to year in each class and in each school. On the basis of these data, it should insist on every school making the best efforts possible to reduce these evils. Similarly, each school should pay adequate attention to individual children. It has been found that wastage is reduced even by a simple act such as a sympathetic enquiry made by a teacher of the parents whenever a child ceases to attend school. What is needed, therefore, is a nation-wide programme of school improvement in which the reduction of wastage and stagnation would figure prominently. The broad outline of such a programme is discussed more fully elsewhere.

7.35 It has to be remembered that wastage and stagnation, like headache and fever, are not diseases in themselves: they are symptoms of other diseases in the educational system. The chief among these are the lack of proper articulation between education and life and the poor capacity of the schools to attract and hold students. To these may be added a third ailment, poverty, which falls outside the system. Urgent action is needed to remove the first two educational weaknesses; the effect of the third can be offset only as the economy of the country improves. The goal of universal retention of pupils, therefore, is the most difficult of all and can be reached only over a period of time. This makes it all the more necessary to organize immediately an intensive programme for the reduction of wastage and to pursue it till the goal is reached. A beginning should be made with class I, where the target should be to reduce the wastage by half before the end of the Fourth Plan and to reduce it to the minimum by the end of the Fifth Plan. In the lower primary stage, all wastage should be reduced to the absolute minimum by the end of the first decade (1966-76) and at the higher primary stage, by the end of the second decade (1976-87).

Enrolment at The Primary Stage

7.41 A process of equalising opportunities in primary education has to be attempted at various levels. When the family is responsible for the primary education of children, inequalities develop between children from the rich and those from the poor families. These can be equalised at the local government level which can strive to reduce the inequalities at the family level. It will, therefore, be a responsibility of the district school boards to try to equalise opportunities for primary education between different villages and towns within their areas and between families in each town and village. But the economic capacities of districts and their loads of the unfinished task are very uneven, It is, therefore, a responsibility of the State Governments to strive to equalise opportunities as between districts through a grant-in-aid based on the principle of equalisation. Finally, similar inequalities appear again at the State level in the development of primary education already achieved, in the magnitude of the unfinished task and in the economic capacity of the States to support a programme of universal education. It is, therefore, the responsibility of the Government of India to strive to equalise opportunities in primary education at the State level. This may be done through the institution of a special grant in aid in the Centrally-sponsored sector to assist the poorer and less developed States to fulfil the Constitutional Directive in time.

7.42 *Enrichment of the Curricula and Improvement of Quality*: Expansion of facilities at the primary stage and the universal enrolment of children and their retention in school till the end of the compulsory period is only one aspect of the fulfilment of the Constitutional Directive. An equally important aspect is qualitative improvement so that the instruction imparted becomes good education and helps children to grow into useful and responsible citizens. The most crucial programme from this point of view is the improvement in the quality of primary teachers, which has already been discussed elsewhere. Another equally significant programme is the introduction of work-experience as an integral part of primary education. Besides this, the teaching of science and mathematics has to be vitalised, the entire curriculum has to be overhauled and improved, and modern methods of teaching and evaluation have to be adopted.

PLANNING AND LOCATION OF SCHOOLS

7.56 *Primary Schools*: At this stage, accessibility is the over-riding consideration and small schools, in spite of their heavier cost and lower efficiency, must be accepted. The optimum size of a school is: for a lower primary school—4 or 5 teachers and an enrolment of 160 to 200, i.e., a school of 4 or 5 classes; and for a higher primary school, a school of 7 or 8 classes, a teacher for each class (excluding the headmaster and an enrolment of 300 to 400). Wherever possible, school of this size (or even bigger ones) should be established. This can be done in all urban areas and in villages of 1,500 persons or more. Since, however small villages predominate, small schools will have to be established, in spite of their comparatively greater cost and lower efficiency. The general rule should be to establish a lower primary school within a mile or so of the home of every child and higher primary school within three miles. Villages with a population of 200 to 300 should have a lower primary school and those with a population of 700 or more should have a higher primary school.

CHAPTER VII: SCHOOL CURRICULUM

8.14 *Standards of Attainment at the Different Stages*: Though the curriculum of the first ten years of general education covering seven years of primary education (four years of lower primary and three years of upper primary) and three years of lower secondary education should be organised as a continuous programme of studies, the standard of attainment at the end of each sub-stage in the total course should be clearly indicated. The standards should be defined in terms of the knowledge, skills, abilities and attitudes to be developed with reference to the overall objectives of school education.

8.15 At the lower primary stage (Classes I to IV) the child should receive instruction in the basic tools of learning such as reading, writing and computation, and learn to adjust himself to his surroundings through an elementary study of his physical and social environment. He should participate in activities which develop his constructive and creative skill and teach him the habits of healthy living. In order that a sound foundation in the mother-tongue may be laid at this stage, no language other than this should be introduced during the first four years. The curriculum of these classes should be gradually expanded and developed in keeping with the child's growth and development.

8.16 At the higher primary stage (Classes V to VII) the study of a second language will be added to that of mother-tongue, arithmetic skill will develop into the acquisition of more difficult mathematical knowledge, environmental activities will lead to the study of natural and physical sciences, history, geography and civics, constructive and creative skills will provide the basis for the practice of simple arts and crafts, and the practice of healthy living will serve as the foundation for physical education.

8.18 We give below what we believe should be the broad areas of curricular studies for the different sub-stages, and shall follow this outline with a discussion of the special features of the curriculum at each sub-stage.

1. *Lower Primary Stage (Classes I-IV)*
   - (a) One language the mother-tongue or the regional language.
   - (b) Mathematics.
   - (c) Study of the Environment (covering Science and Social Studies in Classes III and IV).
   - (d) Creative Activities.
   - (e) Work experience and Social Service.
   - (f) Health Education.
2. *Higher Primary Stage (Classes V-VII)*
   - (a) Two languages—
     - (i) the mother-tongue or the regional language, and
     - (ii) Hindi or English.

     (*Note*—A third language (English, Hindi or the regional language) may be studied on an optional basis.
   - (b) Mathematics.
   - (c) Science.
   - (d) Social Studies (or History, Geography and Civics).
   - (e) Art.
   - (f) Work-experience and Social Service.
   - (g) Physical Education.
   - (h) Education in Moral and Spiritual Values.

8.19 *Curriculum at the Lower Primary Stage*: The first two classes of the primary school should be graded as a single unit, and wherever possible, this arrangement should be extended to cover Classes III and IV. The proposed curriculum for these classes is very simple and reduces the load of formal subjects. Only language and elementary mathematics are to be specially emphasised with a view to developing the basic tools of learning. The study of the environment will be largely informal in the beginning and will be provided by making the child observe his immediate social and physical surroundings and talk in class about what he observes. In Class III environmental studies will gradually lead to social studies and science which may now be treated as regular subjects, but in a very elementary manner. While the activity method will permeate all teaching, special activities in the from of music, art work, dramatics and handwork should be organised for creative self-expression. Health education will stress the formation of good health habits. Work-experience will consist largely of handwork and social service will involve simple activities like cleaning the class-room, decorating the school etc.

8.20 We should like to emphasise one important aspect of education at this stage, viz., reading with understanding. If proper foundations for this are not laid at this level, the entire future education of the child will receive an irreparable set back. Adequate attention has not been paid so far to research in beginning reading, to the evolution of proper methods of teaching reading to young children with phonetic scripts which the Indian languages have, to the preparation of graded vocabularies, to the designing of primers and readers for Class I and to the evolution of tests of reading readiness or competence. It has not yet been possible to organise the proper training of teacher-educators at the primary level in these matters, and the average primary teacher generally tries to teach teaching in rule-of-thumb manner. It is the neglect of this crucial area that is responsible for a good deal of the stagnation at the lower primary stage. We recommend that a study of these problems should be taken up in earnest and that a vigorous programme of improving reading instruction at the lower primary stage should be developed in all parts of the country.

8.29 *Advancement and Enrichment Programmes at Different Stages*: 1. At the primary stage, it is difficult to provide separate advanced courses. Enrichment programmes should, therefore, be created for talented children, so that they may get more challenging and more satisfying learning experiences from their studies. Such programmes may start in Class V or VI. It may, for instance, be in the form of additional science, which may involve more extensive reading, practical work and application of knowledge to life situations. It may also mean additional work in language or art, leading to the development of creative self-expression. It is better if the planning of the enrichment programme is done by teachers and pupils together. General guidelines can be given in the curriculum materials, and the teacher will also need some additional help in the form of special types of work-books and facilities for the establishment of subject clubs. Work under this programme may be done outside the school hours.

2. At the secondary stage, we are not in favour of diversified courses. But we strongly recommend the organisation of courses at two levels—ordinary and advanced—beginning with Class VIII. Advanced courses may be offered in various subjects and should be included in the curriculum on an optional basis.

THREE LANGUAGE FORMULA

8.35 *Implications of the Modified Formula*: At the lower primary stage only one language should be studied compulsorily—the mother-tongue or the regional language, at the option of the pupil. In the case of the vast majority of pupils, the language of study at this stage will be the regional language which will also be the mother-tongue. Some children belonging to the linguistic minorities may also opt for instruction in the regional language because of its great advantages; but they cannot be forced on them, and they have the right under the Constitution to have facilities provided for their primary education through their mother-tongues. The State governments should, therefore, provide primary schools teaching through the mother-tongue for the children of linguistic minorities if they desire to have such an education, subject to the usual condition approved by the Education Ministers' Conference (1949) that the minimum number of such children should be 10 in a class or 40 in the school. It is desirable that such children should have a working knowledge of the regional language also. Facilities for the study should, therefore, be provided, on optional basis, from Class III onwards. We do not favour making the study of religious language compulsory at this stage for children of linguistic minorities, as has been done in some States at present. We also are not in favour of teaching English as a second language at this stage. This has been discussed further in a later section.

8.36 At the higher primary stage only two languages should be studied on a compulsory basis: (1) the mother-tongue or the regional language, and (2) the official or the associate official language of the Union. For almost all the pupils in the Hindi areas and for a majority of them in the non-Hindi areas, English will probably be the second language, but a large proportion of the pupils in non-Hindi areas may also opt for Hindi. In addition, facilities should be provided for the study of a third language on an optional basis, so that the children in Hindi areas whose mother-tongue is not Hindi and the children in non-Hindi areas who have taken English as the second language may study the official language of the Union, if they so desire.

8.37 At the lower secondary stage (Classes VIII—X), a study of three languages should be obligatory; and a student should be under an obligation to study either the official language of the Union or the associate official language which he had not elected at the higher primary stage.

Work Experience

8.73 *Programmes at the Different Stages*: In the lower classes of the primary school, work experience may begin as simple hand-work, the objective being to train children to make use of their hands and thereby help their intellectual and emotional growth. In the senior classes, it may take the form of learning a craft which develops technical thinking and creative capacities in the pupils. Even here, however, some work-experience can be provided in real life situations, such as work on the farms at the time of harvesting or sowing or in a family production unit, and opportunities for this kind of activity should be utilised to the maximum extent possible. As a workshop is proposed to be attached to every school or group of secondary schools in a phased programme spread over the next ten years, work-experience at the lower secondary stage can take the form of workshop training. At the higher secondary stage, where the students will be more mature, and their numbers will be comparatively smaller, work-experience should be made available in school workshops and also on farms and in industrial or commercial establishments.

8.74 The range of possible activities that be provided in a programme of work-experience is very wide, and the choice will be determined merely by the availability of materials and trained instructors.

8.75 *Work-Experience and Basic Education*: We pointed out earlier that the concept of work experience is closely related to the philosophy underlying basic education. The programme of basic education did involve work experience for all children in the primary schools, though the activities proposed were concerned with the indigenous crafts and the village employment patterns. If in practice basic education has become largely frozen around certain crafts, there is no denying the fact that it always stressed the vital principle of relating education to productivity. What is now needed is a reorientation of the basic education programme to the needs of a society that has to be transformed with the help of science and technology. In other words, work-experience must be forward-looking in keeping with the character of the new social order.

8.78 *Implementation*: In implementing the programme of work-experience, three problems have to be tackled: (1) transfer of teachers; (2) provision of necessary formalities including supply of equipment; (3) progressive extension of the programme to all schools.

CHAPTER IX: TEACHING METHODS: GUIDANCE AND EVALUATION

9.30 *Fixing The Minimum Class Size*: We may have a ratio of 40 pupils to one teacher at the primary stage and yet find a class of 10 pupils and another of 80 pupils perhaps in the same district. It is essential that, in addition to the pupil-teacher ratio, the maximum number of pupils to be admitted in a class must also be prescribed, and this maximum should not be allowed to be exceeded in any case. We recommend the following maximum number for the different stages of school education:

Lower Primary	—	50
Higher Primary	—	45
Lower Secondary/Higher Secondary	—	40

9.31 *The Class Size in Classes I and II Bas a Special Significance*: More than half the enrolment at the primary stage is these two classes; and very often, they are large classes of 60 or more. In such cases our first recommendation would be that the needed teachers should be provided and the class size reduced as indicated above. But if this were not possible, we would prefer to break this class into two classes of about 30-35 students and engage them only for three hours a day and request the teacher (with payment of a suitable allowance) to engage two such classes per day. This would be a far better method of education than the present system of herding together 70 or so pupils in one class and keeping them there for six hours a day.

9.32 *Multiple-Class Teaching*: About 40 per cent of our schools are single-teacher schools and even in other schools, the proportion of big schools where one teacher teaches one class is very small. More than half of our teachers, therefore, have to teach more than one class at a time.

9.44 *Guidance in Primary Education*: Guidance should begin from the lowest class of the primary school. It can be used in helping pupils to make a satisfactory transition from home to school; in diagnosing difficulties in the learning of basic educational skills; in identifying pupils in need of special education (e.g., the gifted, the backward, the physically handicapped); in helping potential drop-outs to stay in school; in guiding pupils to develop insight into the world of work and favourable attitudes towards work; and in assisting in plans for heir further education or training. Little has been done so far in the shape of guidance services at the primary stage because of the large numbers of institutions involved, the poor qualifications of the teachers and the absence of resources. It would, therefore, be unrealistic for a long time to come to think of providing qualified counsellors in these schools. Some guidance functions can, however, be performed by well-trained primary school teachers. Community resources can also be mobilised to meet some of the guidance needs of the young pupils.

9.45 Suggestions for making a beginning in guidance in the primary school are outlined below:

1. The training programme for primary school teachers should include familiarising them with simple diagnostic testing with the problem of individual differences and the implications of these differences for classroom practices.
2. There should be at least one lecturer in the training school who should be allowed to deal with the subject of principles of guidance and mental hygiene.
3. Guidance services should be introduced in the training institutions and the schools attached to the institutions so that the trainees may get first-hand knowledge of the problems involved in their organisation.
4. Wherever possible, short in-service courses in guidance should be provided for primary school teachers.
5. Simple literature for the occupation orientation of children may be prepared and made available in the regional languages.
6. At the end of the primary stage, children and parents should be helped in the selection of courses for further education, and the selection should not be based on the examination results alone.

9.66 *The New Concept of Evaluation*: It is not agreed that evaluation is a continuous process, forms an integral part of the total system of education, and is intimately related to educational objectives. It exercises a great influence on the pupil's study habits and the teacher's methods of instruction and this helps not only to measure educational achievement but also to improve it. The techniques of evaluation are means of collecting evidence about the student's development in desirable directions. These techniques should, therefore, be valid, reliable, objective and practicable.

9.69 *Evaluation at the Lower Primary Stage*: One of the main purposes of evaluation at the primary stage is to help the pupils to improve their achievement in the basic skills and to develop the right habits and attitudes with reference to the objectives of primary education. These objectives and their implications for evaluation should be made clear to the teachers... it would be desirable to treat the lower primary stage covering Classes I to IV as an ungraded unit, because this would help the children coming from different backgrounds to advance at their own pace. As the conditions in most primary schools, however, are not favourable to the general adoption of this procedure, we have recommended that the experiment should be tried out in the beginning in Classes I and II, which should be regarded as a single ungraded unit. This will put an end to the existing practice of detentions in Class I and the drop-outs and wastage resulting therefrom, and will also provide for continuity and flexibility in the educational programme of the first two classes. The two-year block may be divided into two groups, one for slow-learners and the other for fast-learners to enable different pupils to proceed at the level of their ability and move from one unit to another. Such a division, however, will be practicable only in a large-sized school with more than one section in each class. If the experiment regarding the ungraded unit succeeds in Classes I and II, it may be extended to the remaining classes of the lower primary stage.

9.70 Teachers should be prepared for the ungraded system through the regular training courses and orientation programmes and should be helped with a supply of diagnostic tests and remedial material. The orientation may be given by the State Institutes of Education. Observation techniques which are more reliable for assessing the pupil's growth at this stage than mere formal techniques of evaluation, should be used by teachers in a planned and systematic manner.

9.71 *Evaluation at the Higher Primary Stage*: At present evaluation in these classes is carried out largely by means of written examinations. We believe that due importance should be given here also to oral tests, which should form a part of the internal assessment. The teacher should be helped in such assessment with a rich supply of evaluation materials prepared by the State Evaluation Organisations, including standardised achievement tests. Diagnostic testing is necessary here and indeed throughout the school stage. In most cases, such testing will be through simple teacher-made diagnostic tests. Cumulative record cards playa vital role in indicating the growth and development of the pupil at each stage, his academic and emotional problems, and his difficulties of adjustment, if any, and the directions in which remedial action is to be taken to solve his problems or difficulties. We are of the opinion that cumulative records intended for primary schools should be very simple so that primary teachers can use them with just a little training.

9.72 *Is a Primary External Examination Necessary*? ... We, therefore, recommend that no compulsory examination should be held at the end of the primary school stage.

Summary

1. The entire pre-university period of education should be treated as one single and continuous unit. It may be subdivided into sub-standards such as pre-primary, lower and higher primary, and lower and higher secondary. But it has to be noted that the similarities between the problems of the different sub-stages are more significant than the differences. (7.01)

2. *Pre-primary Education*: Pre-primary education is of great significance to the physical, emotional and intellectual development of children, especially those with unsatisfactory home backgrounds. An enrolment of five per cent of the population in the age-group 3 to 5 in the pre-primary schools and of 50 per cent in the age-group 5-6 in pre-school classes will be a reasonable target to be attained by 1986.

3. Pre-primary education should be developed on the following lines during the next twenty years:

(1) State-level development centres for pre-primary education should be set up in each State Institute of Education; in addition, a district level centre should be set up in each district for the development, supervision and guidance of pre-primary education in the area.

(2) Private enterprise should be made largely responsible for setting up and running pre-primary centres, the State assisting with grants-in-aid on the basis of equalization.

(3) Experimentation in pre-primary education should be encouraged especially to devise less costly methods of expanding it. This may be done on the Madras pattern. In the alternative, children's play centres should be attached to as many primary schools as possible and should function as pre-school classes.

(4) The State should maintain State and District level play centres, train pre-primary teachers, look after research and preparation of literature on pre-primary education, supervise and guide pre-primary schools and training institutions, assist private agencies with grants-in-aid and run model pre-primary schools.

(5) The programme of pre-primary schools should be flexible and consist of various types of play, manual and learning activities accompanied by sensorial education. (7.03-07)

4. *Expansion of Primary Education*: The objective of primary education should be to prepare individuals to be responsible and useful citizens.

The constitutional directive of providing free and compulsory education for every child upto the age of 14 years is an educational objective of the highest priority and should be fulfilled in all parts of the country through the development of the following programmes:

(1) Five years of good and effective education should be provided to all children by 1975-76.
(2) Seven years of such education should be provided by 1985-86.
(3) Emphasis should be laid on the reduction of wastage and stagnation. The objective should be to ensure that not less than 80 per cent of the children that enter class I reach class VII in a period of seven years.
(4) Children who are not yet fourteen years old at the end of class VII and who do not wish to study further should be retained in the educational system till they complete 14 years of age but should be provided with short vocational courses of their choice.
(5) Each State and district should be required to prepare a perspective plan for the development of primary education in its area in the light of the targets stated above and its local conditions. It should be given full assistance to move forward at its best pace; and care should be taken to see that its progress is not held up for want of financial resources. (7.08-11)

5. *Universal Provision of Schools*: The expansion of primary schools should be so planned that a lower primary school is available within a distance of about a mile from the home of every child. A higher primary school should be available within one to three miles from the home of every child. (7.13)

6. *Universal Enrolment*: A programme of universal enrolment should be organized simultaneously with emphasis on the following:

(1) The present heterogeneity of cohort in class I should be reduced and the bulk of the students in this class should consist of children in the age-group 5-6 or 6-7;
(2) A system of pre-registration should be introduced;
(3) The transfer rate of students from the end of the lower primary stage to the higher primary (which is now about 80 per cent) should be raised to 100 per cent by the end of the Fifth Plan. (7.15-18)

7. *Universality of Retention*: The most important programme to be implemented during the next ten years is to improve the quality of primary education and to reduce stagnation and wastage to the minimum. The target

---

Note: Numbers in brackets refer to Para numbers of the document.

should be to reduce stagnation and wastage by about half by 1976 and to almost eliminate them by 1986.

(1) Stagnation and wastage are very high in class I and their reduction should be a major programme. Of the various measures to be adopted for the purpose, three are very important:

(a) treating classes I and II (and wherever possible even classes I-IV) as one integrated unit;

(b) introducing a year of pre-school education; and

(c) adopting play-way techniques in class I.

(2) Stagnation and wastage in other classes should be reduced by providing various forms of part-time education, by implementing a nation-wide programme of school improvement, and by an intensive programme of parental education.

(3) All children in the age-group 11-14 not attending schools and who have not completed the primary stage of education and become functionally literate, should be required to attend literacy classes for a period of at least one year. The classes should be organized in primary schools and in a flexible manner to suit the convenience of the pupils. They should begin on a voluntary basis; but compulsion may be tried when the local community has become familiar with the concept.

(4) Similar facilities for part-time education should be provided for children who have completed the lower primary stage and who desire to study further. (Their magnitude may be 10 per cent of the total enrolment in 1975-76 and 20 per cent in 1985-86). The curriculum may follow the general education pattern or contain a large vocational element as required by local needs. (7.19-35)

Recommendations

- to transform education relating it to life, needs and aspirations of people;
- education must lead to productivity, and for this, science education and work experience should become integral part of the curriculum;
- social and national integration are essential for a democracy hence common schools, social service, mother tongue as medium of instruction, promotion of national consciousness, etc., were recommended to facilitate in achieving these;
- tolerance to religion in a multi-religious state is also a necessary quality in its citizens which education must help in developing;
- 10 years of general schooling, and two years of senior secondary education in various streams was recommended. The increase of one year of schooling was to improve the quality in every respect;
- vocational education was strongly recommended; at least 20 per cent students were to be diverted to vocational education;

- for higher education, recommendation was a three years of first degree course followed by courses of varying duration for the second degree or research degree;
- part-time and own-time education at all stages of education and with the same status as given to full-time education was also recommended;
- intensive efforts were needed to raise the economic, social and professional status of teachers and to feed back the talented young people into the profession;
- the concept of educated manpower requirement was recommended by this Commission. This meant relating manpower estimates to the output of the educational institution and avoiding unplanned enrollment into the professional/vocational institutions and wasting resources. It also meant providing employment to every graduate/trained personnel;
- arrangements for pre-school education were emphasized specially for those children coming from underprivileged homes and education of girls and handicapped children were also given priority
- the constitutional directive of free and compulsory education up to the age of fourteen, as an educational objective of highest priority, was reemphasized, which needed to be fulfilled by expansion and improvement of quality of primary education in all parts of the country;
- emphasis was also on revision of curriculum, production of good textbooks and teacher's guides, provision of guidance and counseling programme for students, search for talent, improvement of professional skills of teachers, system of evaluation and appropriate buildings and infrastructure needed in the schools;
- reorganization of courses at university level in all areas of studies was yet another important recommendation. Combination of subjects permissible for the first degree should be more elastic than permitted, both in arts and in science, and should not be linked rigidly to the school subjects.
- to develop educational research and relate it effectively to the formulation of educational policies and improvement of education was recommended.
- Agricultural universities and agricultural polytechnics need to be set up in each state for contribution to the development of agriculture.
- vocational, technical and engineering education needs to be imparted after class X or XII organized through polytechnics, IITs and engineering colleges to fulfill the manpower requirements of the country.
- Science education and research are essential for the progress, security and welfare of the nation. Development of science must

derive its nourishment from the cultural and spiritual heritage of the land and not bypass it. While utilizing the scientific manpower, it must aim to achieve highest efficiency—higher than that in the industrially developed countries.

SECOND ALL INDIA EDUCATIONAL SURVEY, 1965*

Findings

Out of 9,82,251 rural habitations identified in the Second Survey, 3,73,086 (37.98%) had primary sections in them. Taking together the habitations with schooling facilities in them and those having it within a walking distance of one mile 8,56,816 (87.23%) were served by primary sections. In terms of population 71.48% of the rural population had primary sections in their own habitation and 94.96% was served by primary sections, located either in the habitation of residence or within a walking distance of one mile.

COMMITTEE OF MEMBERS OF PARLIAMENT TO PREPARE DRAFT OF STATEMENT ON NATIONAL POLICY ON EDUCATION, 1967**

After twenty years of freedom, it was felt urgent to issue a comprehensive resolution on National Policy of Education. The time was also appropriate as the Report of the Education Commission (1964-66), which provided a blue-print of educational development spread over 20 years and which advised the Government on the general principles and policies for the development of education at all stages and in all aspects was before the country. The Commission had recommended that the Government of India should issue a statement on the National Policy of Education, which should provide guidance to the State Governments and the local authorities in preparing and implementing education plans in their areas. And as such a Committee of Members of Parliament was constituted on April, 5, 1967.

A Drafting Committee under the chairmanship of Shri Ganga Sharan Sinha was constituted from amongst the members of the Committee to (i) consider the Report of the Education Commission; (ii) to prepare the draft of a statement on the National Policy on Education for the consideration of the Government of India; and (iii) to identify a programme for immediate action.

Major Recommendation

Education is a powerful instrument of national development—social, economic and cultural. The highest priority should therefore be accorded to the development of a national system of education which will—

* National Council of Educational Research and Training, New Delhi.

** Ministry of Education, Government of India, New Delhi, 1967.

- provide adequate and equal opportunity to every child and help him to develop his personality to its fullest.

A. *Transformation of the educational system*

The most important and urgent reform needed is to transform the existing system of education in order to strengthen national unity, promote social integration, accelerate economic growth and generate moral, social and spiritual values.

2. *The neighbourhood school*: The primary schools should be made the common schools of the nation by making it obligatory on all children, irrespective of caste, creed, community, religion, economic conditions or social status, to attend the primary school in their neighbourhood.

4. *The teaching of languages*: *(a) Classes I-X*: The parent has a right to claim primary education in the mother-tongue of his child. At the secondary stage, the regional language should ordinarily be the medium of education. Only one language, viz., the medium of education, should ordinarily be studied in the first sub-stage of school education covering four or five years. A second language should be introduced, on a compulsory basis, ordinarily at the beginning of the next sub-stage. The study of this language should be continued till the end of Class X. A pupil may begin the study, at his option, of any third language, ordinarily from Class VIII.

6. *Sanskrit*: Facilities for its teaching at the school stage should be provided on a liberal scale and its study encouraged.

7. *Science education and research*: Science and mathematics should be an integral part of general education till the end of Class X; the quality of teaching science should be improved at all stages and scientific research should be promoted.

9. *Work-experience*: Yet another work-experience which may be defined as participation in productive work in school, in the home, in a workshop, in a factory, on a farm, or in any other productive situation, as an integral part of general education at the school stage.

B. *Equalization of educational opportunities*

1. *Pre-primary education*: Greater attention needs to be paid to the development of pre-primary education.

2. *Primary education*: It should be given the highest priority and implemented in two stages. In the first stage, universal education should be provided for all children till they reach the age of eleven years; and in the second, this age-limit should be raised to fourteen years. Primary education should be made immediately free in all parts of the country.

Note: Serial numbers of the recommendation refer to the numbers of the document.

3. *The ten-year school*: It will be advantageous to have a broad uniform educational structure in all parts of the country. The first step is to create the ten-year school providing a common pattern of general education for all children.

8. *Education of girls*: There is still a wide gap in the enrolment of boys and girls at all stages. It is necessary to eliminate this gap at the primary stage, and to narrow it at the other stages.

10. *Education of the handicapped children*: The facilities for the education of the physically and mentally handicapped children should be expanded.

C. *Programmes of qualitative improvement*

3. *Curricula and text books*: There is urgent need to upgrade and improve school curricula, to increase their knowledge content and to provide adequately for the development of skills and the inculcation of right interests, attitudes and values.

5. *Student services, welfare and discipline*: It is desirable to develop programme of student services and welfare at all stages. At the primary stage, provision should be made for free supply of textbooks to all students... .

3

1968 to 1985: Select Documents

NATIONAL POLICY ON EDUCATION, 1968*

This draft on National Policy on Education (1967) was placed before the Central Advisory Board of Education which met in 1967 and discussed the formulation of a National Policy. As a result of these discussions and agreements, Government of India resolved to promote the development of education in the country in accordance with certain principles that embody the Statement of National Policy on Education issued in 1968.

Extracts

2. In the post-Independence period, a major concern of the Government of India and of the states has been to give increasing attention to education as a factor vital to national progress. Problems of educational reconstruction were reviewed by several commission and committees,… .

Some steps to implement the recommendation of these commissions/ committees were taken… . Towards the end of the Third Five Year Plan, a need was felt to hold a comprehensive review of the educational system with a view to initiate a fresh and more determined effort at educational reconstruction, and the Education Commission (1964-66) was appointed to advise the Government on the national pattern of education and on the general principles and policies for the development of education at all stages in all aspects. The Report of the Education Commission has since been widely discussed and commented upon. Government is happy to note that a general consensus on the national policy on education has emerged in the course of these discussions.

3. The Government of India is convinced that a radical reconstruction of education on the broad lines recommended by the Education Commission is essential for economic and cultural development of the country, for national integration and for realising the ideal of a socialistic pattern of society. This will involve a transformation of the system to relate it more closely to the life of the people; a continuous effort to expand educational opportunity; a

* Ministry of Education, Government of India, New Delhi, 1968.

sustained and intensive effort to raise the quality of education at all stages; an emphasis on the development of science and technology; and the cultivation of moral and social values. The educational system must produce young men and women of character and ability committed to national service and development. Only then will education be able to play its vital role in promoting national progress, creating a sense of common citizenship and culture, and strengthening national integration. This is necessary if the country is to attain its rightful place in the comity of nations in conformity with its great cultural heritage and its unique potentialities.

4. The Government of India accordingly resolves to promote the development of education in the country in accordance with the following principles:

(1) *Free and compulsory education*: Strenuous efforts should be made for the early fulfillment of the Directive Principle under Article 45 of the Constitution seeking to provide free and compulsory education for all children up to the age of 14. Suitable programmes should be developed to reduce the prevailing wastage and stagnation in schools and to ensure that every child who is enrolled in a school successfully completes the prescribed course.

System

1.4. The present system of education must be reorganized in the light of contemporary Indian realities and requirements. Subject to the nationally agreed basic concepts of freedom, equality and justice, the system should be flexible and responsive to varying circumstances. Every effort should be made to pursue excellence, without losing sight of the ideal of equality. The system must endeavour to narrow the gulf between the educated classes and the masses and overcome feelings of superiority, inferiority and alienation. With flexibility in the choice, content and duration of courses, the student can choose his own time and channel of study and progress at his own pace. The educational institutions and the community should help each other, the teachers and parents co-operating in providing knowledge and skills and a better future for the children. The school should be closely associated with the development activities of the area.

Universal Elementary Education

Elementary Education for All

2.1. Highest priority must be given to free education for all up to the age of 14 as laid down in the Directive Principles of the Constitution. Education up to this stage should be general and not specialized, and should give pupils a confident command of language and tool subjects and inculcate a scientific attitude. Elementary education should be an integral stage.

Objective and Content of Elementary Education

2.2. The accent in elementary education should be on the development of personality and character. The content of elementary education needs to be restructured keeping in view not only the tradition and values that make up the country's composite culture but also the present realities and the vision of a common future. The content of education at this stage should include language, arithmetic, history, simple elementary sciences with special reference to environment, cultural values and physical education. The curriculum should necessarily include socially useful productive work through purposive manual labour contributing towards goods and services useful to the community. Wherever possible, provision must be made for agricultural or horticultural activity. Thus, education will become functional and related to the lives of the people and the environment. It should promote a scientific temper which results in a capacity for self-criticism and a liberal and human outlook. Flexibility and room for innovation will help the teachers to meet the varying requirements of children.

2.3. There is need for a change in the approach to the learning process in the early years of elementary education. The accent has to be more on creative and joyful activities than formal instruction. Formal instruction must be reduced to the minimum and should not exceed three hours a day. No rigid academic year need be prescribed. The school session should be scheduled according to local needs.

Facilities for Elementary Education

2.4. While it is necessary to expand the facilities for formal education in elementary schools for all children in the age group 6-14, it is also important to formulate schemes of non-formal education for drop-outs and the older children in the age group who have not had any schooling. The aim should be to cover all the children in the age group 6-14 in the next ten years. Steps should be taken to prevent children giving schooling without completing the course. The problem of wastage should be studied in detail and remedial measures taken.

2.5. The curriculum must be capable of catering to the requirements of a wide range of learners and learning circumstances and built around local situations. There has to be a core of basic content for comparability of educational attainment and the acquisition of further skills and knowledge. The core should be minimum. Learning system may be organized through either formal or non-formal arrangements, which may be partly institutional and partly personal. The institutional arrangements should not be so rigid as to exclude those learners who wish to make use of them partially.

Incentives

2.6. Incentives such as mid-day meals, free textbooks, stationery and uniforms should be provided to poorer pupils. Special attention should be given to the education of girls and children of Scheduled Castes and Scheduled Tribes.

School and the Community

2.7. The school should function as a focal centre for the development of the neighbourhood. The community in its turn should involve itself in the educational effort. Skills available within the community should be utilized for education programmes in the school.

Common School System

2.8. Beginning with the elementary stage, steps should be taken towards the common school system. The effort should be to provide education of good quality. It should be ensured that in all schools, the medium of instruction is the regional language and fees and rules of admission are uniform.

Neighbourhood School Plan

2.9. The neighbourhood school plan will be the main feature of the common school system by which the schools in the area will be required to enrol all the children in the neighbourhood. This will promote common interests and social integration.

Culture

Linking Culture and Education

10.1. A positive effort has to be made to ensure the integration of traditional and contemporary cultural elements with formal and non-formal education. The education system has so far not made full use of the rich and varied cultural heritage of the country and vast cultural resources available in communities which are socially and economically backward. All these resources should be drawn upon and woven into the fabric of education, at all stages.

Physical Education

Physical Education as an Integral Part of Education

11.1 Physical education, consisting of sports and games and athletics, including rural sports, indigenous games, yoga exercises and activities promoting a spirit of adventure, should form part of education at various levels. Efforts should be made to locate talent among boys and girls and facilities should be provided to enable them to develop their capacities and attain national and international standards of excellence in sports. Practical knowledge for maintaining one's health and physical fitness should be given at all stages.

Medium of Instruction

Medium and Language Study

12.1. The medium of instruction at all stages shall be the regional language except at the primary stage where it will be the mother tongue.

12.2. Facilities will be provided in schools for teaching English or a foreign language so that pupils can have direct access to a specialized and growing knowledge in the world in their chosen fields.

Educational Opportunities

Problem of Disadvantaged Sections

17.1. While there has been considerable expansion in all sectors of education in our country, imbalances and inequalities still persist. Girls, Scheduled Castes and Tribes, landless labourers, backward classes and urban slum poor generally continue to lag behind in education. Special effort must be made to identify the problems in these cases and to bring all such people into the fold of education.

Talent Search

17.2. Scholarships and fellowships based on merit-cum-means should be expanded at different levels of education. Some of these should be earmarked for rural and backward areas and weaker sections, to ensure that talented students from the weaker sections of the population are identified and helped to acquire good quality education.

Monitoring

17.3. Close monitoring of programmes intended for the disadvantaged classes will be undertaken at the State and national levels at all stages of education so that they may be enabled to reach levels attained by other sections of the population, within the next decade.

Pre-school Education

17.4. Pre-school education for children of first generation learners should be provided through existing schools system.

Regional Imbalances

17.6. Certain States lag behind the rest of India in education. The Centre and States concerned must make special efforts to bring them at par with the other States in education generally and more particularly in universalisation of literacy within the shortest possible time. It has been observed that educational development even within one and the same State is not uniform.

Hence, close monitoring will be introduced during the next Plan period, and emphasis will be laid on area planning to ensure that all relatively backward pockets are assisted to raise their standards.

Education for the Handicapped

17.7. Every effort should be made to expand educational opportunity to cover all handicapped children. For the more severely handicapped children, education may be provided in specially suitable settings for the full development of their potential. The others could be placed in regular schools, and provided with the requisite additional facilities. Appropriate curricula and techniques of teaching suited for handicapped children should be evolved through research and through study of techniques adopted elsewhere.

Teacher Education

18.3. The curriculum of teacher education at the elementary and secondary stages will be suitably changed in order to enable the teachers to play their proper role in reforming education. . .

Review

23.1. The Government of India will review every five years the implementation of the National Policy on education and modify it in the light of experience.

NATIONAL SEMINAR ON PRIMARY AND WORK-ORIENTED EDUCATION, (INTERNATIONAL EDUCATION YEAR) 1970*

The National Seminar on Primary and Work-Oriented Education was organised by NCERT, on November 9-11, 1970 at New Delhi as a part of the programme for the celebration of the International Education Year. Seminar stock of the trends of development in the field of pre-primary and primary education during the sixties and to formulate programmes and policies for the seventies.

Resolutions/Recommendations

1. The programmes of pre-school education should be closely related to the home and community environment of the child.

2. The expansion of the programmes of pre-school education may be left to the care of voluntary agencies. The agencies engaged in pre-school education should try to develop less costly equipment with the help of indigenous materials. Community resources should be fully utilised.

---

* National Council of Educational Research and Training, New Delhi, 1971.

3. Necessary additions/modifications in the primary school teacher training programmes should be made to include principles governing child care and pre-school education so as to enable the primary school teachers to look after pre-school programmes in mixed schools.

4. The state governments should be in a position to provide funds for the purpose of training teachers and specially trained supervisors for pre-primary education.

5. Special attention should be paid to the promotion of the following Gandhian values in primary schools:

(a) The dignity of manual labour through the use of work as a part of the educational programme.

(b) A sense of social awareness and social responsibility through involvement of pupils in community service.

(c) Secular outlook and respect for other religions through an understanding of the fundamental unity of all religions.

(d) Fearlessness, Truth, Non-Violence (Universal Love), Purity, Service and Peacefulness through participation in curricular and co-curricular activities, and through stress on songs, stories and dramas based on Gandhian life and values.

6. While taking step for providing work-experience at the primary stage the following details have to be spelled out:

(a) Formulation of the operational concept of work-experience.

(b) Types of work-experience programmes to be introduced during 1970's in our country.

(c) Minimum work-experience programmes to be introduced in all the schools in the country with stress on structured activities to be introduced in selected schools.

(d) Action programmes pertaining to production of curriculum materials.

(e) The pre-service and in-service training geared to work-experience to be provided to teachers and supervisors.

(f) Steps to be taken for mobilisation of public opinion in favour of work-experience.

7. Work-experience should be socially meaningful. It should be realistic physical work, without over-emphasis on economic aspects at the cost of learning outcomes and it should lead to the development of productive abilities and the total personality of the child.

8. Individual schools might be encouraged to develop their own programmes of work-experience and the results of their programmes might be made available to the various agencies and institutions in the country.

9. The agencies for curriculum development at the centre and state level may start a continuous dialogue on programmes and techniques of curriculum development.

10. In order to improve the competence of teachers, the following steps may be taken:

(a) Suitable in-service and pre-service training courses may be developed by each State Government.

(b) Suitable materials as help books and teacher guides may be developed by State Institutes of Education.

(c) NCERT should take up programmes on development of good techniques of teaching for the primary classes and make the same available to the state level agencies.

11. Efforts may be made to institute the programmes of close supervision of schools to provide guidance to working teachers.

12. The teachers, supervisors and parents may be made conscious of the rate of wastage and stagnation and efforts may be made for identification and proper treatment of potential cases of wastage and stagnation in the school.

13. The possibility of implementing syllabi on health education for the age group of 6-11 and 11-14 along with that of primary teacher training schools developed by the Central Health Education Bureau and the Ministry of Education jointly may be explored.

14. As there were a large number of pupils who were unable to take advantage of the use of full schooling facilities the possibility of providing some part-time education as a temporary measure for such children may be examined. Shift system may be accepted only as a measure of expediency and not as a principle.

15. The government grant policy should develop an incentive to exploit one's own resources of finance, even though by and large the government has to be the main source of financing the primary education in future.

16. The local bodies should exploit the sources of revenue fully for primary education.

17. There is a need for evolving a suitable curriculum for the schools functioning in tribal areas. This curriculum may be science-oriented but culture-based.

18. Steps to improve the Ashram School education may be taken. The teacher-community relationship may be improved.

STUDY GROUP TO PREPARE PROGRAMME OF ACTION FOR DEVELOPMENT OF THE PRE-SCHOOL CHILD, 1972*

CABE in its 35th meeting held in May, 1970 considered the services provided and needed for the pre-school child and made the recommendation, "The Board recognizes the significance of pre-primary

---

* Ministry of Education and Social Welfare, Government of India, New Delhi, 1972.

education and commends the proposal to try out pilot projects by mobilizing local community resources, especially in rural areas".

Accordingly, M/o Education and the Department of Social Welfare jointly set up a Study Group to examine the question and to prepare a programme of action for the development for the pre-school child through the mobilization of local resources, especially in rural areas, with Smt. Mina Swaminathan, as Convener. The report deals with the age group 3-5 only.

Resolutions/Recommendations

1. *Need and significance*: Integrated services combing education, health, nutrition and welfare are essential for the total development of the pre-school child and should receive high priority and adequate resources.

2. *Objective*: The objective of such services should be to promote the optimum physical, mental, emotional and social development of the pre-school child.

3. The different agencies concerned should make concerted and coordinated efforts to provide these services.

4. *Collection of data*: Basic data collected at regular intervals are essential for a proper planning, implementation and evaluation of programmes for the pre-school child. The Department of Social Welfare may be designated and adequately equipped to collect and publish this data annually.

5. *Special features that need emphasis*: In drawing up a programme of services for the pre-school population, special attention needs to be given to the vulnerable groups of children, remedying imbalances in the distribution of services, coordination among the agencies involved in the programme, expansion and reorientation of the training programmes and provision of guidance and supervision.

6. *The new approach*: Strategies that would help in undertaking a sizeable programme within the limited resources available include mobilizing community support and involvement, employing local women in rural areas, part-time employment of educated women and students, maximum utilization of existing institutions and facilities, and adoption of a variety of models.

7. *Targets*: About one million children in the age-group 3-5 are covered at present by existing services. A reasonable and feasible target of enrolment would be to cover 10 per cent or 5 million children by 1981, i.e., one million more children by 1972-74 and a further 3 million by 1981, priority being given to children from the vulnerable sections of the population, i.e., children from the urban slums, tribal areas and under-privileged groups in rural areas.

8. *Need for variety and experimentation*: (a) Flexibility and response to the needs of each situation are essential to maximize the benefits of the

programme. A variety of operational models has been suggested which may be adapted to each situation in the most advantageous manner possible. These include, the Comprehensive Day-Care Centre mainly for urban slums, half-day Balwadis, First Stage Centres, Anganwadis mainly for rural areas, and primary school based centres.

(b) The special needs, difficulties and circumstances of the tribal areas call for an unorthodox approach and increased accent on community participation.

9. *Low cost models*: During the initial period (1972-74) greater emphasis will have to be placed on the low cost models. In the subsequent seven-year period, the improvement in the position expected regarding resources and trained personnel will facilitate the adoption of a larger proportion of the more comprehensive and hence costlier models.

10. *Training of personnel*: The training and orientation of various categories of workers is essential to the success of the programme and should be accorded high priority. An adequate training programme of good quality should be designed for all categories of workers. It will also be necessary to create three new categories of workers: the part-time workers, the local woman worker, and the supervisor.

11. The special features of the training programme recommended include:

(1) Alternations of the primary teacher training curriculum so as to bring primary and pre-school education closer together;

(2) Modification of the pre-primary training course so as to bring it in line with the course of the Bal sevikas;

(3) Provision of new training course for all categories of workers, including sandwich type courses and vacation and orientation courses;

(4) Orientation towards urban, rural and tribal environments; and

(5) Integration of extension, training and research in all training units.

12. *Equipment*: Provision of suitable and adequate play and educational equipment is essential to the success of the scheme. Scales of equipment have been suggested for the different models striking a mean between the optimum desirable and maximum possible. The State and local community should both contribute to provide these.

13. *Methods*: A variety of methods should be adopted to provide the necessary equipment, including mass production, local fabrication, classroom improvization, collection of folk toys, etc., and contributions of simple furnishings by the local community. Assistance should be given to institutions to establish prototype design units and display centres.

14. *Literature*: The existing literature on the subject being meager, immediate steps should be taken to produce the needed literature for

teachers, teacher-trainees, teacher educators, supervisors, administrators and planners, the community and the children themselves.

15. *Research*: Special emphasis should be laid on the development of appropriate programmes of research.

16. *Evaluation*: A programme of evaluation should be built into the different programmes and should be the continuous responsibility of the supervisory staff and of the agencies at the district, State and national levels.

17. *Administration*: Implementation of a comprehensive programme requires a strong administrative machinery at all levels-national, state, district and local (rural and urban).

(a) *National level*: In order to ensure a strong and effective central machinery for coordination of the programmes at the national level, a national committee for the pre-school child should be set up under the chairmanship of the Union Minister for Education and Social Welfare. A Directorate for Pre-school Programme will look after the effective implementation of the decisions of the Committee.

(b) *State level*: The department which would be responsible for the administration of this scheme at the state level will differ from state to state. Where more than one departments are involved, a suitable coordinating machinery will need to be created. A full-time officer of appropriate status will have to be made responsible for the programme.

(c) *District level*: The district being the most appropriate administrative unit for effective coordination in the field, a suitable coordinating committee should be set up with representatives from various agencies engaged in schemes of child welfare. A full time officer of the status of a district officer and working directly under the Collector should look after the implementation of the programme.

(d) Local bodies—Ministry of Education and Social Welfare, Government of India, New Delhi, 1972.rural: Supervisors placed under the control of Zila Parishad or Panchayat Samiti should be provided facilities of transport to enable them to function effectively.

(e) *Local bodies—urban*: A Standing Committee of the municipal authority concerned should supervize the programme in urban areas. A special officer should be entrusted with the execution of the programme.

18. *Estimated costs*: The total costs on the programme during 1972-74 will be Rs. 23.2 crores (Rs. 19 crores recurring and Rs. 4.2 crores non-recurring). This will involve an additional expenditure of Rs. 17.6 crores over and above what is already budgeted for nutrition programmes.

19. *Local community participation*: The maximum amount of community participation should be mobilized for the development of the pre-school child. Such participation would include contribution in cash and kind, contribution in terms of voluntary services and contribution towards buildings, equipment

and feeding programmes. Well-to-do communities should also extend support to those less advantageously placed. In addition, local bodies should explore all avenues to raise resources for pre-school child services.

THIRD ALL INDIA EDUCATIONAL SURVEY, 1973*

Primary Education—Findings

If the figures of the Third Survey have to be compared with the figures of the earlier two surveys, some limitations have to be kept in mind. In those two surveys, the criterion for considering a habitation to be served by a primary section was that a child would require one mile to walk to and fro the school. In the Third Survey, this criterion has been changed to 1 km. Consequently, the comparison will not be very accurate because of different units of distance measurement used in different surveys. Out of 9,53,734 habitations identified in the Third Survey, 4,22,766 (44.33%) have primary sections in them. In all, there are 7,20,809 habitations which are served by primary sections within the habitation itself or by a school located within a walking distance of 1 km. There are 94,433 habitations which are not served by any primary section within a distance of 2 km. In terms of population, 76.12 per cent of the rural population is served by a primary section located in the habitation of residence. Observing the criterion of 1 km walking distance, 90.34 per cent of the rural population is served by primary sections either located in the habitation of residence or within a walking distance of 1 km. On the other hand, 3.42 per cent of the rural population is not served by a primary section located within a walking distance of 2 km.

Table 1: Habitations and Population in Various Population Slabs Served by Primary Sections in them or Within a Walking Distance of 1 km. and 1.5 km. in Rural Areas

Population Slab	*Total No. of Habitations*	*Habitations Served*			*Population Served*	
			Percentage		*Percentage*	
		Number	*1 km.*	*1.5 km.*	*1 km.*	*1.5 km.*
5000 and above	3,838	3,781	97.81	98.51	98.75	98.19
2000 to 4999	30,188	29,831	98.38	98.82	98.89	98.45
1000 to 1999	82,728	81,153	97.29	98.10	98.22	97.39
500 to 999	1,74,142	1,65,102	92.93	94.81	95.07	93.26
400 to 499	73,354	66,831	87.60	91.11	91.17	87.73
300 to 399	93,714	79,329	79.36	84.65	85.02	79.66
200 to 299	1,25,167	97,565	71.83	77.95	78.21	72.20
100 to 199	1,77,923	1,24,868	62.99	70.18	70.50	63.33
Below 100	1,92,680	1,19,823	54.20	62.19	64.28	56.28
Total	9,53,734	7,68,283	75.58	80.56	92.65	90.34

* National Council of Educational Research and Training, New Delhi.

Note: Statement numbers have been changed to conform to this chapter.

Table 2: Population Not Served by Primary Sections either in Their Own Habitations or Within a Walking Distance of 2 km. in Rural Areas

Population Slab	*Population of Habitations in the Slab*	*Population in the Slab not Served by Primary Sections*	*In the Slab (%)*	*Not Served by Primary Sections in them or within 2 km.*	*In Rural Areas in the Country*
5000 and above	2,79,60,686	1,83,523	0.66	1.15	0.04
2000 to 4999	8,30,79,372	4,28,832	0.52	2.70	0.09
1000 to 1999	10,94,82,596	8,84,850	0.81	5.57	0.19
500 to 999	11,59,92,919	25,17,975	2.17	15.84	0.54
400 to 499	3,14,58,821	12,13,776	3.86	7.64	0.26
300 to 399	3,19,55,926	22,13,657	6.93	13.93	0.48
200 to 299	2,98,95,117	29,42,897	9.84	18.52	0.63
100 to 199	2,47,64,924	34,08,617	13.76	21.45	0.73
Below 100	1,07,77,008	20,97,810	19.47	13.20	0.45
Total	46,53,67,369	1,58,91,937	3.41	100.00	3.41

Inter-State Comparisons

Andhra Pradesh: There are 53,231 rural habitations with a population of 3,76,33,301. Of these habitations 56.85% are in the slab 'below 500' and these account for 17.01% of the population. On March 31,1957, 89.89% of the population was served by primary sections. At the time of the Second Survey (31.12.1965), this percentage rose to 97.42%. With the changed distance criterion of 2 km walking distance, the present survey figures reveal that 98.20% of the population has been provided primary education facilities. The total number of habitations which are not served by the primary sections is 7,217 of which, 1,187 are having a population of '300 or more'. The bulk of habitations, not served, belong to the slab 'less than 300' and their number is 6,930.

Assam: There are 29,442 rural habitations with a population of 1,37,45,522. Of these habitations, 68.22% accounting for 33.03% of the population are in the slab 'below 500'. Number of habitations with a population of 'less than 100' is 4,303. In this State the number of small habitations is very large. In the First Survey, i.e. on 31 March, 1957, 82.91% of the population was served by primary sections. At the time of the Second Survey 93.33% of the population was served by primary sections. According to the present data 98.53% of the population is served by primary sections either located within the habitation of residence or within a walking distance of 2 kilometres. In all, there are 964 habitations which are not served by any primary section within a distance of 2 kilometres. Of theses, 870 belong to the slab 'below 500' and 778 are in the slab 'below 300'. If 186 habitations which are not served at the moment by any primary section and which have a population of 300 or more, can be given a primary school, the problem which will remain unsolved will be that of very small habitations only. For these habitations, i.e. those 'below 300', methods other than formal schooling may have to be adopted in order to help children receive education.

Bihar: Total number of rural habitations in Bihar is 1,04,326 and of these 65.41% are in the slab 'below 500' whose population is only 27.05%. Thus, Bihar has also a large number of small habitations. According to the First Survey, 85.90% of the rural population was served by primary sections within a walking distance of one mile. At the time of the Second Survey, with the same distance criterion the percentage of population served by primary sections rose to 97.13% which included 67.13% served by primary sections in their own habitations. According to the present survey, 98.62% of the population is being served by a primary section either in the habitation of residence or by a primary section located in a habitation within a distance of 2 kilometres. Out of 4,365 rural habitations which are not served by any primary section within a distance of 2 kilometres, 4,089 belong to the slab 'below 500'. The major problem of provision of educational facilities at primary stage is of the habitations numbering 3,675 with a population 'below 300'. Presuming that 690 habitations which have a population of 300 or more will be provided with primary schools, some more habitations from the slab 'below 300' will also be covered.

Gujarat: There is one peculiarity about Gujarat. The primary schools cater to classes I to VII and, therefore, the comparable middle classes are included in primary sections only. There are 23,069 rural habitations with a population of 2,04,88,671. The proportion of small habitations, i.e. in the slab 'below 500' is 43.74% which is relatively low. These habitations account for 12.78% of the population. At the time of the First Survey there was no separate state of Gujarat and in the erstwhile state of Bombay 91.58% of the population was served by primary sections. At the time of the Second Survey 97.70% of the population was served by primary sections. Strangely enough the percentage of population served by primary sections at the time of the Third Survey is 96.86% which is lower than what it was at the time of Second Survey. Even though the distance criterion has been changed from 1 mile to 2 kilometres, the percentage of population served has gone down which should have normally increased. Of the total number of 2,597 habitations not served by any primary section within a distance of 2 kilometres, 2,305 belong to the slab 'below 500'. There are 1,883 habitations in the slab 'below 300' which are not served by any primary section. By providing primary schools in 714 rural habitations having a population of '300 or more', some more habitations from lower slabs will be served by these additional schools and the percentage of population served by primary sections will be further increased

Haryana: Haryana State came into being on 1st November, 1966. As such, no data are available for comparison regarding earlier surveys. It was carved out of the erstwhile state of Punjab. At the time of the Second Survey 96.54% of the rural population in Punjab was served by primary sections. In the present State of Haryana there are 7,257 rural habitations of which 2,237 have population of 'less than 500' each. The total population in rural habitations is 89,39,968. Rural population in habitations in the slab 'below 500' constitutes 6.39% of the total rural population. Thus, majority of the population is staying in larger habitations only. The population not served by any primary section within a distance of 2 kilometres is 0.46% only. As a matter of fact 98.24% of the rural population has a primary section either within the habitation of the residence or within a distance of 1 kilometre. Thus, provision of schooling facilities at primary stage has almost reached the saturation point. There are only 50 habitations which have a population of 300 or more and are not served by any primary section within a distance of 2 kilometres. If schools are provided in these 50 habitations, some of the smaller habitations which are unserved yet will also be covered by these schools and the State would be almost free from the need of any further provision of schooling facilities at the primary stage.

Himachal Pradesh: This state has an abundance of small sized habitations. Out of a total of 31,052 rural habitations, 30,157 (97.12%) are in the slab 'below 500'. The number of habitations in the slab 'below 300' is 28,695 which constitutes 92.41% of the total number of rural habitations. Thus, the problem of provision of schooling facilities is more acute in the State because of small sized habitations. At the time of the Third Survey, 16.69% of the rural population residing in 8,570 habitations was not served by any primary section within a distance of 2 kilometres, 175 habitations in the slab '300 or more' do not have primary sections within a walking distance of 2 kilometres and 48 out of these are in the population slab of 500 or more. From the criterion of walking distance of 1 kilometre only 65.37% of the population is served by primary sections. Thus, the State faces an uphill task of providing provision of schooling facilities at the primary stage.

Jammu and Kashmir: There are 13,732 rural habitations with the total population of 40,62,494. This State also has a problem of small sized habitations. 83.80%of these habitations are in the slab 'below 500'. The number of habitations in the slab 'less than 300' is 9,388 which constitute 68.36% of the rural habitations. Population wise 49.66% of the rural inhabitants are in the habitations of size less than 500. 29.62% of the rural population is residing in habitations in the slab 'below 300'. At the time of the First Survey, 71.18% of the population was served by primary sections and this figure increased to 94.58% at the time of the Second Survey. In the present survey 93.36% of the rural population is served by primary sections within a distance of 2 kilometres. On the criterion of 1 kilometre only 85.20% of rural population is served by primary sections. The total number of rural habitations not served by primary sections within a distance of 2 kilometres is 2,085 and out of these 2,029 (97.31%) are in the population slab 'less than 500'.

Karnataka: There are 40,392 rural habitations with a population of 2,37,12,267. Of these, 62.34% are in the slab 'below 500'. At the time of the First Survey, that is, 31st March, 1957, 91.75% of the population in this state was served by primary sections. On 31st December, 1965, that is, at the time of the Second Survey, 97.30% of the population was served by primary sections. In the present survey 97.5% of the population is served by primary sections either within the habitation of residence or within a distance of 2 kilometres. The number of habitations that are not served by primary sections at present is 2,778 of which 2,684 (96.62%) are in the slab 'below 500'. There are 2,526 habitations which are not served at the moment by any primary section and these belong to the slab 'below 300'. Bulk of the habitations which are not served by any school are in this population slab.

Kerala: There are 6,315 rural habitations with a population of 1,92,01,349. Only 8.44% of these habitations are in the slab 'below 500'. At the time of the Second Survey 10,124 rural habitations had been identified and there is a fall in the number of rural habitations in this State. The one peculiarity of the State is that it does not have many habitations of small size. At the time of the First Survey 90.49% of the population was served by primary sections and this figure rose to 92.57% at the time of the Second Survey. At present 97.30% of the population is served by primary sections within a distance of 2 kilometres. There are only 501 habitation which do not have a school within a distance of 2 kilometres. With the distance criterion of 1 kilometre the population served by primary sections is 92.60%. The peculiarity of the State is that the habitations which are not served by primary sections tend to be of larger size. Out of 501 habitations, which are not served at the moment, only 189 belong to the population slab 'below 500' and the remaining ones are in the higher slab of population. There are four habitations in the population slab '5,000 and above', 69 in the slabs '2,000 to 4,999', 107 in the slab '1,000 to 1,999' and 132 in the slab '500 to 999'— which are not served by any school within a distance of 2 kilometres. If these habitations get schools, the problem of smaller habitations also will be solved to some extent.

Madhya Pradesh: There are 1,07,903 habitations in the State with a population of 3,75,89,151. Of these, 70.22% are in the population slab 'below 500' and these account for 39.13% of the rural population. In terms of area Madhya Pradesh is the largest state in India and has a high proportion of small-sized habitations. On 31 March, 1957, 67.78% of the population was served by primary sections located within a walking distance of 1 mile. At the time of the Second Survey 87.88% of the population was served by primary sections. With the changed distance criterion of 2 kilometres 93.3% of the population is served by primary sections. Considering the distance criterion of 1 kilometre only 85.8% of the population is served by existing primary sections. Of the 17,753 habitations which are not served by any school within a distance of 2 kilometres, 17,636 (99.34%) are in the slab 'below 500'. Thus, it is a problem of provision of schooling facilities in small-sized habitations which poses a problem to the State. The number of habitations in the slab 'below 300' which are not served by primary sections within a distance of 2 kilometres is 15,371. These habitations may need some extra effort for the education of the children residing in them.

Maharashtra: There are 65,650 rural habitations with a population of 3,67,42,533. In the Second Survey 65,195 rural habitations had been identified. Of these 65,650 habitations, 43,678 (66.53%) belong to the population slab 'below 500' and these account for 24.13% of the rural population. At the time of the First Survey in the erstwhile State of Bombay 91.58% of the population was served by primary sections within a walking distance of 1 mile. This figure rose to 97.47% at the time of the Second Survey. At present 98.76% of the population is served by primary sections within a distance of 2 kilometres and 95.94% is served by a primary section within a distance of 1 kilometre. In all there are 3,611 habitations, which are not served by any primary section with a distance of 2 kilometres and of these 3,575 (99.00%) are in the slab 'below 500'. Thus, it is essentially a problem of provision of schooling facilities in these smaller habitations in the state and for this, methods other than formal schooling may have to be adopted.

Manipur: At the time of the First Survey 24.88% of the population was served by primary sections within a distance of 1 mile. In 1965, at the time of the Second Survey this percentage rose to 94.50. At present 96.57% of the population is served by primary sections within a distance of 2 kilometres and 95.98% is served by primary sections within a distance of 1 kilometre. The total number of rural habitations in the State is 2,345 with a population of 9,67,227. Of these, 1,747 (74.49%) are in the population slab 'below 500'. The total number of habitations which are not served by any primary section within a distance of 2 kilometres is 272 of which 269 are in the population slab 'below 500'. There are only 36 habitations with a population of 'more than 300' which do not have a school within a distance of 2 kilometres.

Meghalaya: For Meghalaya comparable data for the First and Second Survey are not available because the State was earlier a part of the erstwhile State of Assam. As such, comparisons with earlier figures are not possible. There are 4,841 rural habitations with a population of 9,80,030 of which 4,515 (93.27%) are in the population slab 'below 500'. 87.55% of the population is served by primary sections within a distance of 2 kilometres. 83.66% of the population is served by primary sections within a distance of 1 kilometre. In all, there are 1,235 habitations which do not have a primary section within a walking distance of 2 kilometres and of these, 1,228 are in the slab 'below 500'. Habitations which do not have a primary section within a distance of 2 kilometres and are having a population of 'more than 300' are 47 in number. Thus, the problem is only of provision of educational facilities for small habitations.

Nagaland: There are 1,431 rural habitations in Nagaland with a population of 5,14,850. Of these, 1,149 are in the population slab 'below 500' and these constitute 80.29% of the total number of habitations. 48.13% of the population is staying in these small-sized habitations. At present 98.98% of the population is served by primary sections or schools within a distance of 2 kilometres. On the criterion of 1 kilometre distance 96.25% of the population is served by primary sections/schools. There are only 30 habitations which are not served by any school within a distance of 2 kilometres and of these, 28 are in the population slab 'below 500'. Thus, the problem of provision of schcoling facilities is not a significant one in this state.

Orissa: There are 64,194 rural habitations with a population of 2,14,15,288. At the time of the Second Survey the number of rural habitations identified was 68,369. 51,240 (79.82%) are in the population slab 'below 500' thus, the state has a large number of small habitations. At the time of the First Survey, that is on 31 March, 1957, 87.41% of the population was served by primary sections within a distance of 1 mile. On 31st December, 1965, this figure rose to 91.61%. At present 95.81% of the population is served by primary sections located in the habitation of residence or within a distance of 2 kilometres. On the criterion of 1 kilometre distance 90.54% of the population is served by existing primary sections. The number of habitations which are not served by any primary section within a distance of 2 kilometres is 8,425 and of these, 8,255 (97.98%) are in the population slab 'below 500'. Thus, a large number of habitation which are not served by primary section are small sized ones. The total number of habitations with a population of '300 or more' are 504 in number which are not served by any primary sections. If a provision is made for schooling facilities in these habitations, some additional habitations would also be covered by these schools. Even after this about 7,000 to 7,500 habitations would remain without educational facilities which is a serious problem.

Punjab: The new State of Punjab came into being after data collection for the Second Survey. This will not permit comparisons with the data for the erstwhile Punjab State which included Haryana and parts of the territory that have been transferred to Himachal Pradesh. At present there are 13,156 habitations with a population of 1,10,29,986. Of these, 5,822 (44.25%) are in the slab 'below 500'. There are only 207 habitations which are not served by any primary section within a distance of 2 kilometres and the population in these habitations is only 0.25% of the total rural population. Thus, the problem in the State is not that of provision of additional facilities but is more of additional enrolment.

Rajasthan: There are 40,074 rural habitations with a population of 2,29,10,268. Of these, 23,813 (59.42%) are in the slab 'below 500' and these account for 21.76% of the rural habitations. The total number of habitations identified in the Second Survey was 50,533. On 31st March, 1957, 66.40% of the population was served by primary sections within a distance of 1 mile. At the time of the Second Survey, that is, 31.12.1965 this figure rose to 89.86%. At present 91.38% of the population is served by primary sections within a distance of 2 kilometres. The percentage of population served within a distance of 1 kilometre is 82.91. There are 7,046 habitations which are not served by any primary section within a distance of 2 kilometres. Of these, 5,893 (83.64%) are in the slab 'below 500'. There are quite a few habitations with large population which do not have educational facilities within a distance of 2 kilometres. For example, there are 16 habitations in the slab '5000 or more', 56 in the slab '2000 to 4999', 137 in the slab '1000 to 1999' and 944 in the slab '500 to 999'. These habitations, particularly, the ones in the first two slabs, need a special enquiry as to why these have been left without provision of educational facilities. Rajasthan has to open quite a number of schools at primary stage in order to cater to its population.

Tamil Nadu: There are 43,355 rural habitations in the State having a population of 2,86,81,229. Of these, 24,790 (57.18%) are in the slab 'below 500' accounting for 20.64% of the population. At the time of the First Survey, that is, 31st March, 1957, 94.65% of the population was served by primary sections within a distance of 1 mile. The Second Survey figure was 97.23%. At present 99.35% of the population is served by primary sections within a distance of 2 kilometres. With the criterion as 1 kilometre 93.10% of the population is served by primary sections. In all 1,562 habitations are not served by any primary section within a distance of 2 kilometres. And all these habitations belong to the group 'below 300'.

Tripura: There are 6,050 rural habitations in Tripura with a population of 15,54,446. Of these, 5,244 (86.68%) are in the slab 'below 500'. And these account for 47.48% of the population. On 31st March, 1957, 84.44% of the population was served by primary sections. On 31.12.1965 this percentage rose to 88. At present 94.76% of the population is served by primary sections within a distance of 2 kilometres. Percentage of population served within a distance of 1 kilometre is 82.35.825 habitations are not served by any primary section within a distance of 2 kilometres and out of these, 821 are in the slab 'below 500'. There are only 31 habitations with a population of '300 or more' which are not served by any primary section within a distance of 2 kilometres. Thus, the problem of provision of further facilities is confined to smaller habitations.

Uttar Pradesh: There are 2,37,321 rural habitations with a population of 7,98,62,847. Of these, 1,93,065 (81.35%) are in the slab 'below 500' and these account for 43.76% of the rural population. Thus, it is seen that a very large number of habitations are small-sized. On 31.3.1957, 71.18% of the population was served by primary sections within a distance of 1 mile. On 31.12.1965 this percentage rose to 94.58. At present 94.90% of the population is served by primary sections within a distance of 2 kilometres. Thus, the progress during the period intervening the Second and the Third Surveys is negligible considering that the criteria in the Third Survey is also changed. The population served by primary sections within a distance of 1 kilometre is 81.50% only. There are 19,764 habitations which are not served by any primary section within a distance of 2 kilometres and of these, 18,242 (92.30%) are in the slab 'below 500'. 4,149 habitations with a population of 300 or more each are not served by any primary section within a distance of 2 kilometres. Thus, the State has to put in more effort for opening new schools for provision of schooling facilities at primary stage.

West Bengal: There are 52,270 rural habitations with a population of 3,57,75,402. Of these, 28,473 (54.47%) are in the slab 'below 500' and account for 18.51% of the population. The First All India Educational Survey was not conducted by West Bengal. At the time of the Second Survey 67,703 rural habitations were identified. At that time 97.55% of the rural population was served by primary sections within a distance of 1 mile and the State occupied the second highest figure regarding this percentage and was next only to Gujarat. At present 98.74% of the population is served by primary sections within a distance of 2 kilometres. The population served within a distance of 1 kilometre is 94.23%. In all 1,868 habitations are not served by any primary section within a distance of 2 kilometres and of these, 1,707 (91.38%) are in the slab 'below 500'. There are 557 habitations with the population of 300 or more each which have no primary section within a distance of 2 kilometres. If these habitations are provided with primary schools, some more will be covered by these schools and the problem of provision of schooling facilities at this stage will be further solved.

Union Territories: There are 9 Union Territories in all of which Delhi has been treated as completely urban. Of the remaining 8, Chandigarh, Lakshadweep and Pondicherry are the 3 territories where 100% of the rural population is served by primary sections within a distance of 2 kilometres. In Mizoram 99.76% of the population has schooling facilities within the habitation of residence. There is one habitation with the population of 731 (0.24%) which does not have a primary section within a distance of 2 kilometres. If a school is provided there, this territory will also be in the category of the other three mentioned earlier.

In Goa, Daman & Diu 98.4% of the population is served by primary sections within a distance of 2 kilometres. Thus, there also the problem of provision of schooling facility is not acute.

Dadar and Nagar Haveli has 13.60% of its population which is not served by primary sections within a distance of 2 kilometres. The number of habitations in this category is 79.

Andaman & Nicobar Islands have 17.96% of the population not served by any primary section within a distance of 2 kilometres.

Arunachal Pradesh is the only territory where the proportion of population not served by any primary section within a distance of 2 kilometres is very high, that is, 50.97%. This particular area has a difficult terrain which hinders educational growth.

Villages, Scheduled Tribe Population and Primary Schools

Villages having Scheduled Tribe population up to 15% number 4,20,042 and of these 58.57% have independent primary schools. This percentage falls in the categories where the Scheduled Tribe population is from 16 to 60 percent. It rises again for the two categories where the proportion is 61 to 75 per cent and 76 to 90 percent. In the last category where the Scheduled Tribe population is more than 90%, the proportion of villages having primary schools falls to 35.71% again.

Table 1: Proportion of Scheduled Tribe Population in Villages and Existence of Independent Primary Schools

Proportion (in percentage) of Scheduled Tribes in Villages	*Total No. of Villages*	*Villages having Primary Schools*	
		Number	*Col. (3) as % of Col. (2)*
Up to 15	4,20,042	2,46,021	58.57
16-30	43,488	19,574	45.01
31-45	23,007	10,780	46.86
46-60	18,743	8,524	45.48
61-75	11,689	6,354	54.36
76-90	12,619	6,899	53.67
More than 90	41,632	14,867	35.71
Total	5,71,220	3,13,019	54.80

Enrolment of Scheduled Tribes

In all there are 35,64,810 students belonging to Scheduled Tribes in class I to V. This amounts to 5.81% of the total enrolment in these classes. In rural areas this percentage rises to 6.98% of the total enrolment, but in urban areas this is only 1.96%. That is quite understandable because majority of the Scheduled Tribe population is in rural areas. The total enrolment of Scheduled Tribes in rural areas is 32,87,965 and of these 22,60,250 are boys and 10,27,715 are girls. For urban areas the total enrolment of Scheduled Tribes is 2,76,845 of which 1,62,549 are boys and 1,14,296 are girls. For all areas put together there are 24,22,799 boys and 11,42,011 girls belonging to Scheduled Tribes who are studying in classes I to V.

Table 2: Scheduled Tribe Students in Classes I-V

Area	*Boys*	*Girls*	*Total*	*Col.4 as % of Total Enrolment*
Rural				
Class I	10,26,356	5,46,432	15,72,788	9.04
Class II	5,39,125	2,28,851	7,67,976	7.03
Class III	3,45,134	1,26,577	4,71,711	5.77
Class IV	2,00,546	73,238	2,73,784	4.50
Class V	1,49,089	52,617	2,01,706	4.36
Total	22,60,250	10,27,715	32,87,965	6.98
Urban				
Class I	53,408	38,879	92,287	2.30
Class II	35,413	25,004	60,417	1.98
Class III	29,393	20,186	49,579	1.85
Class IV	24,141	16,519	40,660	1.75
Class V	20,194	13,708	33,902	1.63
Total	1,62,549	1,14,296	2,76,845	1.96
Rural & Urban				
Class I	10,79,764	5,85,311	16,65,075	7.78
Class II	5,74,538	2,53,855	8,28,393	5.96
Class III	3,74,527	1,46,763	5,21,290	4.80
Class IV	2,24,687	89,757	3,14,444	3.74
Class V	1,69,283	66,325	2,35,608	3.51
Total	24,22,799	11,42,011	35,64,810	5.81

NATIONAL POLICY FOR CHILDREN, 1974*

The Government of India enunciated the National Policy for Children on August 22, 1974 and adopted by the Parliament on August 26, 1974.

Resolution

'The nation's children are a supremely important asset. Their nurture and solicitude are our responsibility. Children's programme should find a prominent part in our national plans for the development of human resources, so that our children grow up to become robust citizens,

* Ministry of Education and Social Welfare, Government of India, New Delhi, 1975.

physically fit, mentally alert and morally healthy, endowed with the skills and motivations needed by society. Equal opportunities for development to all children during the period of growth should be our aim, for this would serve our larger purpose of reducing inequality and ensuring social justice.

Goals: The needs of children and our duties towards them have been expressed in the Constitution. The Resolution on a National Policy on Education, which has been adopted by Parliament, gives direction to state policy on the educational needs of children. We are also party to the U.N. Declaration of the Rights of the Child. The goals set out in these documents can reasonably be achieved by judicious and efficient use of the available national resources. Keeping in view these goals, the Government of India adopts this resolution on the National Policy for Children.

Policy and measures: It shall be the policy of the State to provide adequate services to children, both before and after birth and through the period of growth, to ensure their full physical, mental and social development. The State shall progressively increase the scope of such services so that within a reasonable time, all children in the country enjoy optimum condition for their balanced growth. In particular, the following measures shall be adopted towards the achievement of these objectives:

(i) All children shall be covered by a comprehensive health programme.

(ii) Programmes shall be implemented to provide nutrition services with the object of removing deficiencies in the diet of children.

(iii) Programmes will be undertaken for the general improvement of the health and for the care, nutrition and nutrition education of expectant and nursing mothers.

(iv) The State shall take steps to provide free and compulsory education for all children upto the age of 14 for which a time-bound programme will be drawn up consistent with the availability of resources. Special efforts will be made to reduce the prevailing wastage and stagnation in schools, particularly in the case of girls and children of the weaker sections of society. The programme of informal education for pre-school children from such sections will also be taken up.

(v) Children who are not able to take full advantage of formal school education shall be provided other forms of education suited to other requirements.

(vi) Physical education, games, sports and other types of recreational as well as cultural and scientific activities shall be promoted in schools, community centres and such other institutions.

(vii) To ensure equality of opportunity, special assistance shall be provided to all children belonging to the weaker sections of the society, such as children belonging to the Scheduled Castes and

Scheduled Tribes and those belonging to the economically weaker sections, both in urban and rural areas.

(viii) Children who are socially handicapped, who have become delinquent or have been forced to take to begging or are otherwise in distress, shall be provided facilities for education, training and rehabilitation and will be helped to become useful citizens.

(ix) Children shall be protected against neglect, cruelty and exploitation.

(x) No child under 14 years shall be permitted to be engaged in any hazardous occupation or be made to undertake heavy work.

(xi) Facilities shall be provided for special treatment, education, rehabilitation and care of children who are physically handicapped, emotionally disturbed or mentally retarded.

(xii) Children shall be given priority for protection and relief in times of distress of natural calamity.

(xiii) Special programmes shall be formulated to spot, encourage and assist gifted children, particularly those belonging to the weaker sections of society.

(xiv) Existing laws should be amended so that in all legal disputes, whether between parents or institutions, the interests of children are given paramount consideration.

(xv) In organising services for children, efforts would be directed to strengthen family ties so that full potentialities of growth of children are realised within the normal family, neighbourhood and community environment.

Priority in programme formation: In formulating programmes in different sectors, priority shall be given to programmes relating to:

(a) Preventive and promotive aspects of child health.

(b) Nutrition for infants and children in the pre-school age along with nutrition for nursing and expectant mothers.

(c) Maintenance, education and training of orphan and destitute children.

(d) Creches and other facilities for the care of children working or ailing mothers; and

(e) Care, education, training and rehabilitation of handicapped children.

ISHWARBHAI PATEL REVIEW COMMITTEE, 1977

With the formation of the Janata Government in place of Congress Government at the Centre, the Education Minister appointed the Review Committee under the Chairmanship of Dr. Ishwarbhai Patel, Vice Chancellor, Gujarat University to review the syllabus and textbooks prepared by the NCERT for 10+2 system of School Education.

Recommendations

1. *Introduction of Socially Useful Productive Work*: Socially Useful Productive Work may be defined as purposive, meaningful, manual work resulting in either goods or services which are useful to society.

The aim of this curricular area is to provide children with opportunities of participating in social and economic activities inside and outside the classroom, enabling them to understand scientific principles and processes involved in different types of work and in the setting in which they are found in the physical and social environment.

We also prefer the term socially useful productive work to that of work experience, as it is not only more expressive but it focuses attention on the practical aspect of this area of education.

2. *Increased Allocation of Time*: In order to implement the scheme of socially useful productive work we recommend that the time allocation to it should be as under:

(i) In Classes I to IV/V—20 per cent.
(ii) In Classes V/VI to VII/VIII—six hours a week out of a total of 32 hours.
(iii) In Classes VIII/IX to X—six hours a week out of a total of 32 hours.

Although we have stressed the need for flexibility, we wish to make it clear that in this programme of socially useful productive work, if flexibility means a reduction in the allotment of time to work education, then we are against flexibility in this area.

We recommend that if flexibility is to be exercised then it must be to increase the time for socially useful productive work and community science. One way of achieving this is by *implementing such programmes not only during school hours, but also outside school hours and during school holidays and vacations.*

3. *Principles of Basic Education*: The principles of Basic Education as evolved by Mahatma Gandhi and accepted in the Kothari Commission Report with the stress on work education need to find a central place in the educational system. This is the very first step in giving the right direction to our present system of education.

4. *No Home Work*: Home work should banned for classes I to IV/V.

DRAFT NATIONAL POLICY ON EDUCATION, 1979*

The Janata Government decided to revamp the system of education in the country. Accordingly the Government prepared a Draft National Policy on Education in 1979.

* National Council of Educational Research and Training, New Delhi.

Dr. P.C. Chunder, Education Minister, in his Address at Nagpur University in 1977, *inter alia* stated that "...The Janata Party is committed to review all the policies of the earlier Government. I have received hundreds of representations on the subject... What is equally important, the National Policy Resolution itself provides for a quinquennial review which is long overdue. I therefore, feel that it is our duty to review the policy comprehensively and objectively and to make such modifications as therein are justified".

In 1979, Congress Government which came to power again resolved to promote the development of education according to The Government of India Resolution National Policy of Education declared in 1968.

NATIONAL PLAN OF ACTION FOR INTERNATIONAL YEAR OF THE CHILD, 1979*

Education

3.1 The objective of providing free and compulsory education to all children until they complete the age of 14 years as envisaged in the Constitution of India has not been achieved so far. An alarming feature of the present system is the large proportion of drop-outs; out of every 100 children that enter class I, only about 40 complete class V and about 25 complete class VIII.

3.2 As regards pre-school education, the State has not so far assumed responsibility. It is estimated that approximately 4.5 million children are enrolled in some form of pre-schools.[1] The efforts made in regard to pre-school education are sporadic and mostly made by voluntary agencies. However, all these facilities for pre-school education are too inadequate looking to the size of child population. Moreover, parents' perception of the importance of pre-school is also very poor. According to one study, reasons given by parents for sending children to Balwadis were: benefits accruing from school-going habits; keeping the child active and free from mischief; and his being in the company of other children.[2] From certain other studies, evidence is available to show that a majority of parents perceive the pre-school as a place of formal learning supposed to have priority over experiences and socio-emotive relations among children. There are parents who even view the pre-school as an employment agency for the Balsevika. Parents who do not send their children to pre-schools feel that it is an extravagance and that children are more needed in homes and fields.

---

* Department of Social Welfare, Minister of Education and Social Welfare, Government of India, New Delhi, 1978.

Note: Para numbers refer to para numbers of the document.

3.3 Thus, if we look at the overall situation, child education presents a very dismal picture. There is, therefore, an obvious need to raise the status of child education in our country and make the parents aware of the importance of education in the proper development of their children.

3.4 The action programmes as enumerated below if taken up during IYC, will go a long way to promote educational status of children in the country.

Establishment of Pre-Primary and Elementary Schools

3.4.1 During 1978 and 1979, plans for the setting up of pre-primary, primary and middle schools for all children within easy walking distance from their homes should be prepared so that in all uncovered rural, tribal and backward areas, the provision of schools is available by 1980-81 in the context of Government's programme of universalising elementary education.

Action: Department of Education, All State Departments of Education and Local Bodies.

Free Education

3.4.2 From 1979, free education should be provided at least upto class VIII for all children. Efforts may also be made to provide free education upto secondary stage for children of the weaker sections and girls.

Action: Department of Education and State Departments of Education.

Free Education for Weaker Sections

3.4.3 Pre-school education should be made universally available to children of weaker sections of society and those belonging to poverty groups.

Those who did not attend a regular pre-school, should be provided a six-week pre-school education so as to facilitate their adjustment to primary schooling.

Action: Ministry of Education and Social Welfare, State Departments of Education, Directorates of Tribal Welfare, State Harijan Welfare, Social Welfare and Rural Development Departments and Voluntary Agencies.

Improvement in Elementary Education

3.4.4 Efforts should be made to improve the quality of primary education by providing a cheerful atmosphere in the school, by better training of teachers, provision of teaching aids and material as well as facilities for organised games and sports. The pupil-teacher ratio should not be higher than 40 to 1 in primary schools.

Local Panchayats should be encouraged to contribute towards the improvement of primary education in their respective areas.

Appropriate emphasis should be placed on moral and physical education.

Action: Union Ministry of Education and Social Welfare, State Departments of Education and Local Bodies.

3.4.5 Children who are out of the elementary school system including drop-outs and those who cannot attend formal schools due to socio-economic reasons, should be identified and given non-formal elementary education.

Action: Ministry of Education and Social Welfare, State Departments of Education, NCERT, Directorate of Non-formal Education and Voluntary Organisations.

3.4.6 Present school hours at some places are causing under-nourishment in children as they often rush to schools with inadequate food and under intense psychological stress. The school hours should be adjusted in a manner that their food intake is not adversely affected.

Action: State Education Departments concerned.

Incentive for Elementary Schooling

3.4.7 To reduce drop-out rates in primary and middle schools and to improve enrolment of children, particularly among the weaker sections of the community, incentives like school lunch programme, free uniforms and stationery, free medical aid and attendance scholarships should be provided.

Action: State Education Departments and Local Bodies.

Involvement of Local Bodies

3.4.8 Local bodies like Panchayats, Zila Parishads and Municipal Councils should be urged to aid, assist and monitor primary and pre-primary education. The model of 'Kelwani Mandals' in rural Gujarat could be emulated.

Action: State Governments and Local Bodies.

Mobile Schools

3.4.9 In order to offer pre-school and elementary education to unreached children of tribes, migrant labour, construction workers in urban areas and those in sparsely populated tribal areas and the like, voluntary agencies should be encouraged to experiment with some kind of mobile pre and elementary schools on the lines of mobile creches.

Action: CSWB, Voluntary Agencies, State Departments of Education and Social Welfare.

Children's Literature

3.4.10 Massive efforts should be mounted by State Education and Social Welfare Directorates, National Book Trust, Children's Book Trust and Voluntary Agencies to publish attractive, cheap and educative literature for children in all regional languages of India. Efforts should also be made to produce, collect, display and distribute indigenous children's toys and play material.

Action: Department of Education, State Governments, National Book Trust, Children's Book Trust, Voluntary Agencies.

Education of Handicapped Children

3.4.13 Where possible, attempts should be made to enrol handicapped children in pre and primary schools along with normal children. For this purpose selected teachers, one from each school, should be trained in educational problems of different types of handicap such as blind, deaf and orthopaedically handicapped.

Action: Department of Social Welfare, State Departments of Education and Social Welfare, and Voluntary Agencies.

REVISED 20-POINT PROGRAMME, 1982

20-Point Programme initiated in 1975 by Mrs. Indira Gandhi was revised and announced in 1982. The programme devotes point No. 16 to Education.

Point No. 16...Spread universal elementary education for the age-group 6-14 with special emphasis on girls and simultaneously involve students and voluntary agencies in programmes for the removal of adult illiteracy.

Elementary Education: Article 45 of the Constitution promises free and compulsory education for all children in the age group 6-14 years by 1960. We have not been able to fulfill this long standing objective despite concerted efforts. By 1990 all the 16.3 crore children estimated in the age-group 6-14 will have to be enrolled in elementary schools, either in the formal or non-formal system of education. At present 9.3 crore children are attending schools. In the next 10 years, 7 crore additional children will have to be brought to schools. This will mostly benefit the socially and economically backward classes and girls. Out of seven crore children who will be enrolled during the next ten years, 2.5 crores will be boys and 4.5 crores girls. The emphasis will be on enrolling children of Scheduled Castes, Scheduled Tribes and landless labour, especially girls. Appropriate incentives such as free books and stationery, uniforms, attendance, scholarships, etc. will be given to the children of the weaker sections, particularly girls. Against the present enrolment of 125 lakh Scheduled Caste children in classes I-VIII at present to 110 lakhs in 1990. As the children of the weaker sections cannot attend full time formal schools, emphasis will be given to opening of non-formal educational centres.

The quality of education at the elementary stage will be improved. Schools will have to be provided with suitable buildings and adequate equipment. Curriculum will have to be revised to suit local environment. Elementary education has been included as an integral component of the

Minimum Needs Programme and its success will depend on its linkages with several development activities.

The Programme will have to be stepped up in the districts which have the largest proportion of non-enrolled children.

Point No. 17...Expand the public distribution system through more fair price shops including mobile shops in far-flung areas, shops to cater to industrial workers, student hostels and make available to students text-books and exercise books on a priority basis.

The Ministry of Education at present allots paper to the States for the printing of text-books and manufacture of exercise books. The supply of paper to the States will be increased keeping in view the increase in the enrolment in future and the present practice of exercise books at controlled prices will be continued. The following steps will be taken to produce text-books at reduced costs:

(i) Frequent changes in the text-books will be avoided and size of the text-books will be reduced by removing repetitions.

(ii) The orders for printing of text-books will be placed in time to avoid delay in the publication of text-books.

(iii) The number of book banks in schools and colleges will be increased. This ensures free supply of books to the students at the minimum cost to the State.

(iv) Exercise books and text-books will be distributed through school cooperatives. This will save the commissions paid at present to middleman and this will lower the cost of books and stationary to that extent.

CONFERENCE OF EDUCATION SECRETARIES, JANUARY, 1983

A conference of Education Secretaries of all States and UTs was held on 5-6 January, 1983 for the implementation of Point 16 of the New 20-Point Programme.

1. *Universalisation of Elementary Education*

1.1 Since the 1990 date line has to be adhered to, the pace of progress has to be more than doubled in the remaining years. It has also to be recognised in this context that the coverage henceforth will be of difficult target groups who have for various reasons not been able to avail of the facilities in the formal system. There is, therefore, no room for complacency.

1.2. With reference to the special attention for education of girls/women, the conference recommended appropriate inter-sectoral linkages between such programmes (ICDS, Nutrition, health care facilities for children) so as to make optimal use of available services. The Conference recommended in particular that health care of children in schools should get increasing attention and that more schools should be covered under schools health programmes.

1.3. For strengthening the base, States/UTs will have to take various quantitative and qualitative steps. These will include in particular the following:

(a) universal provision of schooling facilities giving preferential coverage to about 40500 habitations which do not have a primary school within 1 km distance.

(b) conversion of all single teacher schools into two-teacher schools.

(c) appointment of additional teachers to cope with additional enrolments.

(d) provision of adequate administrative staff support.

3. *Monitoring and Evaluation*

3.1 The Conference observed that the arrangement for monitoring and evaluation of the two programmes—Universalisation of Elementary Education and Adult Education—was both inadequate and unsatisfactory. Accordingly, it stressed the need for establishment of a suitable mechanism for the purpose at the block, district and State levels. These mechanisms should provide for a regular and timely flow of information and suitable remedial/corrective measures to be initiated on a continuing basis.

4. *Interlinking of Elementary (Both Formal and Non-Formal) and Adult Education with Rural Development, Social Forestry, Handicrafts and Handlooms.*

4.1 The Conference took note of the fact that educational development could not be achieved in isolation without taking into cognizance of the factors determining the life of the child, comprising his first primary physical needs of nutrition immunisation and mother's care as also the sustenance he draws from the natural environment comprising flora, fauna, agricultural crops, animal life and the socio-cultural life-style of the community including varied traditional skills, festivals etc. Educational strategy should be evolved in conjunction with other development sectors which are focusing attention on child and family welfare, environment, social-forestry, agriculture, handicrafts, small-scale industry. It was, therefore, essential for the Departments of Education in the States to keep in touch and structurally inter-link their programmes with other agencies and programmes such as the ICDS, the RIDP, etc. This would ensure an integration so necessary for ensuring organic growth of the student.

It was recommended that educational institutions should draw upon and associate local craftsmen, artists, weavers, potters, blacksmiths and others for training children. There should be no insistence on such skilled workers to be literate.

The Conference was of the view that such an integrated view would help in promoting cohesiveness in society rather than alienating the educated from the community. Also an added advantage would be the availability of additional resources for elementary and adult education from the developmental sector such as National Rural Employment Programme, Social Forestry Programme and others.

5. *Promotion of Population Education*

Concern was also expressed over the need of urgently introducing population education for out-of-school children and in the Adult Education Programme...

6. *Introduction of Ideas of 'Values' of Students*

It stressed that equal attention should be given to value orientation in education of out-of-school children also... .

CENTRAL ADVISORY BOARD OF EDUCATION, 39TH SESSION, JUNE 6-7, 1983

Relevant Resolutions

I. *Spread of universal elementary education for the age-group 6-14*

Consistently with this focus on difficult target groups and/or backward areas, there is need for micro-level planning. For each of the areas/groups so selected for special attention, specific programmes/projects will have to be formulated with reference to their needs, resources, and constraints.

Among the target groups, education of girls requires special attention.

Special attention will simultaneously have to be given to improve the quality and efficiency of education. This will require increased attention to training of teachers, upgradation of syllabi, development of textual materials, provision of teaching aids and equipment and suitable physical facilities.

In order, however, to ensure that systematic teaching and learning take place, the implementation of a liberal policy of promotion will require simultaneously adoption of a non-graded system as well as system of continuous assessment of attainments.

The inadequacy of the formal system to meet the educational needs of those children who, for various reasons, are unable to enrol in the formal system or drop out of it prematurely, was stressed. In non-formal education it is necessary to constantly experiment with different approaches and consequently develop a variety of models.

Note: Sub-head numbers refer to sub-head numbers of the Document.

Non-formal education, while providing the requisite literacy and numeracy, should also attempt at inculcating among the students skills which are useful in the production processes of the community.

Educational strategy should be evolved in conjunction with other development sectors which are focussing attention on child health and family welfare, environment, social forestry, agriculture, handicrafts, and small scale industry. It is, therefore, essential for the Departments of Education in the States to keep in close touch with and structurally interlink their programmes with other agencies and programmes such as the ICDS and the IRDP, etc. This would ensure an integration so necessary for ensuring organic growth of the students. Recognising the need to assist States, which are at varying levels of development, the Board reiterates the following recommendation made in its 37th Session:

"The magnitude of the unfinished task in the provision of universal elementary education, both quantitative and qualitative, varies largely from State to State... A new programme of Central assistance for provision of universal elementary education should be evolved in consultation with the States under which assistance would be made available to a State on the basis of (a) its needs, (b) its ability and (c) its effort".

V. *Women's education*: Special efforts are required for accelerating the pace of education of girls/women.

VI. *Value-orientation in education*: In the context of erosion of values that is taking place and the fissiparous tendencies that have become quite marked in recent years, the Board urges the need for value orientation in education at all levels.

XVI. *A new design of education*: It recommends the evolution of a new design of education for the future which will be relevant and meaningful to the child and the adult.

XVII. *Inter-linking of education and culture with development programmes*: It invites special attention to the recommendations relating to the need for inter-linking elementary, both formal and non-formal and adult education with programme of rural development, social forestry, handicrafts and handlooms.

The Board recommends strongly that skilled artists, craftsmen and other practitioners of traditional skills and crafts be utilised for the school system.

NATIONAL COMMISSION ON TEACHERS-I
CHATTOPADHAYA COMMISSION, 1983-85

Recognising the importance of teachers in developing the nation's human resources, the Government appointed two National Commissions on Teachers, one for the school stage and another for higher education, including technical education in February 1983. The reports submitted in March 1985, received very little attention except the recommendations regarding pay scales of teachers as suggested by the National Commission on Teachers.

Relevant Recommendations

Financial Estimates

10.55 Of the several recommendations that we have made...the ones with large financial implications are the following:

(1) Universalisation of Elementary Education (UEE)

I. *Universalisation of Elementary Education*

10.56 The estimates of additional enrolments to be reached by 1990 through formal and non-formal channels of elementary education have been provided (Table 1).

10.57 We suggest that the cost estimates of the programme be worked out for four levels of projections, namely:

(a) 100 per cent level;
(b) High level (aimed at achieving 75% of the target);
(c) Medium Level (50% of the target); and
(d) Low Level (25%)

Table 1: Estimates of Additional Enrolment to be Reached by 1990 through Formal and Non-Formal Channels of Elementary Education

(in lakhs)

	Enrolment through Formal Channels	*Enrolment through Non-formal Channels*	*Total*
Primary	233.00	78.00	311.00
Middle	288.00	32.00	320.00
Total	521.00	110.00	631.00

NCERT ON CURRICULUM LOAD, 1983-85*

Curriculum Load at the School Level: A Quick Appraisal

The Ishwar Bhai Patel Committee (1977). suggested deletion of some topics from the syllabus. The issue was discussed in various forums even after the implementation of the recommendations of the Patel Committee. NCERT set up a Working Group in 1983 to make a quick appraisal of the curriculum load. The Director of NCERT, also the Chairman of this Working Group submitted the report, which was deliberated by eminent educationists and educational functionaries. Keeping in view the deliberations and also those of the earlier workshops, the Working Group recommends the measures to improve the overall curriculum scenario at the school level.

* National Council of Educational Research and Training, New Delhi, 1985.

Recommendations

1. In order to develop national cohesion, integration, value orientation as reflected in our rich traditions and composite cultural heritage; in order to synthesize the above with modernisation in terms of Science and Technology and to promote a genuine Indian ethos, there is an urgent need to formulate a national core curriculum applicable to all the schools in the country. NCERT should undertake the responsibility of developing the national core curriculum.

2. The national core curriculum, applicable to all the schools in the country should be supplemented by specific curricula to meet the local ecological, sociological, cultural, economic and developmental requirements relevant to states, districts and geographical typogies. It is recommended that national core curriculum should constitute two thirds of the total curriculum. However, the proportion may differ in respect of different subjects and different stages of education.

3. School curriculum should present a happy blend of physical culture, culture and knowledge. The knowledge component should further comprise humanities, science and technology. The relative proportion of each component should vary at different stages of school education.

4. Curriculum should be developed keeping in view the majority of students, teachers and physical facilities available in majority of schools. There is need to check unnecessary disparities and elitism arising from the curriculum.

5. Information load, specially at the earlier stages. should be kept at a minimum. At the higher level also, practice of competitive overloading of information in the textbooks should be avoided. It is recommended that there should not be more than two textbooks of Classes I and II.

6. At least 33 per cent of the instructional time should be allocated for the teaching of mother tongue/regional language at the primary stage because proficiency in language skills will equip the child to learn the content of other subjects with ease. At the primary stage, mother tongue should be medium of instruction.

7. Teaching of formal skills of reading and writing should not be attempted before the age of five. But informal, joyful pre-primary schooling may be introduced, particularly for the first generation learners.

8. The language and the writing style followed in the textbooks should be easily intelligible to students. Books written in simple language help the pupils to learn things better and in less time. The non-language books should reinforce the linguistic abilities of pupils and should in no case pose additional problems of comprehension for them. When books prepared first in one language, are translated into another language, artificial and mechanical translation should be avoided. Where translation needs to be done, the help of practising teachers should be obtained.

9. Quality of education should not be equated with quantum of curriculum content. For the development of creative thinking, it is better to cover a few topics more intensively rather than providing superficial knowledge of too many things.

10. There is a definite place for research in curriculum development, particularly to ensure that the concepts introduced are compatible with the mental development of the child.

11. As the syllabi and textbooks are the concrete manifestations of curriculum, these should be of high quality. There should be a mechanism for determining the suitability of textbooks.

12. Since curriculum development is a continuous process, it should be evaluated periodically and recast in its totality. NCERT should provide academic guidance to the State Education Departments for the evaluation of their curricula, particularly from the point of view of load.

13. Keeping in view the present time allocation of 6 or 7 periods per week, the existing curriculum in social science at the secondary stage in Delhi proves to be lengthy. Besides there are some overlappings in the curriculum in middle and secondary stages. Therefore, the whole course of social science from Classes VI-X should be reorganised so as to remove the overlappings between the curriculum of middle and secondary stages. At the middle/upper primary stage integrated approach should be adopted.

14. The present curriculum in science for Classes VI-X in Delhi has been found to be lengthy. Besides a few topics included in the syllabi of different classes, have been found to be difficult for students. At the secondary stage, Course A in general proves to be difficult for students. The topics found to be difficult should be considered for simplification and deletion from the course. At the middle stage integrated science rather than physics, chemistry and biology as such should form a part of school curriculum.

Facilities

15. Minimum facilities for teaching learning such as Chalk, blackboard, books, source books, maps, charts, models etc. should be provided in every school. Absence of these facilities increases the load of curriculum for pupils and teachers.

16. Overcrowding in classes increases the work load of teachers which affects adversely the quality of curriculum transaction. This may give rise to the problem of curriculum load. The optimum number of pupils in a class should be around 35.

Curriculum Transaction

17. Directorates of Education should ensure 220 working days out of which there should be at least 190 instructional days. Duration of a school day

should be at least six hours, out of which five hours should be available for the transaction of curriculum.

18. Lack of order and system in any aspect of human life makes things heavier and more difficult than they are. This is also true in the case of home work and periodical tests. It should be made obligatory on the part of school to prepare and display in each class an agreed time table for home work assignment and for the conduct of periodical/unit tests. It is further recommended that no formal home work should be assigned at the primary stage.

19. Since the teacher is the major single factor in fostering teaching and learning, it is desirable that he should be suitably trained to discharge his duties effectively. Therefore, curriculum for pre-service training, both for elementary stage and secondary stage, should be simultaneously updated and intensified. Training strategies should be designed in such a way that the trainees are adequately prepared to handle the revised school curriculum. Mushroom growth of substandard teacher training colleges should be checked.

Examinations/Tests

20. There should be no public examination till Class VII. Internal formative and summative evaluation should be carried continuously with a view to diagnose pupil's weaknesses in learning. Subsequently remedial teaching for those pupils who lag behind in some aspect of learning should be arranged. Time spent by teachers on remedial teaching should be considered as part of their regular workload.

STATUS REPORT ON CHALLENGE OF EDUCATION, 1985*

On August 20, 1985 the Education Minister presented, a Status Report on education entitled 'Challenge of Education—A Policy Perspective to the Prime Minister which was debated in the Parliament not only but also there was a nation-wide debate on this report. It was revised in the light of the various observations made, it became the background paper for the formulation of the National Policy on Education. The document *Challenge of Education* provided a critical appraisal of the educational system which *interalia* included Elementary Education.

Extracts

Appraisal of Elementary Education

1. By and large methods of teaching are quite out-moded.
2. New methods of teaching are being ignored in many States.

---

* Ministry of HRD, New Delhi, 1985.

3. Most of the schools do not have even the relatively inexpensive teaching kits developed by NCERT.
4. The programme of Work Experience or Socially Useful Productive Work on which Gandhiji's Basic system of Education laid stress has not been implemented in most of the schools.
5. Overall enrolment position is unsatisfactory.
6. What is more disturbing is the alarming rate of drop-outs.
7. The total expenditure per student per year by the Centre and States has declined in real terms.
8. There is total dependence on Government in running the schools.
9. There is hardly any effort on the part of a village or the Community leadership or at the level of block or district, to set up or even to help the proper running of schools.
10. No systematic study of the effectiveness of Non-Formal education is available.

General Appraisal

1. The drop-out rates among urban children is lower than in the rural areas.
2. Despite considerable acceleration in recent years girls education is still far behind the boys.
3. The share of Elementary Education in funds allocation has gone down considerably. From 56 per cent in the First Plan it has gone down to 36 per cent in the Sixth Plan...

Factors Facilitating Educational Restructuring

4.17 Teachers have a special responsibility in every society and the way it is discharged sets the tone for the education of the young. Their commitment to give it their best in moulding the tender minds entrusted to them must be seen beyond question...

4.23 The decision to set up pace setting Model Schools in the Central Sector in every district of country reflects not only the extent of Central Government to education but also its concern for equity. Through these schools, the most meritorious children particularly of rural areas, will be able to get quality education irrespective of the economic status of their parents.

Universalisation of Elementary Education

4.72 As for the issues of access, equity and minimum threshold, availability of good quality elementary education to all children irrespective of their caste, sex, creed, economic status and region is a commitment enshrined in the Constitution. As discussed at length earlier, this commitment, which was to be fulfilled by 1960, is still to be realised.

An Alternative Model for Elementary Education

4.75 It has been argued that, under Indian conditions, no single approach is likely to make much headway in the near future in imparting education beyond the age of 11, particularly among the poor, in the rural areas. A holistic model has, therefore, been proposed in which, with the help of Anganwadis under the Integrated Child Development Scheme Programme, pre-primary education would be provided for three years and thereafter, in continuation and conjunction, at the same location, primary education would be organised.

4.76 As far as access and equity at the secondary level is concerned, Scheduled Castes, Scheduled Tribes and girls present a major challenge. What alternatives could be devised by way of vocational training in place of the formal education under the 10+2 model so that skills relevant to the rural environment and employment opportunities could be imparted, needs careful consideration. Not many ideas have emerged in this regard this far. Some of the suggestions received relate to the desirability of linking post-elementary training with TRYSEM and community Polytechnics, establishment of a peripatetic system of education supported by distance learning and publication and free distribution of specially designed books for continuing education.

Social Relevance, Diversification and Quality

4.102 A decenteralised system with the district or block as the unit of planning will be able to ensure that the children at two ends of the spectrum of competence will be looked after properly. Those who are physically or mentally handicapped and others who are specially talented and, therefore, capable of joining the reservoir of national talent for the development of the national economy, will need very different treatment and facilities.

Design for an integrated strategy of education

4.144 In broad terms, the tasks of evolving the New Education Policy would consist of laying down a long-term strategy for... Universalisation of Elementary Education... .

CHALLENGE OF ACTION: A POLICY PERSPECTIVE 1985*

This document represents an important stage in the process of reviewing and shaping the educational system. The review as pointed out the limitations and constraints as also pointers to the direction of future initiatives, based essentially on the views and suggestions from all

* Minister of Education, Government of India, New Delhi, 1985.
Note: Para numbers refer to para numbers of Chapter 4 of the document.

interested in education. This document ultimately became the basis of the National Policy on Education, 1986.

Extracts—Goal Orientation for Educational Planning

4.6 A recapitulation of the goals of education, emphasised by the Indian Constitution and enunciated, from time to time, by thinkers, planners, policy-makers and educationists, indicates that this basic issue should be considered from three inter-related approaches.

4.7 First of all, it is necessary to define the role of the educational system in totality since it has an institutional character of its own which goes beyond its main function of imparting education to pupils. The system is expected to generate new knowledge in all fields within the reach of the human mind. In addition, it has to evolve principles, methodologies and guidelines for the application of knowledge for benefiting society. It is also expected to provide knowledge and skills for solving the problems of development. It must also enable the students to develop an understanding and a perspective of the physical and social environment. Research and development and extension, therefore, have to be accepted as essential ingredients of the educational process.

4.8 Secondly, emphasis has to be laid on the socio-economic well-being competence and creativity of the individual, which encompasses:

(i) physical, intellectual and aesthetic development of personality;
(ii) inculcation of a scientific temper and democratic, moral and spiritual values;
(iii) development of self-confidence to innovate and face unfamiliar situations;
(iv) creation of an awareness of the physical, social, technological, economic and cultural environment;
(v) fostering a healthy attitude to dignity of labour and hard work;
(vi) a commitment to principles of secularism and social justice;
(vii) dedication to uphold the integrity, honour and foster the development of the country; and
(viii) promotion of international understanding.

4.9 In addition to developing the personal attributes listed above, education has to assume the responsibility for imparting knowledge about concepts and facts relating to different subjects and for developing skills in the area of languages and communication, as also interest in hobbies, games and sports.

Financial Constraints

4.49 It is hardly necessary to establish the relevance of financial constraints in the context of educational planning. Whether one looks at the question of equity or coverage or quality or diversification, the provision of sizeable financial resources appears inescapable. There is no point in discussing universalisation of elementary education (UEE), vocationalisation of education, removal of illiteracy, qualitative improvement of school and higher, particularly technical education, or of establishment of institutions of excellence unless a system is evolved for allocation of funds on the basis of an objective determination of norms of per unit cost in various streams.

4.50 In addition to facing these issues, it appears necessary that adequate thought should be given to the scope of raising funds for education; by levy of appropriate cess on consumption or imports; earmarking of resources for manpower development in all large projects; and mobilization of private resources. It will also have to be decided as to what should be the proportion between Central and State funding and what steps should be taken for the enforcement of earmarking conditions for various educational programmes. As the major reason for those who are opting out of education at the school level is poverty, it would be unrealistic to expect them to contribute significantly to resources for education. Secondly, now that education is a concurrent subject, the Central share for education will have to be enhanced; otherwise, it will not be possible to establish any correlation between responsibility and performance. Thirdly, except for school and vocational levels, the pricing of education at other levels will have to be reconsidered and quantum and nature of subsidisation will have to be related either to merit or the dictates of social justice.

4.58 Even within the education sector, problems are created by departmental jealousies. It is recognized that the types of courses offered in Arts, Humanities and even Science, particularly at the undergraduate level, are unsuitable for adequately increasing either the functional efficiency or employability of students. Yet, the desired composite courses have not been introduced because of the insularity of academics belonging to different disciplines.

4.59 A detailed analysis of the constraints of educational planning has been attempted essentially to underline that if the initiative for reorientation remains confined only to educational planners and administrators and the total system remains unconcerned and unchanged, the chances of success of the new policy initiative will be greatly compromised.

Perspective of Policy Formulation

4.60 Having described the goals of education and discussed some of the factors which would facilitate or impede the initiative for radical restructuring of education, it appears necessary to proceed with the description of a broad perspective with reference to which the new policy framework will have to be evolved. There are serious difficulties in presenting a comprehensive and detailed projection of the future scenario, not merely because of inadequacies of data pertaining to education but also because of lack of clarity about the overall scenario at the efficacy of health and family welfare programmes, volume and composition of GNP changes expected in the employment market because of modifications in policies with reference to the choice of technologies and the impact of modernisation on the process of urbanisation and participation of women. However, for the present paper, it would be adequate to present a broad picture since it would yield the insights relevant to policy planning and also pinpoint the issues on which a view has to be taken through interaction and discussion.

4.61 The age-specific population in age-group 6-14 in the year 1981 is calculated to be approximately 15 crores. In 1981, 9.3 crores pupils were enrolled in elementary education, 0.95 crore in secondary and 0.31 crore in higher education. Assuming that the growth rate of age-specific population in years 6-14 age-group in the 'eighties can be contained around 1.5 per cent per annum, it is estimated that by 1990-91, the population in this age-group would be 17.4 crores. If the past pattern of educational development continues, particularly in terms of the growth of enrolment and its retention rate, 11.2 crores children will be enrolled in the elementary education under formal system, while another 1.15 and 0.38 crores will be in secondary and higher education levels respectively.

4.62 However, it is expected that in the 'nineties the growth of age-specific population in years 6-14 age-group will further slow down. On the assumption of 1 per cent per annum growth the age-specific population in 2000 AD, is estimated to be 19.25 crores. Assuming that the universal elementary education is achieved by 1990, out of the total age-specific population of 17.4 crores, 11 crore pupils should be in primary stage and the remaining 6.4 crores in the middle stage. It may be noted that this achievement implies that the primary education will be 1.5 times and the middle 3.2 times of its present size. Such an expansion will have a significant impact on the educational expenditure as well. It is estimated that in terms of 1980-81 prices, and assuming the per unit costs of 1977-78 to stay put, the budgetary requirements for the year 1990-91 will be doubled to Rs. 3200 crores (the 1980-81 expenditure being Rs. 1537 crores). On the basis of 8 per cent per annum rate of inflation the budget in current prices would be more than four times the 1980-81 allocations. In 1981 the number of teachers engaged in elementary education was 21.7 lakhs. At the existing pattern of educational development, their number will be 29 lakhs by 1990. However, if universalisation of elementary education is achieved by 1990, the total requirement of teachers for elementary education would increase to nearly 44 lakhs.

4.63 In addition, the universalisation of elementary education by 1990, will also imply that even at the existing transition rates, the enrolment in the secondary and higher education level will increase to nearly twice of their

1980-81 enrolments. However, keeping in view the fact that the per unit cost of secondary and higher education are several times higher than the per unit cost of elementary education, the overall impact on the educational budget would be tremendous. It may be recalled that these implications have been worked out without taking into account the expenditure which would have inevitably to be incurred on improving the quality of education.

4.64 The upshot of the above scenario is that any substantial improvement in education coverage as well as retention, which constitutes the core of universalisation of elementary education efforts, will not only require significant increase in educational expenditure on elementary education but will also have a multiplier effect on the total educational budget through increased enrolments in the secondary and higher education. Hence, policy deliberations vis-a-vis universalisation of elementary education need to be matched with hard financial decisions.

4.65 Alternatively, other educational approaches, such as non-formal/ distance education and vocationalisation have to be worked out in detail for a large scale implementation, and replication.

4.66 The above scenario underlines the immensity of the quantitative tasks of education on the basis of conservative assumptions. This re-emphasises the importance of taking up programmes for population control on a massive scale through adult education as well as school and college education so that small family norm becomes deeply embedded in the consciousness of the community. Otherwise, a situation might arise in which, due to sheer weight to numbers, the system might cross the bounds of financial feasibility at even the present levels of participation and attainment.

4.67 ...It is apparent that the objectives of education cannot be attained unless qualitative changes are introduced in the system. To a great extent these would be in the nature of behavioural, conceptual, methodological and organizational modifications. It has, however, to be recognised that these will not bear any fruit unless educational institutions attain a minimum threshold of essential facilities in terms of buildings; black-boards; charts and posters; drinking water and bathroom facilities; laboratories; science kits and libraries; and minimum contingencies for organising Socially Useful Productive Work, nature studies, games and sports and cultural activities.

Approaches to Resource Mobilisation for Education

4.68 Providing these facilities will involve additional expenses. At least for schools and for institutions of excellence, the expenditure will have to be met fully between the state and central governments. In the case of other institutions and the general run of students, except, of course, the disadvantaged section who have to be brought at par with others, the possibility of rationalising the fee structure may have to be considered. This will, apart from augmenting internal resources, also change the perception about the value of education.

4.69 Other suggestions received in this connection are: requiring development sectors to allocate a percentage of their budgets for education; including manpower development as an item in the cost structure of public sector projects; realisation of at least a part of the real cost of education in professional institutions from those employing their products; levy of cess on imports; encouraging private entrepreneurs to contribute to educational development, particularly in respect of vocational and professional streams, by giving suitable rebates in taxes; and setting up of training institutions in collaboration with public and private enterprises, a surcharge on land revenue and on municipal house-tax.

4.70 The problem of resources for education has already reached the proportions of a crisis for the central as well as the state government. Over the years, despite the recognition of its crucial role in human resource development, education has been treated as a residual sector to be taken care of, largely by the states, out of the resources accruing to them through the Finance Commission awards and Central Assistance for plan expenditure under the modified Gadgil formula. Now, however, education is being encouraged to assume its assigned role in the process of development, a new strategy for raising and sharing resources has, therefore, to be devised. If investing in education is costly, not doing is costlier. A possible approach to this could be the setting up of a high powered joint commission of the centre and states for studying the problem of resources for education and working out a strategy for mobilising these on a long-term basis.

Elements of a Strategy for Educational Planning

4.71 Any strategy for educational planning will have to deal with problems of (a) access; (b) equity and minimum threshold; (c) social relevance, diversification and quality; and (d) methodology and management.

Universalisation of Elementary Education (UEE)

4.72 As for the issues of access, equity and minimum threshold, availability of good quality elementary education to all children irrespective of their caste, sex, creed, economic status and region is a commitment enshrined in the Constitution. As discussed at length earlier, this commitment, which was to be fulfilled by 1960, is still to be realised. A section of educational planners have, however, been arguing that this will stand fulfilled as soon as the enrolment reaches a particular participation ratio. This view is difficult to accept. Education is not a ritual. It cannot be taken as having been delivered till a child has reached the level of attainment envisaged as a norm for a 14 year old boy or girl. With drop-out rates ranging around 77%, enrolment, by itself, loses its meaning, except as a frame of reference.

4.73 It has been explained already that this state of affairs is attributable largely to general apathy towards education, poverty, irrelevance of educational content, lack of women teachers and allocation of inadequate resources. There has been uneven development of education not only between states but also between the Scheduled Castes and Scheduled Tribes and girls on the one hand, and the generality of children in rural and urban areas, on the other. Measures such as mid-day meals, free supply of uniforms and books, and even central assistance to the nine educationally backward States for the appointment of women teachers in single teacher schools, have not yielded significant results as yet. Consequently, new approaches such as the setting up of part-time schools and non-formal education centres have been proposed to provide flexibility in the school routine for accommodating boys involved in income generating activities or family occupations and girls preoccupied with domestic chores, especially the care of siblings. Other suggestions received for consideration include payment of opportunity-cost compensation to parents who forego the support of children while they are at school and greater involvement of the community for the maintenance of physical facilities, effective management of schools, and exercise of evaluative control on the teachers. Another suggestion favours augmentation of the association of women with children's education in the formal as well as non-formal streams through relaxation of qualifications and age-bar, training and appointment of women from the same village on contract basis and enhancement of the visibility of school by making it a centre of community participation. It has also been proposed that the educated employed in rural areas should be trained and assisted to become educational entrepreneurs to help the students, in return for payment on unit basis, to attain, through intensive coaching, educational levels certified by external examinations to be equivalent to class V or class VIII.

An Alternative Model for Elementary Education

4.74 Some studies have shown that the children who are involved in pre-primary education through Angan-Wadis under the Integrated Child Development Scheme tend to participate in education to a much greater extent at later stages. Based upon this experience and also keeping in view the compulsion of girls to look after their domestic chores, a wholly different approach to elementary education has also been suggested.

4.75 It has been argued that, under Indian conditions, no single approach is likely to make much headway in the near future in imparting education beyond the age of 11, particularly among the poor, in the rural areas. A holistic model has, therefore, been proposed in which, with the help of Angan-Wadis under the Integrated Child Development Scheme programme, pre-primary education would be provided for three years and thereafter, in continuation and conjunction, at the same location, primary education would be organised. This would be evaluated by a public examination on the basis of which admissions would be made for further continuation of education from clas VI to X. In this model, girls would be able to come to the school with siblings, who would be taken care of in Angan-Wadis, while they would be studying in higher classes, and non-formal education would be taken up for classes VI to X, to the extent necessary, through the enlargement of the Open School system. This model also envisages that children should enter the vocational stream at a stage earlier than the 10+ level; otherwise they are unlikely to take to vocationalisation with any real interest.

4.76 As far as access and equity at the secondary level is concerned, Scheduled Castes, Scheduled Tribes and girls present a major challenge. There is a general disinclination amongst all communities to send girls to far away schools, particularly if these have a co-educational system. Resource constraints, however, do not permit either the opening of separate schools for boys and girls or the setting up of a much larger number of schools, to bring them closer to village habitations. What alternatives could be devised by way of vocational training in place of the formal education under the 10+2 model so that skills relevant to the rural environment and employment opportunities could be imparted, needs careful consideration. Not many ideas have emerged in this regard till date. Some of the suggestions received relate to the desirability of linking post-elementary training with TRYSEM and Community Polytechnics, establishment of a peripatetic system of education supported by distance learning and publication and free distribution of specially designed books for continuing education.

4

Commissions and Documents on Elementary Education: 1986-1996

NATIONAL POLICY ON EDUCATION, 1986*

The document *The Challenge of Education—A Policy Perspective* and Prime Minister's speech under the title *Revamping the Educational System* was the basis of discussion at the Conference of State Education Ministers, (29-30 August, 1985). The document was distributed by the Ministry, inviting suggestions and comments from all sections of the people. Thereafter in April 1986, the Ministry of Human Resource Development prepared a revised document, '*National Policy on Education, 1986 - A Presentation*'. Which was discussed at the meetings of the State Minister of Education, the National Development Council and the Central Advisory Board of Education. The 'Draft National Policy on Education, 1986 given below, was finally adopted by the Lok Sabha on May 8, 1986 and the Rajya Sabha on May 12, 1986.

Extracts

1.1 Education has continued to evolve, diversify and extend its reach and coverage since the dawn of human history. Every country develops its system of education to express and promote its unique socio-cultural identity and also to meet the challenges of the times. There are moments in history when a new direction has to be given to an age-old process. That moment is today.

The 1968 Education Policy and After

1.4 The National Policy of 1968 marked a significant step in the history of education in post-Independence India. It aimed to promote national progress, a sense of common citizenship and culture, and to strengthen national integration...

---

* Department of Education, Ministry of Human Resource Development, Government of India, New Delhi, 1988.

1.5 Since the adoption of the 1968 Policy, there has been considerable expansion in educational facilities all over the country at all levels. More than 90 per cent of the country's rural habitations now have schooling facilities within a radius of one kilometre. There has been sizeable augmentation of facilities at other stages also.

1.10 In the Indian way of thinking, a human being is a positive asset and a precious national resource which needs to be cherished, nurtured and developed with tenderness and care, coupled with dynamism. Each individual's growth presents a different range of problems and requirements, at every stage—from the womb to the tomb. The catalytic action of Education in this complex and dynamic growth process needs to be planned meticulously and executed with great sensitivity.

The Essence and Role of Education

2.1 In our national perception education is essentially for all. This is fundamental to our all-round development, material and spiritual.

2.4 In sum, Education is a unique investment in the present and the future. This cardinal principle is the key to the National Policy on Education.

National System of Education

3.2 The concept of a National System of Education implies that, u to a given level, all students, irrespective of caste, creed, location or sex, have access to education of a comparable quality. To achieve this, the Government will initiate appropriately funded programmes. Effective measures will be taken in the direction of the Common School System recommended in the 1968 Policy.

3.3 The National System of Education envisages a common educational structure. The 10+2+3 structure has now been accepted in all parts of the country. Regarding the further break-up of the first 10 years efforts will be made to move towards an elementary system comprising 5 years of primary education and 3 years of upper primary, followed by 2 years of High School.

3.7 Minimum levels of learning will be laid down for each stage of education. Steps will also be taken to foster among students an understanding of the diverse cultural and social systems of the people living in different parts of the country. Besides the promotion of the link language, programmes will also be launched to increase substantially the translation of books from one language to another and to publish multi-lingual dictionaries and glossaries. The young will be encouraged to undertake the rediscovery of India, each in his own image and perception.

3.10 The Nation as a whole will assume the responsibility of providing resource support for implementing programmes of educational transformation, reducing disparities, universalisation of elementary education, adult literacy, scientific and technological research etc.

A Meaningful Partnership

3.13 The Constitutional Amendment of 1976, which includes Education in the Concurrent List, was a far-reaching step whose implications - substantive, financial and administrative - require a new sharing of responsibility between the Union Government and the States in respect of this vital area of national life.

Education for Equality

Disparities

4.1 The new policy will lay special emphasis on the removal of disparities and to equalise educational opportunity by attending to the specific needs of those who have been denied equality so far.

Education for Women's Equality

4.3 The removal of women's illiteracy and obstacles inhibiting their access to, and retention in, elementary education will receive overriding priority, through provision of special support services, setting of time targets, and effective monitoring. Major emphasis will be laid on women's participation in vocational, technical and professional education at different levels. The policy of non-discrimination will be pursued vigorously to eliminate sex stereo-typing in vocational and professional courses and to promote women's participation in non-traditional occupations, as well as in existing and emergent technologies.

The Education of Scheduled Castes

4.4 The central focus in the SCs' education development is their equalisation with the non-SC population at all stages and levels of education, in all areas and in all the four dimensions—rural male, rural female, urban male and urban female.

4.5 The measures contemplated for this purpose include:

(i) Incentives to indigent families to send their children to school regularly till they reach the age of 14;

(ii) Pre-matric Scholarship scheme for children of families engaged in occupations such as scavenging, flaying and tanning to be made applicable from Class I onwards. All children of such families, regardless of incomes, will be covered by this scheme and time-bound programmes targetted on them will be undertaken;

(iii) Constant micro-planning and verification to ensure that the enrolment, retention and successful completion of courses by SC students do not fall at any stage, and provision of remedial courses to improve their prospects for further education and employment.

(iv) Recruitment of teachers from Scheduled Castes;

(v) Provision of facilities for SC students in students' hostels at district headquarters, according to a phased programme;

(vi) Location of school buildings, Balwadis and Adult Education Centres in such a way as to facilitate full participation of the Scheduled Castes;

(vii) The utilization of N.R.E.P. and R.L.E.G.P. resources so as to make substantial educational facilities available to the Scheduled Castes; and

(viii) Constant innovation in finding new methods to increase the participation of the Scheduled Castes in the educational process.

The Education of Scheduled Tribes

4.6 The following measures will be taken urgently to bring the Scheduled Tribes on par with others:

(i) Priority will be accorded to opening primary schools in tribal areas. The construction of school buildings will be undertaken in these areas on a priority basis under the normal funds for education, as well as under the N.R.E.P., R.L.E.G.P, Tribal Welfare Schemes etc.

(ii) The socio-cultural milieu of the STs has its distinctive characteristics including, in many cases, their own spoken languages. This underlines the need to develop the curricula and devise instructional materials in tribal languages at the initial stages, with arrangements for switching over to the regional language.

The Handicapped

4.9 The objective should be to integrate the physically and mentally handicapped with the general community as equal partners, to prepare them for normal growth and to enable them to face life with courage and confidence. The following measures will be taken in this regard:

(i) Wherever it is feasible, the education of children with motor handicaps and other mild handicaps will be common with that of others.

(ii) Special schools with hostels will be provided, as far as possible at district headquarters, for the severely handicapped children.

(iii) Adequate arrangements will be made to give vocational training to the disabled.

(iv) Teachers' training programmes will be reoriented, in particular for teachers of primary classes, to deal with the special difficulties of the handicapped children; and

(v) Voluntary effort for the education of the disabled, will be encouraged in every possible manner.

Reorganisation of Education at Different Stages

Early Childhood Care and Education

5.1 The national policy on Children specially emphasises investment in the development of the young child, particularly children from sections of the population in which first generation learners predominate.

5.2 Recognising the holistic nature of child development, *viz.*, nutrition, health and social, mental, physical, moral and emotional development. Early Childhood Care and Education (ECCE) will receive high priority and be suitably integrated with the Integrated Child Development Services programme, wherever possible. Day-care centres will be provided as a support service for universalisation of primary education, to enable girls engaged in taking care of siblings to attend school and as a support service for working women belonging to poorer sections.

5.3 Programmes of ECCE will be child-oriented, focused around play and the individuality of the child. Formal methods and introduction of the 3 R's will be discouraged at this stage. The local community will be fully involved in these programmes.

5.4 A full integration of child care and pre-primary education will be brought about, both as a feeder and a strengthening factor for primary education and for human resource development in general. In continuation of this stage, the School Health Programme will be strengthened.

Elementary Education

5.5 The new thrust in elementary education will emphasise two aspects:

(i) universal enrolment and universal retention of children up to 14 years of age, and
(ii) a substantial improvement in the quality of education.

Child-Centred Approach

5.6 A warm, welcoming and encouraging approach, in which all concerned share a solicitude for the needs of the child, is the best motivation for the child to attend school and learn. A child-centred and activity-based process of learning should be adopted at the primary stage. First generation learners should be allowed to set their own pace and be given supplementary remedial instruction. As the child grows, the component of cognitive learning will be increased and skills organised through practice. The policy of non-detention at the primary stage will be retained, making evaluation as disaggregated as feasible. Corporal punishment will be firmly excluded from the educational system and school timings as well as vacations adjusted to the convenience of children.

School Facilities

5.7 Provision will be made of essential facilities in primary schools, including at least two reasonably large rooms that are usable in all weather, and the necessary toys, blackboards, maps, charts, and other learning material. At least two teachers, one of whom a woman, should work in every school, the number increasing as early as possible to one teacher per class. A phased drive, symbolically called Operation Blackboard will be undertaken with immediate effect to improve Primary Schools all over the country. Government, local bodies, voluntary agencies and individuals will be fully involved. Construction of school buildings will be the first charge on NREP and RLEGP funds.

The Future

12.1 The future shape of education in India is too complex to envision with precision. Yet, given our tradition which has almost always put a high premium on intellectual and spiritual attainment, we are bound to succeed in achieving our objectives.

12.2 The main task is to strengthen the base of the pyramid, which might come close to a billion people at the turn of the century. Equally, it is important to ensure that those at the top of the pyramid are among the best in the world. Our cultural well-springs had taken good care of both ends in the past; the skew set in with foreign domination and influence. It should now be possible to further intensify the nation-wide effort in Human Resource Development, with Education playing its multifaceted role.

PROGRAMME OF ACTION FOR IMPLEMENTATION OF NPE, 1986*

The Government of India itself prepared a 'Programme of Action' for the implementation of National Policy on Education (NPE), 1986. Twenty-three Task Forces were constituted and each was assigned a specific topic covered by NPE. The Task Forces examined the subjects assigned and elaborated upon the implications of specific statements on NPE. The Task Forces submitted their reports in July 1986 which were further considered in Conference of the Education Secretaries of the State Governments and the Union Territories on July 20, 1986 and Meeting of the CABE on August 1-2, 1986. All the suggestions emerging were taken into account, and the final Programme of Action was placed before the Parliament on August 8, 1986. The Lok Sabha and the Rajya Sabha approved the Programme of Action on August 22 and August 23 respectively.

---

* Department of Education, Ministry of Education, Government of India, New Delhi, 1986.

INNOVATIONS IN EDUCATION, 1986*

The Post-Independence period has seen fast expansion of education in the country. As against 1,50,000 elementary schools. 4,000 secondary schools and 214 intermediate/junior colleges in the country in the year 1947, the total number of institutions has increased respectively to 6,35,000, 55,000 and 4,000 in 1983-84. The enrolment also increased nine times at elementary, 25 times at secondary and 20 times at intermediate levels during the same period. The Education Departments of Centre and States spent Rs. 5517 crores in 1983-84 as against total expenditure of 55 crores in 1947. Despite significant expansion in physical facilities and increase in expenditure, the education sector faces many challenges. The literacy rate is barely 36 per cent, and about 50 million children remain to be enrolled in elementary education by the end of Seventh Five Year Plan. Improvement in the quality of education is an area of immediate concern. In the context of resource constraints for education should call for special emphasis.

Several States/organisations experimented with innovative methods to make education cost-effective, purposeful and suitable to the convenience of learners.

School Education

Innovative Project/Practices mainly related to Elementary Education:

1. Pilot Project Schools (Meghalaya)
2. Innovations in the Teaching of Mathematics in Primary Schools (Nagaland)
3. Schools Adoption by Training Institutes (Punjab)
4. Integrated Education of the Disabled (Rajasthan)
5. Correspondence-cum-Contact Course for Higher Grade Teachers (Tamil Nadu)
6. Chief Minister's Nutritious Meal Programme (Tamil Nadu)
7. Problem of Wastage and Stagnation and its Eradication (Uttar Pradesh)
8. Using the Environment and Local Resources for Science Education at the Primary Stage (NCERT, New Delhi)
9. Training of In-Service Teacher Education Personnel in Environmental Studies for Primary Schools (NCERT, New Delhi)
10. Guidance at the Elementary School Stage (NCERT, New Delhi)
11. Radio Pilot Project (NCERT, New Delhi)
12. Nutrition, Health, Education and Environmental Sanitation (NHEES) UNICEF Assisted Project, (NCERT, New Delhi)

---

* Department of Education, Ministry of Human Resource Development, Government of India, New Delhi, 1986.

13. Primary Education Curriculum renewal (PECR) a UNICEF Assisted Project (NCERT, New Delhi)
14. Early Childhood Education Project (ECE) and Children's Media Laboratory (CML) a UNICEF Assisted Project (NCERT, New Delhi)
15. Education of Special Groups

FIFTH ALL INDIA EDUCATIONAL SURVEY, 1986-89*

For proper planning of school facilities at all levels, the first all India Educational Survey was conducted by the Ministry of Education in 1957 and after that by National Council of Educational Research and Training in 1965, 1973, 1978 and 1986 respectively. The Fifth Survey provides data as on 30 September, 1986.

Relevant Findings

2. *Schools*

2.2 Among the total 735785 schools, there were 529392 (71.95%) primary schools, 138687 (18.85%) upper primary schools, 52208 (7.09%) secondary schools and 15498 (2.11%) higher secondary schools. Of these, 475938 (89.90%) primary schools, 112836 (81.36%) upper primary schools, 38720 (74.16%) secondary schools and 7225 (46.62%) higher secondary schools were located in rural areas.

2.3 Of the 529392 primary schools, 219837 (41.53%) were government schools, 251699 (47.54%) local body schools, 44701 (8.44%) private aided schools and 13155 (2.49%) private unaided schools. In most of the States the majority of the primary schools were government or local body schools.

2.4 The number of primary schools increased by 11.54 per cent, upper primary schools by 23.38 per cent, secondary schools by 42.35 per cent and higher secondary schools by 48.60 per cent over the period 1978-86. The increase for the total number of schools was 16.03 per cent during the foresaid period.

2.7 As regards facilities for teaching physical education/Yoga, 13513 (2.55%) primary schools, 16869 (12.16%) upper primary schools, 36312 (69.55%) secondary schools and 12503 (80.67%) higher secondary schools had teachers exclusively for physical education/Yoga.

3. *Educational Facilities*

3.1 *Primary Stage*: Out of total habitations, 502806 (51.36%) habitations covering 80.34 per cent rural population had primary schools/sections. The corresponding percentage at the time of the Fourth Survey (1978) were

---

* National Council of Educational Research and Training, New Delhi, 1989.

46.80 and 78.53 respectively. 94.60 per cent rural population was served by primary sections located either within the habitation or up to a walking distance of one km as against 92.82 per cent population in 1978.

The country had 530176 (54.15%) habitations with population 300 or more. Of these, 76.98 per cent had the facility for primary stage within the habitation of residence and 94.01 per cent had the facility either within the habitation of residence or within a walking distance of one km.

3.2 *Upper Primary Stage*: Only 129710 (13.25%) habitations covering 35.98 per cent rural population had upper primary schools/sections within the habitation of residence. The corresponding percentages for the Fourth Survey (1978) were 10.74 per cent and 33.47 per cent respectively. 85.39 per cent rural population had the facility for upper primary stage either within the habitation of residence or within a walking distance of 3 km as against 78.83 per cent population in 1978.

4. *Enrolment*

4.1 The enrolment in class I-V was 86683289 including 6679707 (77.06%) enrolment in rural areas. Enrolment of girls in classes I-V was 35676643 (41.16%). The percentage increase in enrolment over the period 1978-86 was 26.36 per cent.

Enrolment in classes VI-VIII was 27200656 including 9642537 (35.45%) girls. The corresponding enrolment for the rural areas was 17795293 (65.42%). The percentage increase in enrolment over the period 1978-86 was 51.46 per cent.

4.2 Enrolment of Scheduled Castes was 15039683 in classes I-V and 4064405 in classes VI-VIII. The S.C. enrolment in classes I-V and VI-VIII was 17.35 per cent and 14.94 per cent, of the corresponding total enrolments. The enrolment of Scheduled Tribes was 6995848 in classes I-V, 1377992 in classes VI-VIII. These enrolments were 8.07 per cent and 5.07 per cent of the corresponding total enrolments.

4.3 Gross Enrolment Ratio for classes I-V (6-11 years) was 93.63 as against 81.65 in 1978. These ratios for boys and girls were 106.42 and 79.89 respectively. The Gross Enrolment Ratio for classes VI-VIII (11-14 years) was 48.51 as against 37.94 in 1978. These ratios for boys and girls were 60.61 and 35.57 respectively.

4.4 Enrolment in class VIII as percentage of enrolment in class I at the national level was 31.11. These percentages for States and Union Territories ranged from 82.08 for Goa to 15.88 for Andhra Pradesh.

5. *Teachers*

5.1 There were 3692751 teachers in schools as against 2940337 in 1978. There has been an increase in number of teachers to the tune of 25.58 per cent.

Of the 3692751 teachers, 1530145 (41.44%) were in primary schools, 1011049 (27.38%) in upper primary schools... 28.76 per cent teachers in primary schools, 33.27 per cent in upper primary schools... The corresponding percentages for S.C. teachers were 11.22 8.60... respectively and for S.T. teachers were 5.99 and 4.61 respectively.

5.2 Of the 3692751 teachers in schools, 1865503 (50.52%) were working at the primary stage, 921612 (24.96%) at the upper primary stage... Women teachers constituted 30.56 per cent, 32.18 per cent, of teachers working at primary, upper primary. 86.66 per cent teachers at the primary stage, 87.33 per cent at the upper primary stage were trained.

5.3 The pupil-teacher ratio for the primary stage at the national level was 44. Among the States and Union Territories it ranged from as low as 15 in Sikkim to as high as 61 in Gujarat. The pupil-teacher ratios for the upper primary stage was 29 respectively.

5.4 Among the primary schools, 148033 (27.96%) were single-teacher schools and 171389 (32.38%) were two-teacher schools. In the States of Arunachal Pradesh (55.25%). Jammu & Kashmir (58.67%), Karnataka (62.33%), Meghalaya (53.33%), Rajashtan (54.63%) and in Union Territory of Dadar & Nagar Haveli (66.94%), the single teacher schools constituted more than 50 per cent of the primary schools.

6. *Facilities*

6.1 Among the primary schools, 71495 (13.50%) were without building, that is, they were run in thatched huts, tents or in open space. Of the rest, 385120 (72.75%) primary schools had pucca or partly pucca buildings. Among upper primary schools 121707 (87.76%) had pucca or partly pucca buildings and 11280 (8.13%) schools had kachcha buildings.

6.2 Further among the primary schools, 40732 (7.69%), 200077 (37.79%) and 134551 (25.42%) had zero instructional room, one instructional room and two instructional rooms respectively. In case of upper primary schools, 3192 schools had no instructional room and 24909 had one or two instructional rooms.

NATIONAL CURRICULUM FOR ELEMENTARY AND SECONDARY EDUCATION: A FRAMEWORK, 1988*

For implementing the directions given in NPE, 1986 regarding 'Reorienting the Content and Process of Education', NCERT revised the earlier curriculum.

* National Council of Educational Research and Training, New Delhi, 1988.

Main Features

Framework

The national curricular framework for elementary and secondary education is envisaged in the context of the National System of Education as elaborated earlier. The basic features and the main thrusts of the curricular framework are as follows:

(i) Emphasis on the development of human resources for the realisation of the national goals of development.

(ii) Broad-based general education to all learners at the elementary (primary and upper primary) and secondary stages.

(iii) A common scheme of studies for elementary and secondary stages.

(iv) The common core components comprising the following:

- The history of India's freedom movement;
- The constitutional obligations;
- Content essential to nurture national identity;
- India's common cultural heritage;
- Egalitarianism, democracy and secularism;
- Equality of the sexes;
- Protection of the environment;
- Removal of social barriers;
- Observance of the small family norm; and
- Inculcation of the scientific temper.

(v) Emphasis on defining Minimum Learning Outcomes (MLOs) for each area of learning at all stages of education.

(vi) Provision for flexibility in terms of selection of content/components and learning experiences which would facilitate the attainment of minimum learning outcomes laid down for each stage of school education.

(vii) Emphasis on child-centred and activity-based processes rather than the teacher-centred approach during the transaction of curriculum.

(viii) Recasting of the examination system and introduction of continuous and comprehensive evaluation that incorporates both scholastic and specific objectives for each stage of education, to precisely stated specific objectives of each subject area in the form of expected learning outcomes indicating what exact behaviour a learner would be able to demonstrate after the curriculum transaction. Thus, the curriculum organisers are required at the outset to indicate overall objectives of curriculum which would coincide with the overall aim of school education. It is necessary to further formulate carefully the stage-wise objectives keeping in view the developmental characteristics and level associated with different stages of education. Each subject area would have its own specific objectives clearly defined in terms of behavioural outcomes. Put differently, efforts should be directed at the achievement of a particular set of objectives for which specific learning experiences are provided under a particular subject area. However, it should not be forgotten that human learning makes one unified whole and that separate subject area has been created only for the sake of convenience.

For education to help our country to express and promote its unique socio-cultural identity, to meet the challenges of the times and to develop appropriately its human resources, the objectives will have to be formulated with utmost care keeping in view the national priorities and values enshrined in our Constitution, socio-economic and cultural considerations, position of physical resources, global inter-relationships, pedagogical concerns and nature and level of learners. needless to mention objectives related to Common Core Components should be given a central place.

General Objectives of Education

School curriculum, on the whole, should aim at enabling the learners to acquire knowledge, develop concepts, and inculcate skills, attitudes, values and habits conducive to the all-round development of their personality and commensurate with the social, cultural, economic and environmental realities at national and international levels.

School curriculum should, therefore, help to promote development in the learner of:

- Language abilities and communication skills needed for social living and further learning;
- Competencies that facilitate mathematical operations and their applications in day-to-day life and learning;
- Knowledge, attitudes and habits necessary for keeping physically fit and strong in conformity with normal development pattern;
- A proper understanding about the role and importance of sex in human life, and healthy attitude towards sex and members of opposite sex;
- Qualities that make a man socially effective and happy in various social settings such as friendliness, cooperativeness, comparison, self-discipline, self-criticism, self-control, humour, courage, love for social justice, self-control, etc.;
- Moral and character values such as honesty, truthfulness, dependability, courtesy, fearlessness, compassion, etc.;
- Pre-vocational/vocational skills, willingness to work hard, entrepreneurship and dignity of manual work necessary for increased productivity and job satisfaction;
- Ability to appreciate and discover beauty in various life situations and integrate it into one's own personality;
- Understanding of the environmental and its limited resources and the need for conservation of natural resources and energy;

- Appreciation of various consequences of large families and over population and need of checking population growth;
- Understanding of the diverse cultural and social systems of people living in different parts of the country and the country's composite cultural heritage;
- Appreciation for the need of a balanced synthesis between the change-oriented technologies and the continuity of country's cultural heritage;
- Knowledge of national symbols and desire and determination to uphold the ideas of national identity and unity;
- Capability of appreciating and tolerating differences and diversities of various sorts and the capacity to choose between alternative value systems;
- An awareness of the inherent equality of all and need of global fraternity with a strong commitment to humane values and to social justice;
- Scientific temper characterised by spirit of inquiry, courage to question and objectivity leading to elimination of obscurantism, superstition and fatalism;
- Knowledge of scientific methods of inquiry and its use in solving problems;
- Appreciation of sacrifices and contribution made by the freedom-fighters and social workers in the country's freedom struggle and social regenerations and readiness to follow their ideals;
- Appreciation of and readiness to practice in life the national goals of socialism, secularism, democracy and non-violence;
- Divergent and independent thinking and ability to discover new relationships and combinations;
- Qualities and characteristics necessary for self-learning and for life-long learning leading to creation of a learning society.

Objectives at Various-Levels of Education

The emphasis on the 'child-centrered approach' to education necessarily implies that objectives of education to be achieved at a particular stage/class level should be determined carefully, keeping in view the norms of development—physical, mental, social, emotional and moral of children of relevant age groups. Exact expected learning outcomes related to each objective for a particular class should be precisely worked out.

Most of the objectives indicated above will continue through various classes. However, the level of achievement with regard to a particular objective will be rising from one class to another class in a spiral fashion. Thus, there will be sort of learning continuum so far as targets of achievement with regard to a particular objectives are concerned, and it will reach its terminal point at a particular class level depending on the nature of the concerned objectives.

Subjects at Various Stages and Time Allocation

Elementary Allocation (8 Years)	*Time Allocation*
Primary Stage (5 Years)	
(a) One language-the Mother Tongue/Regional Language	30%
(b) Mathematics	15%
(c) Environmental Studies I & II	15%
(d) Work Experience	20%
(e) Art Education	10%
(f) Health and Physical Education	10%
	100%
Upper Primary Stage (3 Years)	
(a) Three Languages	32%
(b) Mathematics	12%
(c) Science	12%
(d) Social Sciences	12%
(e) Work Experience	12%
(f) Art Education	10%
(g) Health and Physical Education	10%
	100%
Secondary Stage (2 Years)	
(a) Three Languages	30%
(b) Mathematics	13%
(c) Science	13%
(d) Social Sciences	13%
(e) Work Experience	13%
(f) Art Education	9%
(g) Health and Physical Education	9%
	100%

EDUCATION FOR ALL BY 2000, 1990*

UEE is the important goals of educational development. The goals of free and compulsory education for all children up to age of 14 years as stipulated in Article 45 of the Constitution was to be achieved by 1960, but revised several times. The date according to the National Policy on Education

* *Education for all by 2000: Indian Perspective*, National Institute of Educational Planning and Administration, New Delhi, 1990.

Notes: 1. All figures, including costs and norms, are based on official (published and unpublished) sources of the Ministry of Human Resource Development, Department of Education.
2. Original Table numbers have been changed to conform to this Chapter number.
3. Para numbers refer to the para numbers of the document.

(1986) is 1995. The document under reference does not subscribe to the problem and attempts to indicate possible directions and broad resource requirements.

It covers an analytical study of various aspects of education with reference to Indian situation. And in this context it attempts to lay emphasis on 'special requirements of different disadvantaged groups such as Women, Scheduled Castes and Scheduled Tribes'. The process of education including content, evaluation and teacher education are examined and discussed.

EXTRACTS

3. Goals and Targets

Unrealistic Targets in the Past

A review of the progress of basic education shows that goals and targets were fixed in the past on the basis of an inadequate understanding of the significance of education. These targets did not take into the account the problem of availability of resources, and the conflicting claims of social and economic planning.

Realistic Targets

If right from the beginning, it is apparent that goals are unrealistic and unachievable, they do not lead to the kind of motivation and resource mobilisation required. The right approach, therefore, is to set realistic targets - realistic not defined as easily achievable, but as achievable with conceivable maximum input of meticulous planning and resources financial as well as human.

We shall, therefore, proceed to propose realistic targets that we believe can be achieved by the year 2000, keeping in view the past trends, the contemporary situation, and the future prospects of availability of resources and other favourable environment, as also the constraints. The targets will be presented in more precise and specific terms. Although it is a plan for ten years, it would be useful to set separate targets for the first five and the second five years to enable mid-term appraisal and corrective action. This will also coincide with the Eighth and the Ninth Five Year Plan periods.

Identification of Educational Inputs

For ideal planning, educational inputs provided by other sectors should also be taken into account.

Limited Specificity and Disaggregation in Target Fixing

Different targets for different States and areas could be attempted, but this would make the whole exercise too cumbersome to be meaningful. It is, therefore, proposed that the national targets may have limited specificity and disaggregation with the further requirement that more detailed disaggregated targets will be set for each state, each district, each development block and each unit of microplanning. In this disaggregated target-setting at various levels, the following important considerations will be kept in view:

(1) Separate targets for rural and urban areas should be fixed.

(2) Separate targets for the disadvantaged sections of the society will be fixed gender-wise.

(3) The low participation in education of girls and women is the most significant factor to be taken into account. Any target for a group may be achieved with continued inequity between males and females of that group, so long as the targets do not clearly indicate the levels to be achieved separately for both genders. That is why it has been suggested that the group-wise disaggregated target will also be gender-wise.

(4) Access to educational facilities, participation in education and achievement in education are distinct, though interrelated. These aspects should be separately considered for fixing targets and appropriate planning.

Targets at National Level

The mechanism of micro-level planning will result in separate targets for each planning unit—state, district, block, and village. In a truly decentralised approach of planning, realistic targets fixed by all the villages of the block should lead to the target of the block, the targets of all the blocks in a district should lead to the target of the district and so on. However, such a process will not only be time-consuming, it would also lack a national goal reference. By expecting certain national level targets on the basis of disaggregation, we are also hoping to oblige the national and state level planners to pay higher attention to areas and groups and within them to girls/women, receiving special attention.

A. *Access*

1. By the year 1995, primary schools or their alternatives will be provided to every child in the rural areas within a distance of one km.
2. By the year 2000, upper primary schools or their alternatives will be provided to every child in the rural area within a distance of three km.

According to the All-India Educational Survey (1986), 94 per cent of the rural population is being served by a primary school within one km and 85.39 per cent of the rural population is being served by an upper primary school within a distance of three km. In view of this, it should not be difficult to provide a school or an alternative education centre in the next 5 years to the remaining 6 per cent of the rural population for primary education, and the remaining 14.61 per cent for upper primary education in the next 10 years. In this we are assuming a growth rate of slightly above one per cent, which is not very high.

B. *Participation*

3. Primary education through schools or alternatives will be provided to:

(a) Eighty per cent of all children up to the age of 11 years by 1995, which will necessarily include at least 70 per cent belonging to every identified disadvantaged group; and

(b) Ninety-five per cent of all children up to the age of 11 years by the year 2000, which will necessarily include 85 per cent girls belonging to every identified disadvantaged group.

Taking into account the current lower participation rate of the children of disadvantaged groups as compared to the total participation of children, different levels of participation are proposed for children of disadvantaged groups and for the overall participation.

4. Upper primary education through schools or alternatives will be provided to:

(a) Sixty per cent of all children up to the age of 14 years by 1995, which will necessarily include at least 65 per cent of girls belonging to every identified disadvantaged group; and

(b) Seventy-five per cent of all children up to the age of 14 years by 1995, which will necessarily include at least 65 per cent of girls belonging to every identified disadvantaged group.

The drop-out rate is extremely high in the early stages of primary education and is considerably less between the completion of primary and the start of the upper primary education. Of those who complete primary education roughly 75 per cent continue studies for upper primary education. Most of the children who continue studies for upper primary education usually complete that stage. Keeping this in view, the targets for participation in upper primary education have been kept at approximately 75 per cent of those for primary education. As implicit assumption is that if the existing transfer rate for primary to upper primary is 75 per cent, it is likely to go up and similarly the drop-out rate at the upper primary stage would also be reduced. The effect of the level achieved in 1995 at the end of the primary stage will usually be seen at the end of the upper primary stage after three years. However, in view of the improved environment for education, it has been visualised that improved transfer to and retention in upper primary education will not be sequential but partly contemporaneous with improvement in primary education.

C. *Achievement*

(a) Seventy per cent of children, including at least 60 per cent girls of every disadvantaged group, pursuing elementary education, will achieve the minimum levels of learning by the year 1995; and

(b) Eighty per cent of children, including at least 70 per cent girls of every disadvantaged group, pursuing elementary education, will achieve the minimum levels of learning by the year 2000.

These targets highlight the new approach and thrust in the plan for Education for All by the Year 2000. Minimum levels of learning will be clearly defined and laid down for the end of primary education and upper primary education. To enable the monitoring of progress of children towards these levels, the teachers will be suitably oriented to appreciate the concept of minimum levels of learning, to work towards their achievement, to design and administer tests, and to ensure progress...

13 Resources for Education

Inadequacy of resources constitutes a major bottleneck in realising any plan targets. Elementary education suffered in India, apart from several factors, because of insufficient allocation of financial resources. While finances are an important constraint, they are not the only constraints, but one among many. Resources are a necessary, although not a sufficient, condition in achieving the educational goals.

A quick glance at the trends in public expenditure on education shows that over the years, it has increased as a proportion of GNP. At the inception of planning (1950-51) India was spending 1.2 per cent of GNP on education, and according to the latest available statistics (1986-87), this increased to approximately 4 per cent. The share of elementary education also increased from an insignificant level of 0.48 per cent of GNP in 1950-51 to 1.7 per cent in 1986-87.

Future Requirements

Elementary Education

According to population projections, the target population for elementary education, i.e., of the age-group 6-14, will be 163 million in A.D. 2000; 102 million of the age-group 6-11, and 61 million of the age-group 11-14. How much would it cost to provide primary education to 95 per cent of children of the age-group 6-11, and upper primary education to 80 per cent of children to the 11-14 age group, as pragmatically suggested in this document? It is proposed that 70 per cent of the children will be provided formal education. Further, it is felt that the number of over and under-age children in elementary education would come down gradually, to levels of 25 per cent in primary education and 15 per cent in upper primary education.

In the absence of recent estimates on expenditure per student, we shall consider here the salary of teachers in estimating the requirement of resources. After all, teachers' salaries constitute about 95 per cent of the total recurring expenditure. The average salary of teachers in primary schools is found to be Rs. 24,000 per annum and in the upper primary schools Rs. 36,000 per annum. Assuming teacher-pupil ratios of 40 and 35 in primary and upper primary schools respectively, the total number of teachers required in A.D. 2000 is estimated at 2.1 million in primary and 1.1 million in upper primary schools. Accordingly, the teacher costs worked out to Rs. 91.2 thousand million - Rs. 50.9 thousand in primary schools and Rs. 40.3 thousand million in upper primary schools. To this, we add 5 per cent non-teaching recurring cost, i.e. Rs. 0.46 thousand million. Thus, the total recurring cost amounts to Rs. 91.7 thousand million.

Now, this is only recurring expenditure, and it does not cover expenditure on capital items; it also does not make any allowance for improvement in the quality of education. This is the level of resources required for elementary education by A.D. 2000.

One may briefly note that the additional resources required, in the context of several measures of improvement in quality as suggested in the present document, would be quite substantial. The Working Group on Resources for Education for the Eighth Five Year Plan (1990-95) has estimated the requirements for a few such items. The Group estimated the indirect expenditure on administration and supervision, quality improvement, stipends, scholarships and other incentives, at Rs. 2067 million, the cost of construction of classrooms for additional children at Rs. 11.095 million, and the cost of construction of the backlog of schools, based on the Fifth All-India Educational Survey, at Rs. 38,561 million. In addition, for Operation Blackboard, an additional amount of Rs. 15,139 million was estimated as the requirement and in all Rs. 88 thousand million. It is assumed that during 1995-2000 an additional amount of Rs. 23 thousand million would be required. Thus, on an average, Rs. 11.2 thousand million would be required for formal elementary education as non-recurring expenditure every year during 1991-2000. These estimates exclude normal recurring expenditure in the form of teacher cost etc., that we have estimated separately.

Thus, in all putting recurring and non-recurring expenditures together, elementary education requires about Rs.800 thousand million during the next ten years; in other words the total expenditure should gradually increase to Rs. 103 thousand million in A.D. 2000 at 1989-90 prices.

Non-formal Education

It is being planned that 30 per cent of the children of the age group 6-14 would be provided education through the non-formal channel.

We believe that the non-formal system of education should be comparable with formal system as far as the quality and content are concerned. Then only vertical mobility of the students into the formal system of education would be possible. This obviously requires more resources.

At present it is estimated by the Ministry of Human Resource Development (Department of Education), that a centre for non-formal education costs about Rs. 12,000 per year and it provides education to 20 students. Within two years of non-formal education, one is expected to have acquired an education equivalent to compulsory elementary education. The unit costs of non-formal education for two years per student works out to Rs. 1200 (at current 1989-90 prices). Accordingly it is estimated that non-formal education will require Rs. 52.6 thousand million in A.D. 2000 at 1989-90 prices. It amounts to about Rs. 500 thousand million for the 10 years until A.D. 2000.

In all, the requirements of elementary education, including non-formal education, in A.D. 2000 would be in the order of Rs. 156 thousand million at 1989-90 prices. Given the earlier trends, it seems to be a gigantic task. Between 1960-61 and 1970-71, the real expenditure on elementary education was doubled; and between 1970-71 and 1980-81 it increased by about 40 per cent. The present estimates suggest that these trends would be substantially reversed: the total expenditure should be doubled by the turn of the century.

Minimum Level of Resources

Thus, the requirement of resources for a few major programmes is estimated here. It should also be noted that the estimates are based on some crude and quick calculations. More importantly, these estimates allow for mere enrolment in the system by A.D. 2000. Hence, they should be viewed as the minimum level of resources required.

It is clear that the estimates made here do not cover several programmes and policies suggested in this document, such as training of teachers, administrators, voluntary agencies, mothers, community leaders, public provision of incentives to school children, particularly, of the weaker sections, establishment of special organisations like National Testing Service, central, state and district boards of education, village education committees, school complexes, and mechanisms of monitoring, etc. These are only illustrative. If one were to cost each item, assuming that reliable estimates of unit costs of the items are available, it is likely that the actual level of requirement of resources would be of a very high order.

Generating Non-Conventional Resources

While every effort should be made to generate additional resources for education, it is also required that non-conventional strategies need to be devised in mobilising and effectively utilising monetary, physical, and human resources. As an example, a few strategies relating to human resources are out-lined below. However, it may be noted that these strategies do not necessarily mean that the level of resources required for education could be substantially lowered.

Human Resources

The stupendous task of Education for All will require massive human resources. For this, we have to diversify the sources. Some of them are as follows:

Local Community

The local community is a tremendous fund of human resources, if imaginatively used. Our present approach of looking towards outside sources will have to change to enable us to properly identify and utilise the local human resources. The teachers and instructors for NFE and adult education can be drawn from the community. They will have a greater motivation and involvement. Volunteers from the community can be identified and their assistance obtained. Persons in the community with special skills and expertise can be identified and used as a resource person for development of those specified skills.

The concept of Village Education Committee also reflects the utilization of local human resources for management and supervision, which the existing hierarchical and bureaucratic system is unable to perform satisfactorily. In framing curriculum and preparation of textual materials, we are adopting a decentralised approach and also desire that the local needs and environment should be properly linked.

Support of Voluntary Organisations

The support of voluntary organisations and social action groups may be enlisted for motivating and enabling the community to get fully involved in EFA, working as a catalyst for changing the culture of educational management in which community and teachers will have a more central role and to identify, promote and encourage more voluntary groups and social activists in areas where they are required. A well-designed policy to approach the human resources in colleges, universities, research institutions, and other institutions of higher learning, national laboratories, etc., and to motivate them to spare their free time and knowledge for elementary education is required. There are a number of other important sources from which valuable human resources can be drawn for educational effort, including educated people.

Concluding Observations

It will be against the spirit of the Constitution to allow elementary education to suffer from inadequacy of resources. As far as funding elementary education and literacy programmes is concerned, it should be viewed in the framework of the Constitution. It is not just the Department of Education, but all the government departments which should be made to allocate substantial resources for elementary education, as no sector can develop significantly with illiterate masses. In fact, the whole nation should feel responsible for the development of education in the country.

In the system of central planning we are used to in this country, only the resources required from the government or public sector agencies are taken into account. However, for an activity like education, there are considerable costs borne by the children and their parents. Individuals have to spend on books, stationery, uniform, transport, etc. These costs are not included in the financial implications presented here, except for the provision of incentives like books and uniforms to the weaker sections. The Constitution has directed that education for children in primary and upper primary levles of education should be free. This has been so far taken, in practice; to mean that schools should not charge any fees. The cost incurred by parents for education of their children has been ignored and has not been considered as a violation of the directive of free education. In view of the paucity of resources, it may be pragmatic to continue this approach and let the parents bear costs of this nature, while underscoring that ideally these costs should be borne by public funds.

We may also have to move from the concept of exclusive responsibility of the government for education to shared responsibility between the government and the community. This would not be difficult, keeping in view the tradition in India of community support to education from ancient times. The scope for better utilisation of non-financial resources available within and outside the education system should be explored, and the provision for meeting the costs to utilise them, which would obviously be small, should be made.

Serious efforts should be initiated to encourage individuals and organisations through task incentives and other measures to make large endowments and donations to the education sector. However, given the earlier experience, mobilisation of cheap local resources, revision of the fee structure in higher education, and voluntary donations and endowments, etc., should be viewed only as peripheral sources of mobilisation of additional resources for marginal improvements in the system. After all, they cannot become primary and reliable sources of revenue for large-scale improvements in the system. The Government cannot but continue taking more responsibility for elementary education.

For safeguarding democracy and strengthening the foundations of the integrated nation, it is necessary not to compromise with the requirements of these basic needs in education. It should be noted that without adequate resources, financial, physical, and human, our target of Education For All will remain unachieved even by the turn of the country. If we have to enter the twenty-first century without the burden of the unfulfilled goals originally proposed by the Constitution-makers of India, substantial resources should be allocated to elementary and adult education programmes.

COMMITTEE TO REVIEW THE NATIONAL POLICY ON EDUCATION (1986), 1990-91*

The Government formed in 1989 decided to review the implementation of the National Policy on Education and appointed on may 7, 1990, a committee with Acharya Ramamurti as its Chairman. The Committee submitted its report entitled *Towards an Enlightened and Humane Society* to the Minister of State, Ministry of Human Resource Development on December 26, 1990. The report was tabled in Parliament on January 9, 1991. However, no action could be taken on the report as the National Front Government was very short-lived.

Terms of Reference

- To review the National Policy on Education, 1986, and its implementation;
- to make recommendations regarding the revision of the Policy; and
- to recommend action necessary for implementation of the revised policy within a time frame.

Government of India Resolution No. F.-1-6/90 PN (D.I.) dated 7th May, 1990

Despite efforts at social and economic development since attainment of Independence, a majority of our people continue to remain deprived of education, which is one of the basic needs for human development. It is also a matter of grave concern that our people comprise 50 per cent of the world's illiterate and large sections of children have to go without acceptable level of primary education. Government accords the highest priority to education—both as a human right and as the means for bringing about a transformation towards a more humane and enlightened society. There is need to make education an effective instrument for securing a status of equality for women, and persons belonging to the backwards classes and minorities. However, it is essential to give a work and

---

* *Towards an Enlightened and Humane Society*: NPE, 1986, A Review, Part I, 1990. Committee for Review of National Policy on Education, Government of India, New Delhi, 1991.

Note: Para numbers refer to para number of the document.

employment orientation to education and to exclude from it the elitist aberrations which have become the glaring characteristic of the educational scene. Educational institutions are increasingly being influenced by casteism, communalism and obscurantism and it is necessary to lay special emphasis on struggle against this phenomenon and to move towards a genuinely egalitarian and secular social order. The National Policy on Education, 1986 (NPE), needs to be reviewed to evolve a framework which would enable the country to move towards this perspective of education.

Government have, therefore, decided to set up NPE Review Committee.

3. The Department of Education should coordinate with the other concerned departments and secure adequate resource allocation for the above-mentioned programmes based on parameters which indicate the status of girls' education in a given habitation/village. For instance, priority needs to be given to the habitations/villages having enrolment and retention rates for girls in schools below the average rates of the States.

4. To achieve the above purpose, planning for educational development of any given region would have to be necessarily conducted at the Block or sub-Block level. This task would be facilitated if it is undertaken through the proposed Educational Complexes in which there will be Block-level representatives of the various agencies/departments concerned with social welfare and development, along with teachers, Anganwadi workers and representatives of poor women's groups and Panchayati Raj institutions.

5. Teachers, Anganwadi workers, village-level functionaries of other departments, and representatives of women's groups and community-level organisations should play an important role in making micro-level information available to the Educational Complex for prioritisation of action in this regard.

Early Childhood Care and Education (ECCE)

6. The policy framework on women's education must bring out the criticality of the link between ECCE and girls' accessibility to elementary education.

7. Comprehensive and effective ECCE services should be provided in proximity to every primary and middle school and be programmatically linked with elementary education.

8. Priority should be given to child-care programmes catering to the 0-3 age group, particularly among the underprivileged sections of society.

9. The timings of the ECCE centres should include the school hours so that the girls in the 6-14 age group are relieved from the responsibility of sibling care.

10. While the Anganwadis (ICDS) should continue to be given importance, other models which are sensitive to local needs should also be encouraged.

11. The management of Anganwadis and other ECCE programmes should be decentralised and be made participative, as recommended in the chapter on ECCE.

12. In order that child-care facilities and pre-school and primary education of girls are prioritised in the village and the community, the Anganwadi workers and poor women's groups should be represented on the Village Education Committees.

Regional Disparities

13. The issue of regional disparities needs to be incorporated into the operational design for universalising girls' access to elementary education.

14. Any effective strategy for raising the educational status of women in India would have to give priority to the educationally backward districts.

15. Educational planning at the level of Educational complexes will depend on block-level or sub-block level profiles. These profiles should be based on micro-level information collected from habitations/villages. Teachers, Anganwadi workers, other village-level functionaries and representatives of poor women and other community level organisations should be involved in making such information available.

16. Decentralised and participative mode of planning and management offer an effective basis for responding to the challenge of regional disparities in education, including girls' education. Diverse strategies and disaggregated time-frames, worked out locally, constitute the twin instrumentalities to achieve the goal of universalisation.

Content of Education and the Gender Bias

17. The curriculum in schools should include:

- Increase in the visibility of women and projection of a positive image of the role of women in history, their contribution to society in general and the Indian context in particular. For instance, social history should project the contribution that women have made in the national movement. All such issues should be carefully incorporated in the training and orientation of teachers, educators and administrators.
- Special efforts should be made to strengthen mathematics and science education among girls. Girls' schools should give greater importance to mathematics and science than at present.
- Undifferentiated curriculum for boys and girls.
- Elimination of negative stereotypes and biological and social concepts which have a sexist bias.
- Outmoded traditions and myths that hinder positive development of women and their role in national life should be objectively discussed in the class-room in a gender perspective. Similarly the portrayal of

women in our epics and mythology needs to be critically examined in the class-room.

- Basic legal information including protective laws regarding women and children and extracts from the Constitution to make the children aware of the fundamental rights and other basic concepts therein.
- Specific measures to improve the participation of girls in physical training and sports should be undertaken.

Stereotypes in Text-books and the 'Hidden Curriculum'

18. It is recommended that all school text-books, both by NCERT/SCERTs and other publishers, be reviewed to eliminate the invisibility of women and gender stereotypes, and also for the proper incorporation of a women's perspective in the teaching of all subjects. This review should also cover all the supplementary reading material and library books being recommended for schools, particularly those supplied by Operation Blackboard.

Scope of Article 45 of the Constitution

104. The scope of the Constitutional Directive (Article 45) of providing within a specified time-frame, free and compulsory education for all children until they complete the age of fourteen years, should be enlarged to include ECCE.

Operational Design

105. Since ECCE is a cross-sectoral programme, addressing the intersecting needs of children, women and girls, ECCE as a component should receive due attention in all dimensions and stages of education, such as women's education, education of Scheduled Castes and Scheduled Tribes, elementary education, vocational education, content and process, teacher training, higher education etc.

Priority

106. ECCE should be included in the Minimum Needs Programme.

Role and Responsibility of Various Departments

107. The Department of Women and Child Development in the Ministry of HRD at the Centre (and the Departments of Social Welfare in the States) should be held accountable for the implementation of ECCE in all aspects of its operational design, as recommended in the POA.

108. This Department must also accept the nodal role of stimulating, co-coordinating and monitoring the ECCE work undertaken by other agencies/departments such as Labour, Works and Housing, Tribal Welfare, Irrigation, Rural Development, Forest etc.

109. The Department of Women and Child Development (and its counterparts in the States) should seek the setting up of an Inter-Ministerial Committee.

Strategies and Measures for Achieving UEE

169. Make each school, primary or middle, fully responsible, accountable for formulating and implementing strategies for UEE in villages/habitations/*mohallas* in the area under its coverage. For this purpose, vest the school with the necessary authority and autonomy to decide upon their mix of strategies and measures (e.g. adult education, para-schools, Operation Blackboard). Provide each school through the avenue of the Educational Complex adequate funds and intellectual resources to implement its programme of universalisation.

170. Authorise the school Head Master/Head Mistress to recruit para-teacher (*Shiksha Karmis*) for reaching out either to unserved habitations or to those children who cannot attend the school in the day hours. The issues of emoluments, rules governing their probationary period and eventual absorption in the school, and their training in an 'Internship Model' have already been dealt with in this chapter.

171. Encourage innovation by teachers themselves in building up diverse models of child-centred approach to education and create mechanisms of collating, integrating and disseminating the growing expense of the teaching community within and among Educational Complexes.

172. In order to increase the relevance of education from the standpoint of working children, especially girls, it would be necessary to emphasise vocationalisation of the entire educational process up to Class VIII level.

173. The goal of universalisation of education may be viewed in two phases—the first phase of Universalisation of Primary Education (UPE) and the second phase of UEE. While the school shall be expected to undertake micro-planning for UPE in association with the Educational Complex in the first phase itself, UEE may be allowed to grow organically out of the development of Primary Education. In the second phase, after achieving the goal of UPE, micro-planning for UEE would also become necessary and viable.

174. Adopt the principle of differentiated or disaggregated targets and pluralistic educational strategies for achieving UEE. This mode of decentralised and participative planning provides scope for gender specific, community-wise, Block-level and District-level, and regional parameters to inform the planning process. The National and State targets of UEE as well as resource allocation shall emerge from collation and integration of the disaggregated targets.

175. Monitoring of the move towards UEE shall be integral to the planning process and may operate at three independent but co-ordinated levels:

(a) Within the Educational Complex, of individual schools;
(b) Within the district, of individual Educational Complexes; and
(c) Within the State, of individual District Boards of Education.

Resources for Education

15.2.0 Though education has been in the Concurrent List in the Constitution since 1976, it remains primarily a State activity. Bulk of the investments is made by the State Governments. Free and compulsory education is expected to be provided by the States for all children up to 14 years of age. In most States education is free in the entire school stage. Up to class XII education is free for girls in all the States...

15.8.1 The total Central and State Plan expenditure has also been falling. It was only 3.55 per cent for the Seventh Plan.

15.8.2 The share of Elementary Education has come down from the level of 56 per cent in First Plan to 29 per cent in the Seventh Plan.

Resources for Education as envisaged in the National Policy on Education, 1986

15.10.1 The National Policy on Education, 1986, spells out the approach to mobilisation of resources for Education as follows:

> ...The Government and the community in general will find funds for such programmes as the universalisation of elementary education; liquidating illiteracy, equality of access to educational opportunities to all sections throughout the country.

15.11.2 The Seventh Plan document lays down the strategy and pattern of growth of Education as follows:

> "Enrolment in elementary education (Class I-VIII) is expected to increase by 25 million and cover 92 per cent of the population in the age-group 6-14 years by 1989-90. In addition, non-formal systems will be used to bring closer the objective of universalisation of elementary education. Secondary school enrolment is expected to go up by 5 million partly through better utilisation of existing schools, and with a special emphasis on vocationalisation. Special efforts will be made to improve the quality of education. As part of this drive, model schools will be set up in each district to impart quality education to promising children, particularly those coming from rural areas. Adult literacy programmes will be pursued with the objective of covering all illiterates in the age-group 15-35 by 1990. In higher education and technical education, the emphasis will be on consolidation and improvements in quality."

Recommendations of the Eighth Finance Commission

15.12.2 The State Governments gave requests to the Eighth Finance Commission aggregating to nearly Rs. 4,000 crores—for appointment of additional teachers, provision of furniture and equipment, construction of buildings, provision of mid-day meals etc. The then Ministry of Education also emphasized the need for clearing the backlog of *pucca* buildings for primary and middle schools, conversion of single teacher schools into two-teacher schools, provision of adequate inspecting staff and administration facilities. The Ministry also assessed the financial requirements for this purpose as over Rs. 3,000 crores. The Eighth Finance Commission disposed of the matter as follows:

> "It seems to us that lack of *pucca* buildings for the primary schools and the existence of single-teacher primary schools constitute two basic weaknesses in the education system. Presently, 185,666 primary schools accounting for 40.88 per cent of total number of primary schools in all the 22 States are functioning in thatched huts, tents, etc. We have decided that the States in which the percentage of primary schools without *pucca* buildings exceeds 40 per cent, should be helped with upgradation outlays to bring down the percentage of such primary schools to the all-India average, i.e. 40 per cent. We have assumed a unit cost of Rs. 40,000 for a school building of two class-rooms. We have added 30 per cent to the unit cost for the hill States. We have thus allocated Rs. 164.39 crores for the construction of 38,946 additional school buildings in 11 States to bring them to the all-India average of 60 per cent building satisfaction in respect of primary schools.
>
> Another facet of the education sector, which caused us concern, was the preponderance of single-teacher primary schools in some States. Out of the 454,213 primary schools in the 22 States, 165,848 schools function as single-teacher schools. Thus, they form 36.5 per cent of the total number of primary schools. We have decided to extend our support to those States where the proportion of single-teacher schools exceeds 35 per cent, which is the all-India average. The States wherein the proportion of single-teacher primary schools exceeds 35 per cent are Andhra Pradesh, Gujarat, Himachal Pradesh, Jammu & Kashmir, Karnataka, Madhya Pradesh, Maharashtra, Meghalaya, Orissa, Rajasthan and Tripura. We have provided outlays for the appointment of 45,255 additional teachers to bring these States to the all-India level. In the computation of upgradation outlays, we have adopted State specific emolument - levels for each of the 11 States. We have thus provided Rs. 122.01 crores. With this provision, it should be possible to raise the number of primary schools with two

teachers or more, in the 11 States, to 65 per cent which is the all-India average. We have provided a total sum of Rs. 286.40 crores for upgradation of the education sector."

Recommendations of the Ninth Finance Commission in its first report (1989-90) and second report (1990-95)

15.12.8 In its second report (for 1990-95) the Ninth Finance Commission has followed the normative approach according to which needs and capacities of different governments are assessed normatively and such normative assessments are taken as the basis far determining the volume and pattern of federal transfers. So far as education is concerned the factors that have been taken into consideration for the purpose of assessing expenditure are the following:

Primary Education

- Expenditure per child in the age group of 6-10 (taken as a dependent variable).
- Proportion of enrolment in primary stage to the population in the age group 6-10.
- Students-teacher ratio in primary state.
- Differences in the average salaries of primary school teachers across the States.

Strategies for Raising Resources

15.13.1 ...Primary Education is yet to reach the level attained during the first plan. This pattern is not consistent with the Constitutional mandate for achieving universalisation of Elementary Education. Nor is it consistent with the need for providing a meaningful vocational bias for School Education... .

CENTRAL ADVISORY BOARD OF EDUCATION, 46TH SESSION, 1991*

The 46th meeting of CABE was held at New Delhi on March 8-9, 1991 under the Chairmanship of Shri Rajmangal Pandey, Minister of Human Resource Development.

Proceedings and Recommendations

Elementary Education: The working group report on elementary education was presented by Dr. L.P. Pandey, the Rapporteur of the group.

Education Minister, Karnataka said the CABE should recommend adoption of mid-day meal programme. He said that the experience of the

* Ministry of Human Resource Development, Government of India, New Delhi, 1992.

States which had adopted such a programme had been very positive. In response to this, Anil Bordia explained that CABE had always endorsed the idea but had also consistently taken the stand that the responsibility for this should not lie with the school system, as the work relating to procurement of foodgrains, their storage, cooking, distribution, accounting, monitoring, etc., greatly interfered with the task of teaching/learning in schools.

Prof. D.S. Kothari said that while he fully agreed with the MLL approach and concept, there was need for a re-examination of the recommendations of the R.H. Dave Committee in regard to specific skills and competencies before adopting them. He also advised that inculcation of values and other non-cognitive and affective areas should also be emphasised.

Some other members also made observations on different aspects of the report of the working group. CABE adopted the Report of the working group with the following additional observations:

(a) The specific levels of skills and competencies recommended by the R.H. Dave Committee should be got thoroughly reexamined by the Ministry before accepting the Report;

(b) Operation Blackboard should continue in the Eighth Plan and expanded to the upper primary stage. Funds for appointment of teachers provided by the central Government during the Seventh Plan should continue to form part of the Centrally-sponsored Schemes during the Eighth Plan. A time-bound programme should be taken up for provision of infrastructure and basic facilities for primary education based on well laid down norms; and

CENTRAL ADVISORY BOARD OF EDUCATION WORKING GROUP ON ELEMENTARY EDUCATION, 1991

The working group on Elementary Education discussed only Minimum Levels of Learning, Micro-Planning and Non-Formal Education.

Minimum Levels of Learning

The major concern behind the need to have minimum levels of learning was to reduce the existing disparities and improve the level of achievement in rural areas, socially and economically backward areas and thus work towards the establishment of equity and social justice. It is in this context that the Minimum Essential Levels of Learning were proposed. One of the factors which affected the quality of primary education was an over-ambitious and excessively heavy curriculum that had little relevance to the lives and needs of the majority of students and had compelled a joyless rote memorisation and over-emphasis on text-books. What was required was a curriculum that equipped children to acquire mastery over competencies and skills essential for them to function as literate adults in their communities even if they do not get the opportunity for further studies. Another important feature of the MLL is achievability. Reduced quantum of learning will enable children to learn to mastery levels, even while permitting the teacher to relate text-book information and objective reality into a meaningful process of understanding and application through experimentation, exploration and activity-based teaching. The reduced quantum will thus not only permit a greater joyousness in the class-room but also by virtue of a good mastery over the earlier learning units, the ability to progress faster through later stages of education.

The strategy of Minimum Levels of Learning will provide the common basis for both formal and non-formal modes of imparting primary level education. This strategy can, therefore, be effectively utilised for establishing comparability and equivalence of achievement between the formal and the non-formal system, at least in the essential subjects of study such as Language and Mathematics.

An important aspect of the MLLs was that it took into account the existing disparities between regions, districts, and States in achievement levels. The strategy for introducing MLLs, therefore, envisaged that each region would examine the MLLs in relation to its existing conditions and achievement levels and modify them suitably before accepting them as expected goals of performance. Thus, in areas with significantly lower achievement levels, intermediate levels of MLLs could be set with time-bound targets. Different regions could thus have differentiated MLLs. The endeavour of this strategy would be to direct better results where levels of learning were lower and to consciously accelerate the pace of development in the interior regions thereby reducing disparities and equalising the minimum standards over the entire country.

Continuous and comprehensive evaluation forms an important part of the strategy of MLLs. Having set MLLs as the performance goal, continuous and comprehensive evaluation would ensure the attainment of competencies and skills through continuous and periodical evaluation and corresponding remedial measures as well as summative assessment of performance from stage to stage.

After the detailed discussion, the Committee recommends as follows:

(i) The strategy of Minimum Levels of Learning (MLL) should be accepted as an important component of all educational planning for universalisation of elementary education, including non-formal education;

(ii) Steps should be taken to widely disseminate the strategy and concept of MLL, highlighting its inbuilt flexibility and the active involvement in a decentralised manner of teachers, educationists, parents, etc.;

(iii) Concrete measures should be initiated as early as possible to implement the whole strategy in order to improve the quality of achievement coupled with equity and social justice;

(iv) The State Governments and Voluntary Organisations, universities and other institutions should be provided assistance, financial and academic, to operationalise the strategy; and

(v) Since the ultimate objective is universalisation of elementary education, a similar exercise should be initiated for the upper primary level so that improvement in attainment, together with social justice and equity is ensured at the upper-primary level also.

Micro Planning

At the outset, the Working Group wanted to be fully apprised of the main parameters of micro-planning. These were explained as follows:

Efforts have been made in the past to bring elementary education system closer to the community. The modalities created over the years have continued to serve the well-to-do sections of the society, which co-opted into their fold, the influential teachers and other persons concerned with delivery of basic education services. This powerful section has protected the disfunctionality of the school system and has not made much contribution to enhancing the participation of children in the elementary educational system. The disfunctionality of the elementary education system has consequently reached an alarming stage. In large parts of the country, schools are running in an unsatisfactory manner, children drop-out in large numbers, and the levels of their learning are well below the expected norms. A significant percentage of children has remained altogether deprived of the benefits of elementary education.

The situation has to change. A widespread mobilisation has to be generated to energies the hitherto deprived sections in the countryside. Mobilisation could be generated with the help of mass-media, traditional and folk forms of communication and person to person contact by committed activists. Such a communication strategy should highlight the present status of elementary education and indicate areas in which useful intervention can be made. The mobilisation which has got generated in several parts of the country under the National Literacy Mission, should also be harnessed in this behalf. Simultaneously with the creation of an environment, large-scale programme of training and orientation should be taken up for village youth and women. The purpose behind this should be to explain the responsibility of the village community towards elementary system and engendering a confidence among them to secure accountability of the elementary system to the Village Education Committee. The trained women and youth will need to work in rapport with the local level Panchayati Raj structure as well as with teachers and AE/NFE instructors.

The latter *viz.* elementary school teachers and AE/NFE instructors, should be given confidence that the process of micro-planning is not a confrontation with them but a new kind of mutually beneficial partnership. This group (comprising oriented women and youth) could take the shape of *Mahila Samooh* (as has happened in several hundred villages in Rajasthan where the Women's Development Programme is being implemented), or Village Education Committee (VEC). This *Mahila Samooh* or VEC will not be a structure only in name as in some States. This organisation will have its own inner strength. It must take the form of *Lok Shakti/Stree Shakti*. This group (MS or VEC) will need to be provided a support system in the form of school complexes or a block level education organisation which is permeated by a similar spirit.

The elementary education system (Primary and upper primary school as well as the NFE Centre) will be accountable to this kind of a village education structure. In concrete terms, accountability will imply an effective say (without interference in academic aspects) in the running of elementary education programmes. While on the one hand, this MS/VEC will secure accountability of the elementary education system, it will, on the other hand, help the schools and NFE centres in their work. The group will undertake school mapping to ensure that practically every child of the village has access to elementary education; it will monitor from day to day and week to week the rate of participation of children in the elementary education system to ensure retention and active participation; and it will also take interest to see that the shortcomings and difficulties, found by teachers are resolved and the children have satisfactory achievement in cognitive as well as non-cognitive areas.

The Working Group endorses the micro-planning approach for improvement of elementary education programmes and calls upon all State Governments to take steps for its careful implementation. It requests the Central Government, NIEPA and NCERT to actively associate themselves with the State Government in effective implementation of this approach as early as possible. In doing so, the State Government. may have to incur a good deal of expenditure, which should be built into various schemes of the Central and State Government. and the additionality required should be separately provided as a Centrally-sponsored Scheme. The Working Group is also of the view that the monitoring of the present status of elementary education and in particular of microplanning, NFE programme, achievement related progress of pupil's etc. should be effectively monitored.

School Calendar

The Group felt that School Calendar should match the major agricultural activities, socio-economic factors of the region. This would improve attendance of children in schools on the one hand and control teacher absenteeism on the other.

Recommendations and Observations of CABE on Elementary Education

The Working Group Report on Elementary Education was presented by Dr. L.P. Pandey, the Rapporteur of the group.

Education Minister, Karnataka said the CABE should recommend adoption of mid-day meals programme for improving enrolment and retention. He said that the experience of the States which had adopted such a programme had been very positive. In response to this, Shri Anil Bordia explained that CABE had always endorsed the idea of provision of mid-day meals to children but had also consistently taken the stand that the responsibility for this should not lie with the school system, as the work relating to procurement of foodgrains, their storage, cooking, distribution, accounting, monitoring, etc., greatly interfered with the task of teaching/learning in schools.

Prof. D.S. Kothari said that while he fully agreed with the MLL approach and concept, there was need for a re-examination of the recommendations of the R.H. Dave Committee in regard to specific skills and competencies before adopting them. He also advised that inclucation of values and other non-cognitive and affective areas should also be emphasised.

Some other members also made observations on different aspects of the report of the working group. CABE adopted the Report of the working group with the following additional observations:

(a) The specific levels of skills and competencies recommended by the R.H. Dave Committee should be got thoroughly re-examined by the Ministry before accepting the Report;

(b) Operation Blackboard should continue in the Eighth Plan and expanded to the upper primary stage. Funds for appointment of teachers provided by the Central Government during the Seventh Plan should continue to form part of the Centrally-sponsored Scheme during the Eighth Plan. A time bound programme should be taken up for provision of infrastructure and basic facilities for primary education based on well-laid down norms; and

(c) The Central and State Governments should be called upon to fully implement the law relating to child labour while efforts are made to provide education to all working children.

COMMITTEE ON MINIMUM LEVELS OF LEARNING (MLL) AT PRIMARY STAGE, 1991

The need to lay down Minimum Levels of Learning (MLLs) arised from the need for provision of equal access and conditions for success to all children irrespective of caste, creed, location or sex. Ministry of Human Resource Development, Department of Education, NCERT, set up a committee in January 1990, under the chairmanship of Prof. R.H. Dave to study afresh the learning outcomes defined in the existing curriculum and to lay down Minimum Levels of Learning that all children who pass the primary stage of education must achieve.

The terms of reference of the committee were as under:

1. Draw up Minimum Levels of Learning for Classes III and V.
2. Recommend a procedure for comprehensive learner evaluation and assessment.
3. Look into the non-cognitive areas of learning and suggest concrete ways in which teaching in these areas can be improved.

The committee was further informed that the terms of reference related to both formal and non-formal systems of education.

Meaning of Minimum Levels of Learning (Extracts from Chapter 2).

Minimum Levels of Learning can, perhaps, be specified in a variety of ways. For instance, MLLs can be stated as expected learning outcomes defined as observable terminal behaviours. One may also go for a taxonomic analysis of learning objectives such as knowledge, comprehension, application, analysis, synthesis, evaluation and so on and accordingly indicate the expected learning outcomes. One can also state the MLLs in terms of learning competencies expected to be mastered by every child by the end of a particular class or stage of education. These different approaches for stating the MLLs are not mutually exclusive. Of the various alternatives available, the committee has chosen to state the MLLs in terms of terminal competencies. Each competency can be further delineated in terms of sub-competencies while specifying the content inputs or while designing specific measures of learning.

It may be noted that the set of MLLs would actually represent the rational criteria adopted for judging the adequacy of the curricular inputs provided and the learning outcomes to be expected. There can be no finality with respect to any set of MLLs. This applies to the set of MLLs developed by the committee also. Two basic considerations kept in view while formulating the MLLs are: (i) the cognitive capabilities of the children at different classes or grades corresponding to different stage of development; and (ii) the empirical reality in terms of enabling environmental conditions that characterise the primary education programme.

Action Plan for Implementation (Text—Chapter 8)

1. Introduction of MLLs in primary schools and NFE centres in the country will require a carefully worked out strategy with necessary phasing. The overall implementation plan may be divided into three or more phases. In

the first phase this curriculum plan may be introduced in only a few selected districts or blocks in two or three states after making a thorough preparation. In this phase, a few innovative centres and on-going reform projects may also be encouraged to follow the MLL approach in order to raise the standard of achievement. Even some individual specialists working in places like teachers' colleges and universities may be encouraged by the Ministry of Human Resource Development to introduce MLLs in selected schools and NFE centres.

2. The chief purpose of this phase should be to understand how the proposed MLLs function in both formal and non-formal delivery systems, what kind of orientation and aids are needed for the teacher in order to achieve the desired level of mastery by the students, what kind of modifications and adaptations are needed in the existing textbooks, how exactly should the system of evaluation and monitoring be evolved and made genuinely functional in different settings and what other administrative and academic measures would be required to succeed in attaining the ultimate goal of enhancing the quality of learner achievement. The second and third phases should aim at further refinement of MLLs and other related aspects and systematic expansion of the implementation programme.

3. It is proposed that in the first phase the number of blocks of different districts and states be kept as small as possible, say, about 4 to 6. However, all schools and NFE centres in the block concerned should be selected for implementation. For comparison purposes, matching samples from neighbouring blocks or districts may be taken. In any case, pre-testing must be carried out to establish benchmark data. Appropriate preparatory steps for making this phase most effective should be taken with full participation of local authorities including teachers, headmasters, supervisors and community members. The district level authorities including the office of DEO, DIET (where established) and other concerned agencies should take the responsibility of organizing, coordinating, implementing and evaluating the programme together with local agencies in charge of both formal education and NFE centres. The district should ultimately be treated as a unit of operation for this innovation and for carrying out various tasks involved at the stages of preparation, implementation, monitoring, evaluation and further expansion in cooperation with local authorities on the one hand, and state agencies including SCERT and State Education Department as well as national authorities on the other.

4. In the ultimate analysis, every district should ensure that the minimum essential standards of achievement laid down at the national level in terms of MLLs as a basic and common criterion of reference should be attained by all as early as possible and even go beyond. different districts and schools within them may need different time frame and resources for

obvious reasons and may set their own intermediate phases for moving towards the standards set by the MLLs. However, within the time span of a few years, to be determined locally, all districts in a given state and all states of the country must ensure the achievement of atleast the minimum levels of learning for almost all children. In certain special programmes and projects such as those launched or being planned in Andhra Pradesh, Bihar, Orissa, Rajasthan and Uttar Pradesh, entire district may be selected to introduce the MLL approach and intensive efforts be made to produce transactional and evaluation materials, etc., from the resources available for these programmes.

5. In order to assist the teacher, who will play the most central role in this programme, it will be necessary to prepare teachers' handbooks in different curriculum areas. The handbooks should provide all explanatory notes and illustrative material relating to MLLs and their effective use in teaching and testing. The handbooks should also indicate how existing textbooks could be used to achieve MLLs until such times that the textbooks are revised, if necessary, in relation to this approach. Suggestions for the use of supplementary textual materials, teaching-learning aids and activity-based methods should be made in the handbooks such that student learning becomes meaningful, effective and cheerful. Besides the handbooks for teachers of primary schools and instructors of NFE centres, those for supervisors and other local functionaries should also be prepared to improve the efficiency of their respective tasks in the context of the MLL approach.

6. While the draft MLLs are laid down nationally, they allow full flexibility for the use of local illustrations, materials and environment for the purpose of establishing their relevance and functionality in the local context. This particular aspect should be clearly shown in the handbooks so that the process of decentralization operates maximally within the national curricular framework. Moreover, this aspect should be sufficiently stressed in the training and retraining of teachers organized on the basis of MLLs. In course of time, integrated instructional materials may be produced which would include textual material, pupils, worksheets, unit-wise evaluation exercises and reinforcement materials, on the basis of specific competencies indicated in the MLLs. It should be worthwhile to examine, in this context, the primers produced under the IPCL programme of adult education.

7. As proposed separately, a continuous and comprehensive scheme of evaluation should be made an integral part of the MLL approacn to quality control right from the first phase of implementation. Teaching and evaluation should be intertwined in various ways including the incorporation of diagnostic testing, remedial teaching, mastery learning and criterion-referenced evaluation including pre-testing and post-testing for monitoring the progress. For these purposes, a large pool of test items, units

tests and other evaluation instruments such as those for vocabulary tests, dictation exercises, mental mathematics and application tests should be prepared and thereby teachers should be given further concrete help in making her/his work optimally efficient and effective. Supervisors can also use this pool of test materials for spot checking of student achievement and district level agencies can utilize them for conducting criterion-referenced testing for the comparison of standards and other such purposes.

8. Based on MLLs handbooks, textual materials and items pools, and appropriate orientation of teachers should be organized before Phase I begins and should likewise be repeated before launching Phases II and III under the expansion programme. Similar orientation should be provided to supervisors and other concerned personnel in relation to their respective responsibilities. For all these functionaries a systematic plan of recurrent orientation during the entire implementation programme should be meticulously followed. The recurrent training should be of short duration and should be functional and task-oriented.

9. Efforts should be made to involve the local community in a variety of ways. Where local education committees exist, their cooperation and active participation should be sought, cooperation of those parents (among others) whose children do not attend school regularly should be sought by establishing contact with them and regular attendance of their children ascertained so that they do not lag behind in attaining the expected mastery of MLLs. If there are voluntary agencies or individual volunteers in the community or neighbouring communities who can provide guidance and support to the school especially in regard to raising the quality of education, their involvement and participation should also be explored. Such agencies and individuals may include, among others, retired educators or other professionals, personnel from a primary or secondary training college nearby, and officials of health department and other such agencies in a village who are motivated enough to extend a helping hand to the school or the NFE centre from time to time. In brief, full utilization of human, physical and even financial resources available in the local environment (whether village, town or city) should be made for effective implementation of MLLs.

10. Similarly, for the purposes of getting internal support and mutual reinforcement, networking of neighbouring schools may be introduced where feasible. Such school-clusters or complexes, as proposed by the Education Commission in the sixties, could work cooperatively for sharing experiences and materials, solving certain problems of instruction, evaluation and monitoring among themselves, reducing time and cost by producing tests, remedial materials, etc., cooperatively and thus, helping one another in improving the quality of the learning process. If the networking or clustering approach is followed, it should be seen that

the size of these groups is kept manageable, say, clusters of some 5 to 10 schools in a compact area within a block. Teachers and headmasters may form their councils to run the networks and set agenda and targets for their cooperative work in the light of their felt needs.

11. The implementation strategy, to be effective, will need a sound monitoring system accompanied by a resource support system. This should be established at the district level. Sufficient preparatory work should be carried out at the initial stage, a detailed design of implementation charted out and necessary financial provision made so that the implementation programme once started moves further with full steam and necessary helps in the form of training, materials, evaluation instruments for pre-testing and stage-wise assessment surveys, etc., the motivation and enthusiasm of all concerned is sustained and any unforeseen obstacles and bottlenecks are removed in time. This system should also be responsible for the review of MLLs, etc., at the end of Phase I of the implementation programme.

12. At the national level, the Department of Education of the Ministry of Human Resource Development (MHRD), Government of India, should continue to play a leading role at the implementation stage together with NCERT, NIEPA and NEO (National Evaluation Organisation, when established). It is recommended that the MHRD may undertake the following responsibilities, among others:

(i) It should coordinate the task of ensuring quality with equity in close cooperation with the state and district level authorities as part of the national programme of universalizing elementary education and providing 'Basic Education for All'. The MHRD should mobilize resources in cooperation with various agencies, motivate the people concerned and ensure political will for implementing the initial and subsequent phases of MLLs in all primary schools and NFE centres in the country as a time-bound programme;

(ii) It should periodically review and monitor progress of implementing this programme at the national level and introduce modifications so that eventually the ultimate goal of quality education for all children is accomplished. Towards this end, it should conduct achievement surveys, especially in the languages, mathematics and basic concepts of general or environmental studies (social, civic and scientific aspects) and take follow-up action on their findings leading to a drastic reduction, if not elimination, of unjustifiable disparities in the standard of achievement at the primary stage that exist between states, among districts within states, between urban and rural areas, and between boys and girls. For carrying out this work NEO may be established as early as possible;

(iii) Once the task of laying down MLLs for the primary stage takes shape, the MHRD should immediately undertake a similar exercise for the upper primary stage comprising Classes VI to VIII without which the work done for the first five classes will remain incomplete and will have less chances of success. In fact, this exercise should be extended in course of time up to the end of general education which includes Classes IX and X as well; and

(iv) The NCERT, NIEPA and pertinent agencies in the states should be involved in the implementation of MLLs while the MHRD should continue to play its vital role as an initiator, catalyst and cooperator with regard to resource mobilization and monitoring of results. The NCERT may set up a special unit for organizing different phases of implementation, for orienting teachers and other educators, for developing handbooks and other instructional materials aligned with MLLs, for producing pools of test materials and remedial exercises, and for several other such purposes. The task of achieving quality coupled with equity for millions and millions of children who are expected to receive primary education through formal or non-formal delivery systems is by no means easy. Keeping in view the magnitude and complexity of the task, MLLs Implementation Unit should have a sufficient number of competent and dedicated people representing subject specialities such as language, mathematics and general studies as well as pedagogical specialities such as teacher training, preparation of handbooks and other materials, instructional processes, evaluation and monitoring.

13. After examining the experience of Phase I and introducing necessary changes in MLLs and other related aspects, Phase II may be launched to include the whole district or clusters or districts for implementation of MLLs in selected places. If the experience is positive and resources are available, this programme may be introduced in about 50 districts chosen from different states. All important steps such as those indicated in the previous paragraphs of this chapter should be taken in order to ensure that the ultimate goal of raising the quality of learning to the mastery level for practically all children in these basic subjects of study is in no way compromised. Again, after analysing the experiences and outcomes of the second phase and making necessary modifications in the MLLs as well as the implementation strategy, Phase III may be launched to extend the programme to all districts in every State/UT in the country. Needless to state that on the basis of the experience thus, gained improving quality and enhancing equity in primary education, further cycles of reform should be undertaken periodically in the light of new needs and developments at the local, national and international levels.

14. A comparative analysis of competencies included in the curricula of literacy and post-literacy programmes of adults may also be carried out to understand the extent to which basic parity exists between different delivery modes all of which are aimed at basic education. Such an analysis may ultimately lead to establishing a common or comparable set of minimum learning competencies for all adults and children in the perspective of life-long learning.

COMMITTEE TO REVIEW NPE (1986) AND REPORT OF THE COMMITTEE TO REVIEW THE NPE (1990-91), 1991*

The National Policy on Education (NPE) was followed up by an elaboration through the Programme of Action (PoA) adopted by Parliament in August 1986. Para 11.5 of NPE envisages a review of the implementation of various parameters of the Policy every five years. The Central Government had in May 1990, appointed a Committee to review NPE, 1986 (NPERC), under the Chairmanship of Acharya Ramamurti. The Committee submitted its report on December 26, 1991 which was tabled in both the Houses of Parliament on January 9, 1991. CABE in its meeting held on March 8-9, 1991 examined the procedure to be adopted for consideration of the report of the NPERC and decided that a CABE Committee be constituted by the Chairman, *viz.*, Union Minister of Human Resource Development, to consider the recommendations of the NPERC. Accordingly, the Chairman of the CABE appointed a Committee on July 31, 1991, under the Chairmanship of Shri N. Janardhan Reddy, Minister of Education.

Early Childhood Care and Education (ECCE)

The scope of Article 45 of the Constitution need not be enlarged. (Para 8.8)

ICDS and other CSS relating to ECCE should continue as Centrally-sponsored Schemes during the Eighth Five Year Plan. The Anganwadi workers should play an expanded role and should be the focal point for a number of activities and support services for women and children, such as child care, family welfare, nutrition and health. The recruitment and training of Anganwadi workers should be so organised as to ensure that they have the necessary skills and motivation to discharge the expanded role. (Para 8.8)

The other recommendations of the NPERC which broadly relate to implementation modalities should be taken into account for reviewing PoA. (Para 8.8)

---

* *Report of the CABE Committee on Policy*, Department of Education, Ministry of Human Resource Development, Government of India, New Delhi, 1992.
Note: Para numbers in brackets refer to para numbers of the document.

Universalisation of Elementary Education (UEE)

What is needed is not so much a Constitutional amendment as suggested by the NPERC as the manifestation of a national will to achieve UEE. The Central and State Governments should bestow over-riding priority to adult literacy and UEE, and provide to the programmes in these two areas total support—financial, administrative and political—a support which is commensurate with the priority. (Para 9.2)

No further refinement of the policy relating to access and enrolment is required; what needs to be done is large scale operationalisation of important components of the strategy outlined by NPE/PoA such as community mobilisation, school mapping and micro-planning. (Para 9.5)

MLL should be a thrust area. (Para 9.6)

The NPE approach to non-formal education is more practical and realistic than that of the NPERC. (Para 9.13)

Expeditious and effective action is required to tone up the management system and the learning environment of NFE so as to ensure that the quality of NFE is comparable with that of formal system in all respects. The Centre and the States should closely and continuously monitor NFE programmes in order that the programmes are effective. (Para 9.13)

Operation Blackboard being one of the priority strategies for UEE, should continue during the Eighth Plan, in an expanded and extended form. (Para 9.15)

Till operational models of an educational complex are developed, tested and tried out, it is not feasible to link the Scheme of Operation Blackboard with the educational complex; nor is it feasible to entrust the planning and monitoring of UEE to the educational complex, as suggested in R.Nos. 169, 171, 173 and 175 by the NPERC. (Para 9.15)

Para 5.12 of NPE, which laid the targets for UPE and UEE, needs to be revised. Every effort should be made to ensure that the constitutional obligation of providing free and compulsory education up to the age of 14 years becomes a reality before we enter the twenty-first century. (Paras 2.6 and 9.17)

The following points deserve priority during the Eighth Five Year Plan in the area of UEE:

- (i) Universal enrolment of all children, including girls and persons belonging to SC/ST;
- (ii) Provision of primary school for all children within one kilometre of walking distance and of facility of non-formal education for school drop-outs; working children and girls who cannot attend schools;
- (iii) Improvement of ratio of primary school to upper primary schools from the existing 1:4 to 1:2, this being a pre-condition for larger

opportunity for widening girls' participation at upper primary stage;

(iv) Reduction of drop-out rates between Classes I to V and I to VIII from the existing 45 per cent and 60 per cent to 20 per cent and 40 per cent respectively;

(v) Improvement of school facilities by revamped Operation Blackboard to be extended to upper primary level also;

(vi) Achievement of minimum levels of learning by approximately all children at the primary level and introduction of this concept at the upper primary stage on a large scale;

(vii) Local level committee, with due representation to women and teachers, to assist in the working of primary education and to oversee its functioning; and

(viii) Improvement of the monitoring system for universalisation of elementary education to see to the achievement of above-mentioned goals.

NPE and PoA may be revised accordingly. (Para 9.18)

NATIONAL PLAN OF ACTION, 1992*

IV.1. Major Goal

Universal enrolment, retention, minimum level of learning, reduction of disparities and universalisation of effective access of schooling.

IV.1.1. Objectives

(a) Universal enrolment of all children including girls, using both full time formal schools and part time non-formal arrangements.

(b) Reduction of drop-out rate between class I to V and I to VIII from the existing 45 per cent and 60 per cent to 20 per cent and 40 per cent respectively.

(c) Achievement of minimum level of learning by approximately all children at the primary level and introduction of this concept at the upper primary state on large scale.

(d) Reduction in disparities by emphasis on girl's education and special measures for children belonging to Scheduled Castes/Scheduled Tribes (SCs/STs).

(e) Expansion of Early Childhood Development activities including appropriate low cost family and community based interventions.

---

* *National Plan of Action: Commitment to the Child*, Department of Women and Child Development, Ministry of Human Resource Development, Government of India, 1992 (Reprint 1996).

Note: Para numbers refer to para numbers of the document.

(f) Universalisation of effective access to schooling. The two broad strategy frames for reaching the targets are:

(i) Micro-planning through people's participation and decentralisation; and

(ii) Introducing Minimum Levels of Learning (MLL) in schools. Micro-planning would be area specific, population specific through mobilising community participation, decentralising educational administration, re-orienting and strengthening local administrative and resource support systems, ascertaining educational requirements of the area, bringing to school all children who can be enrolled, seeing that all children regularly and actually participate in primary education and planning for the improvement of the schools. Minimum levels of learning strategy focuses on learning acquisition in schools and outcomes and is proposed to be implemented through an assessment of the existing level of learning achievement; a definition of the MLL for the area and the time frame for achieving it; reorientation of teaching practices to competency based teaching; introduction of evaluation of student learning; review of textbooks and revision, if required and the provision of inputs to improve learning acquisition to the MLL including provision of physical facilities, teacher training, supervision, evaluation etc.

Activities

(i) Seek people's participation by arousing them to the need for education, creating a sense of responsibility towards children's education and empowering them to take accountability of the school system.

(ii) Community mobilization and environment building will use folk and traditional media, people-to-people discussions, group meetings etc.

(iii) Village Education Committees (VEC) will be formed in each village, with adequate representation of women and the disadvantaged groups to interact with teachers, provide support to the school, ensure regular participation of all children through parental motivation and take accountability over the running of the school.

(iv) Efforts will be made to involve suitable NGOs or field level organisations/project management and to strengthen them adequately for such provision of support to the VEC. Capacity building at local levels will be an essential activity in all areas adopting the micro-planning strategy.

(v) In the next 5 years, efforts will be made to shift educational planning to the district level, by setting up District Boards of Education and District Institutes of Education and Training (DIETs).

(vi) An effective MIS will be created to provide information required for decision making planning and management to the district levels and information for monitoring district plans of the State and national levels.

(vii) The accent during the next 5 years will be upon opening of new primary schools according to the norm in the unserved habitation, and the provision of non-formal education programmes for smaller habitations and for children who cannot benefit from the school system.

(viii) In order to increase enrolment at the upper primary stage, the infrastructure at the upper primary stage will be considerably expanded.

(ix) The existing norm of providing an upper primary school within 3 km walking distance, for all practical purposes, denies education at this level to a large section of girls. This norm will be relaxed and the existing ratio between primary and upper primary schools will be improved to 1:2.

(x) Provisions will be made to add additional rooms and provide additional teachers to existing schools through the scheme of Operation Blackboard and the existing norm for the minimum-2 classrooms and 2 teachers-will be raised successively.

(xi) Non-formal education (NFE) will be developed as a complementary system to the formal education system such that there will be parallel administrative apparatus for NFE; greater attention to the interests of the learner and its quality will be comparable with formal system and conform to the MLLs laid down for the primary stage.

(xii) Mechanisms will be developed for entry from non-formal to the formal system and vice-versa.

(xiii) The NFE programme will include a substantial enhancement in costs per learner on the reasoning that it is not possible to reach out to the marginalised groups with marginalised funding.

(xiv) In order to ensure that regular in-service training and academic supervision is provided to teachers, a beginning will be made to create Teachers' Centres for every cluster of 20-25 primary schools to provide a forum to teachers to get together, discuss issues, resolve common problems and receive academic guidance to build upon their capacities and skills.

(xv) A programme of in-service training of teachers will be coordinated by this block level team to infuse a level of competency in teachers to effectively transact curriculum and textual material.

(xvi) At the State level the existing Councils of Educational Research and Training (SCERT) will be restructured so that they become institutions principally for resource support to elementary education, non-formal education and early childhood education.

(xvii) Resource support through researches and studies will be encouraged by continuing support to Colleges of Teacher Education and Institutes of Advanced Studies in Education.

(xviii) District specific plans will be developed as projects, with specific activities, clearly defined responsibilities, definite time-schedules and district specific targets. Apart from effective UEE the goals of each project will include the reduction of existing disparities in educational access, the provision of alternative systems of comparable standards to the disadvantaged groups, bringing about a substantial improvement in the quality of schooling facilities, obtaining a genuine community involvement in running of schools, and building up local level capacity to ensure effective decentralisation of educational planning.

(xix) A monitoring system will be developed to obtain timely and reliable information on enrolment, retention, completion and achievement. In addition the qualitative monitoring of achievement will also be introduced.

Objective

For Reduction in Disparities by emphasis on girls' education, and special measures for children belonging to SCs/STs.

Activities

(i) An effort will be made to provide a comprehensive system of incentives and support services for girls and children of the economically weaker sections of society.

(ii) A provision of services such as establishment of Day Care Centres for pre-school children and infants, provision of free uniforms, text books and stationery as attendance incentives to girls, coordination of support services such as drinking water, fodder and fuel.

(iii) A similar incentive as appropriate, will be provided in the non-formal system, also, in addition to provision of free text books and stationery to all NFE learners.

Objective

For Early Childhood Education

Expansion of early childhood development activities including appropriate low-cost family and community based interventions.

Activities

(i) During the Eighth Five Year Plan, the ICDS will be expanded and will be the main scheme for early childhood activities.

(ii) The contribution of ICDS to basic education will be enhanced by adjusting it to school timings and by strengthening its educational component.

(iii) Other existing schemes for early childhood education will be improved so as to become holistic schemes providing nutrition and health care as well as education.

(vi) Emphasis and efforts will be made on training of personnel, production of sufficient play way learning material for children, creation of a system of monitoring and supervision, and development of effective rapport between ECCE and community and the primary schools.

NATIONAL PLAN OF ACTION FOR THE SAARC DECADE OF GIRL CHILD, 1991-2000 AD, 1992*

II. Overall Development of the Girl Child

1. Major Goal: Universal access to basic education and completion of primary education by at least 80 per cent Primary School-age children through the following objectives-(a) Universal access and enrolment; (b) Drop-out and retention; (c) Achievement of minimum levels of learning; and (d) Reduction of disparities.

A. Universal Access and Enrolment

Interventions

(i) Universal provision of adequate educational facilities within easy reach of the girl child will be ensured. A school or an alternative system within one kilometre will be provided.

(ii) Primary education will be made cost-free through universal coverage of programmes of mid-day meals, books, uniforms, provision of transportation etc. Innovative schemes like the Savitri Bai Phule Foster

* Department of Women and Child Development, Ministry of Human Resource Development, Government of India, New Delhi, 1992 (Reprint 1996)
Note: Para numbers refer to para numbers of the document.

Parent Scheme in Maharashtra will be encouraged to reduce the burden of parents in educating the girl children.

(iii) Opening of primary schools (classes I-VIII) in every village and making women panchas and panchayats responsible for ensuring enrolment and attendance of girls will be attempted.

(iv) Provision of Early Childhood Care and Education (ECCE) and universalisation of ICDS for facilitating readiness for children and for releasing girl children to attend schools will be ensured.

(v) Support services like day care centres, supply of drinking water, cheap fuel and fodder and other development inputs will be provided to free the girls especially in rural areas to attend school.

(vi) Non-formal Education (NFE) will be developed as a complementary system to the formal education system to cater to the large number of girls who are either non-enrolled or drop-outs from the formal system.

(vii) The NFE programme is an attempt to reach out to those out of schools. Hence, mobile school services will be created with counterparts at State and District level.

(viii) An element of education for responsible parenthood will be introduced in all courses and programmes.

(ix) Mechanisms will be developed for entry from non-formal to the formal system and vice-versa.

(x) Legal measures will be adopted to compel employers to send their girl child workers to the schools set up for the purpose.

B. Drop-out and Retention

Interventions

(i) Drop-out rate is higher amongst girls, still higher among rural girls and highest among tribal girls. Therefore, special efforts will be made to check the problem of drop-outs amongst these groups.

(ii) Communities will be mobilised to create a positive climate for girls' education among rural people.

(iii) Provision of women teachers particularly at the upper primary level will be ensured.

(iv) Support facilities will be provided to enable girls to continue at school.

(v) Health and nutrition approach will be the other major correlates of girls' education. School, therefore, has to become the local point for convergence of education and health services especially for girls in the age group 6-14 years.

(vi) Ancillary facilities like drinking water, urinals and lavatories will be provided.

(vii) Efforts will be initiated to sensitize the education structure to region and habitation specific issues.

(viii) Special efforts will be made to encourage SC/ST girls, by extending to them incentives like free uniforms, book allowances, hostel facilities etc.

(ix) Awards will be given for primary school teachers and fellowships for rural girls.

(x) Vocationalisation of secondary education will be encouraged.

(xi) For implementing Universalisation of Primary Education (UPE) programmes especially in rural areas, data disaggregated by age, sex, caste/tribe will be collected block-wise for decentralised, micro-level participatory planning and management.

(xii) ECCE services will be extended, on a preferential basis, to SC/ST and other economically deprived sections in rural areas.

(xiii) Efforts will be made for sensitization of policy planners, leaders, teachers, administrators, curriculum developers, text book writers and parents.

C. Achievement of Minimum Levels of Learning

Interventions

(i) Innovative projects will be developed aimed at location specific curriculum.

(ii) Teaching materials will be developed through action research by primary teacher trainees in rural areas.

(iii) Minimum levels of learning essential for gender sensitive educational planning will be ensured.

D. Reduction of Disparities

Interventions

(i) 'Education for Women's Equality' will be the main strategy to be adopted under the revised Plan of Action of National Policy on Education (NPE) -1986. Special efforts will be made to remove disparities in the provision of education and promotion of equality between sexes.

(ii) Efforts will be made to provide a comprehensive system of incentives and support services for girls and children of the economically weaker sections of society.

(iii) A similar incentive as appropriate will be provided in the non-formal system.

REVISED NATIONAL POLICY ON EDUCATION, 1992*

The recommendations of the Ramamurti Review Committee (appointed by National Front Government in May, 1990) Report were examined by the Janardhana Committee appointed by the Central Advisory Board of Education in July 1991. The Janardhana Committee submitted its recommendations in January 1992. The CABE considered the Janardhana Committee Report in the first week of May 1992 and finalised the revised National Policy on Education. It was presented in both Houses of Parliament on May 7, 1992 by the Human Resource Development Minister Arjun Singh. In his statement the Minister said the National Policy on Education (1986) has stood the test of time and enunciated a comprehensive framework to guide the development of education. He further observed that while the framework continues to be relevant, the development during the past few years and the experience in implementation of the policy has necessitated certain modifications.

Part V

Reorganisation of Education at Different Stages

Early Childhood Care and Education

5.1 The National Policy on Children specially emphasises investment in the development of the young child, particularly children from sections of the population in which first generation learners predominate.

5.2 Recognising the holistic nature of child development, *viz*., nutrition, health and social, mental, physical, moral and emotional development. Early Childhood Care and Education (ECCE) will receive high priority and be suitably integrated with the Integrated Child Development Services programme, wherever possible. Day-care centres will be provided as a support service for universalisation of primary education, to enable girls engaged in taking care of siblings to attend school and as a support service for working women belonging to poorer sections.

5.3 Programmes of ECCE will be child-oriented, focused around play, and the individuality of the child. Formal methods and the introduction of the 3 R's will be discouraged at this stage. The local community will be fully involved in these programmes.

5.4 A full integration of child care and pre-primary education will be brought about, both as a feeder and a strengthening factor for primary

---

* Ministry of Human Resource Development, Government of India, New Delhi, 1992.

Notes: 1. Para numbers refer to para numbers of the document.
2. The Modified paragraphs are given in italics.
3. Table numbers have been changed to conform to this chapter.

education and for human resource development in general. In continuation of this stage, the School Health Programme will be strengthened.

Elementary Education

5.5 (Revised Para) *The new thrust in elementary education will emphasise three aspects: (i) universal access and enrolment, (ii) universal retention of children up to 14 years of age; and (iii) a substantial improvement in the quality of education to enable all children to achieve essential levels of learning.*

5.5 (NPE, 1986) The new thrust in elementary education will emphasise two aspects: (i) universal enrolment and universal retention of children up to 14 years of age, and (ii) a substantial improvement in the quality of education.

Child-Centred Approach

5.6 A warm, welcoming and encouraging, approach, in which all concerned share a solicitude for the needs of the child, is the best motivation for the child to attend school and learn. A child-centred and activity-based process of learning should be adopted at the primary stage. First generation learners should be allowed to set their own pace and be given supplementary remedial instruction. As the child grows, the component of cognitive learning will be increased and skills organised through practice. The policy of non-detention at the primary stage will be retained, making evaluation as disaggregated as feasible. Corporal punishment will be firmly excluded from the educational system, and school timings as well as vacations adjusted to the convenience of children.

5.7 (Revised Para) *Provision will be made of essential facilities in primary schools. The scope of Operation Blackboard will be enlarged to provide three reasonably large rooms that are useable in all weather, and blackboards, maps, charts, toys, other necessary learning aids and school library. At least three teachers should work in every school, the number increasing, as early as possible, to one teacher per class. At least 50 per cent of teachers recruited in future should be women. The Operation Blackboard will be extended to upper primary stage also. Construction of school buildings will be a priority charge on JRY funds.*

5.7 (NPE, 1986) Provision will be made of essential facilities in primary schools, including at least two reasonably large rooms that are usable in all weather, and the necessary toys, blackboards, maps, charts, and other learning material. At least two teachers, one of whom a woman, should work in every school, the number increasing as early as possible to one teacher per class. A phased drive, symbolically called *Operation Blackboard* will be undertaken with immediate effect to improve Primary schools all over the country. Government, local bodies, voluntary agencies and individuals will be fully involved. Construction of school buildings will be first charge on NREP and RLEGP funds.

5.8 (Revised Para) *Modern technological aids will be used to improve the learning environment of NFE-Centres. Talented and dedicated young men and women from the local community will be chosen to serve as instructors, and particular attention paid to their training. All necessary measures will be taken to ensure that the quality of non-formal education is comparable with the formal education. Steps will be taken to facilitate lateral entry into the formal system of children passing out of the non-formal system.*

5.9 (NPE, 1986) Modern technological aids will be used to improve the learning environment of NFE centres. Talented and dedicated young men and women from the local community will be chosen to serve as instructors and particular attention paid to their training. Steps will be taken to facilitate their entry into the formal system in deserving cases. All necessary measures will be taken to ensure that the quality of non-formal education is comparable with formal education.

5.10 Effective steps will be taken to provide a framework for the curriculum on the lines of the national core curriculum, but based on the needs of the learners and related to the local environment. Learning material of high quality will be developed and provided free of charge to all pupils. NFE programmes will provide participatory learning environment, and activities such as games and sports, cultural programmes, excursions, etc.

5.11 (Revised Para) *The Government will take over-all responsibility for this vital sector. Voluntary agencies and Panchayati Raj institutions will take much of the responsibility of running NFE programmes. The provision of funds to these agencies will be adequate and timely.*

5.11 (NPE, 1986) Much of the work running of NFE centres will be done through voluntary agencies and Panchayati Raj institutions. The provision of funds to the agencies will be adequate and timely. The Government will take over-all responsibility for this vital sector.

A Resolve

5.12 (Revised Para) *The New Education Policy will give the highest priority to solving the problem of children dropping out of school and will adopt an array of meticulously formulated strategies based on micro planning and applied at the grass roots level all over the country, to ensure children's retention at school. This effort will be fully coordinated with the network of non-formal education. It shall be ensured that free and compulsory education of satisfactory quality is provided to all children up to 14 years of age before we enter the twenty-first century. A national mission will be launched for the achievement of this goal.*

5.12 (NPE 1986) The New Education Policy will give the highest priority to solving the problem of children dropping out of school and will adopt an array of meticulously formulated strategies based on micro planning, and applied at the grass-roots level all over the country, to ensure children's retention at school. This effort will be fully coordinated with the network of non-formal education. It shall be ensured that all children who attain the age of about 11 years by 1990 will have had five years of schooling, or its equivalent through the non-formal stream. Likewise, by 1995 all children will be provided free and compulsory education up to 14 years of age.

PROGRAMME OF ACTION ON NATIONAL POLICY ON EDUCATION, 1992*

The Revised Policy Formulations were placed in Parliament on May 7, 1992. In July 1991, CABE Committee on Policy was constituted to review the implementation of the various parameters of the NPE, 1986, taking into consideration the report of the Committee for Review of the NPE (NPERC) and other relevant development since the Policy was formulated. The Janardhana Reddy Committee (JRC), in its report submitted in January, 1992, came to the conclusion that while very little of the NPE, 1986 required reformulation, the Programme of Action (PoA) needed to be revised considerably. In its 47th meeting (May 5-6, 1992), the CABE considered the JRC report and formulated the RPF. The PoA, 1992 was evolved through the consensual process.

Recommendations

The PoA's recommendations cover the following areas:

1. Education for Women's Equality; 2. Education of SCs and STs and other Backward classes; 3. Minorities' Education; 4. Education of the Handicapped; 5. Adult and Continuing Education; 6. *Early Childhood Care and Education*; 7. *Elementary Education*; 8. Secondary Education; 9. Navodaya Vidyalayas; 10. Vocational Education; 11. Higher Education; 12. Open Education; 13. Delinking Degrees from Jobs and Manpower Planning; 14. Rural Universities and Institutes; 15. Technical and Management Education; 16. Research and Development; 17. The Cultural Perspective; 18. Development of Languages; 19. Media and Educational Technology; 20. Sports, Physical Education and Youth; 21. Evaluation Process and Examination Reforms; 22. Teachers and Their Training; 23. Management of Education.

---

* Department of Education, Ministry of Human Resource Development, Government of India, New Delhi, 1992.

Note: Para numbers refer to para numbers of this document.

Elementary Education

Taking into account the experience gained in the implementation of NPE, 1986 and PoA, the following strategies are proposed:

(a) *Access and Enrolment*

In order to ensure universal access and enrolment of SC children in rural areas, henceforth, in opening primary and upper primary schools priority would be given to the needs of SC habitations and hamlets. As far as possible pre-primary section will be an integral part of such schools.

Every Scheduled Tribe habitation will be provided with a primary school or other suitable institution before the end of the Eighth Five Year Plan in order to ensure universal enrolment and participation.

In tribal areas educational plan will be implemented in an integrated manner. Pre-school education (through Balwadis), Non-Formal Education, elementary education and adult education will be organically linked and integrated to ensure achievement of total literacy of the entire population. This integrated Educational Complex will be responsible for total education within its area serving all children in the age-group 3-14 and adults in the age-group 15 and above.

For SC children access and enrolment will be assured primarily in the formal school. Where SC children are not able to attend the formal school provision for non-formal and distance education centres will be made to ensure universal access and enrolment.

It will be the responsibility of the teachers to organise drives at the beginning of every academic session to enrol all school-age children specially girls belonging to SCs, STs and other backward sections. For this purpose active assistance of voluntary agencies and local communities shall be taken. Traditional and folk media can be very effective in reaching parents and children in remote areas to motivate them.

(b) *Participation*

Adequate incentives will be provided for the children of SC, ST and other backward sections in the form of scholarships, uniforms, textbooks, stationery and mid-day meals.

All schools, NFE centres and pre-school centres in SC/ST habitations will be equipped with necessary and essential infrastructural facilities in accordance with the norms laid down for Operation Blackboard and for achieving Minimum Levels of Learning (MLL).

Operation Blackboard shall cover within a period of two years all schools in tribal areas and Harijan Bastees irrespective of the date on which the school was set up.

The indigent families among SC/ST will be given incentives to send children, particularly girls, to schools.

(c) *Achievement*

Children from tribal communities will be taught through the mother tongue in the earlier stages in primary school. Teaching/learning material in the tribal languages will be prepared providing for a transition to the regional language by Class III.

The home language of children of SC/ST may be different from others. Therefore, standard teaching/learning material will be re-written to make them intelligible to the SC/ST children especially in areas where the standard language and the learners' dialect are different.

It will be ensured that MLL already set-up for primary schools will be achieved, that the necessary standards of 3 Rs. are acquired by all children in SC/ST communities. Effective methodologies for measurement of MLL will be implemented.

3. Long-Term Programmes include

(a) *Early Childhood Care and Education Centres*

Early Childhood Education Centres will be set up in primary schools in areas pre-dominantly inhabited by educationally backward minorities. Socially Useful Productive Work (SUPW) should be introduced in such schools. The Department of Education, Ministry of Human Resource Development should prepare a scheme of assistance to State Governments in this regard. However, the State Governments will be encouraged to start their own programmes in ECCE. (Action: Department of Education, Ministry of HRD).

(b) *Primary Education*

(i) Institutional system for compilation of statistical information required by Commissioner for Linguistic Minorities regarding educational facilities. (Action: State Govts./UTs);

(ii) Eliminating delay in sanctioning of linguistic minority teachers' posts and appointment of teachers by delegation of powers to District Collectors (Action: State Govts./UTs);

(iii) Survey on availability of text-books in minority languages and setting up of printing facilities in minority languages. (Action: State Govts./UTs);

(iv) Survey on availability of teacher training facilities for teachers in minority languages and measures to enhance such capacity wherever necessary. (Action: State Govts./UTs); and

(v) Efforts will be made to utilise 15 per cent of the curricular time for training in local crafts/trades and to arrange evening classes for children of artisans/agricultural labourers. (Action: State Govts./UTs).

Early Childhood Care and Education (ECCE)

Integrated Child Development Service (ICDS)

The ICDS is currently the biggest programme of early childhood development with 2.90 lakh Anganwadis serving nearly 140 lakh children and about 27 lakh mothers; 91.5 per cent ICDS projects are located in rural and tribal areas and 8.5 per cent in urban slums. Besides the ICDS, by the end of 1991-92 there were 12,470 creches with a coverage of about 3 lakh children below 5 years, 4395 ECE centres in 9 Educationally Backward (EB) States and the Balwadi Nutrition programme serving nearly 2.30 lakh children in the age-group of 3-5 years.

Over the recent years, a number of initiatives have been taken to make the programmes more focussed. The measures under ICDS, include emphasis on practical training for Anganwadi Workers, and extension work by Anganwadi training centres, which are required to adopt 10 Anganwadis each for developing them as model Anganwadis. To build up resource capabilities in the field, action is afoot to develop CDPO's office into resource centre. Instructional materials for Anganwadi Training Centres are also under preparation. Effort are also being made to distribute education-cum-play materials to Anganwadis to improve their pre-school education component. Initiative has also been taken to improve the scheme of creches by reviewing norms for voluntary and community participation. A scheme has been worked out by the Department of Women and Child Development for converging the services under DWCRA, ICDS, pre-school education and related schemes of the Departments of Health, Family Welfare, and Rural Development.

Targets and Phasing

The aim of ECCE is that every child should be assured access to the fulfillment of all basic needs. As such efforts will be made towards universalisation of ICDS by A.D. 2000. By the end of the Eighth Plan, 3.75 lakh Anganwadi centres would be established and by A.D. 2000 seven lakh Anganwadi centres. Anganwadis will be gradually converted into Anganwadis-cum-creches. By the end of Eighth Plan, 25 per cent of Anganwadis will be converted into Anganwadis-cum-creches. Qualitative improvement of ongoing ECCE programmes would receive high attention. New cost-effective designs of ECCE will also be encouraged and supported.

Strategy of Implementation

The ECCE involves the total development of child, i.e. physical, motor, cognitive, language, emotional, social and moral. The age span under consideration in ECCE is from conception to about 6 years. Even a modest development process during this period includes care of mother during pregnancy (ante-natal health check-up, nutritional support, control of anaemia, immunization for prevention of tetanus following delivery, etc.), hygienic and skilled birth attendance, nutritional care of mother during lactation, correct infant feeding practices, immunization of infant from communicable diseases, mothers' education in the child care, early childhood stimulation and health nutritional support throughout. Thus, ECCE is a complex integral function.

Elementary Education

Four Categories Districts

(i) High literacy districts in which access and enrolment are almost universal and community awareness for education is already high;

(ii) Total literacy campaign districts in which community mobilisation for educational needs has been successfully generated by the National Literacy Mission;

(iii) Low literacy districts in which the provision of education facilities is unsatisfactory and the delivery system functions without any community involvement; and

(iv) Externally assisted project districts with a different management structure and sufficient financial support.

The strategies with regard to access, participation, achievement, environment building, community participation, etc. will be different for the four categories of districts.

District Planning

Under this broad strategy of district planning and based on the experience gained in implementation of NPE, and the RPF, the following strategies are proposed:

(i) Adoption of alternative channels of schooling like voluntary schools and NFE centres for those who cannot avail of conventional full-time schooling;

(ii) Microplanning through involvement of teachers and the community in order to design and implement a family-wise, child-wise plan of action for universal access/enrolment and participation.

(iii) Making parents aware about their responsibility for ensuring the completion of elementary education by their children and for providing at home the facilities and encouragement needed for this purpose;

(iv) Establishment of linkages between programmes of pre-school and primary education, and between programmes of literacy and UEE, in total literacy campaign districts;

(v) Improvement of school facilities through revamped Operation Blackboard and connecting it to MLL strategy. It will be extended to upper primary stage;

(vi) Decentralization of educational management for making the schools function so as to ensure universal enrolment, retention and achievement; and

(vii) Introduction of MLLs at primary and upper primary stages including coverage of the non-formal education channel.

Strategies

- Revision of process and content of elementary education to make teaching-learning child-centred, activity based and joyful.
- Introduction of continuous and comprehensive evaluation with focus on remedial measures.
- Modification of teacher training programmes in view of changed strategies and programmes.
- Improvement of the monitoring system for UEE.
- Launching a National Mission to achieve the goals envisaged in the revised policy.

Provision of Universal Access

Existing schemes will be suitably modified and measures will be taken to incorporate the new policy formulations.

Formal Schooling

New primary schools according to the norms, will be opened in unserved habitations. NFE centres will be opened in smaller habitations and for children who cannot benefit from the school system. In addition, a new scheme of Voluntary Schools will be launched to achieve universal access for children in different areas.

Primary Schools: In 1986, it was estimated that there were approximately 32,000 habitations with a population of 300 or more that required primary schools. Though many new schools have been opened, new habitations have also come into existence and it is estimated that 35,000 new schools will be required. These schools will be opened by the State Governments following the norms specified under Operation Blackboard.

(i) Provision of NFE centres will be based on the Microplanning exercise carried out for UEE. NFE centres will invariably cater to the needs of children, especially girls, who are not able to or who cannot attend the formal school;

(ii) The community will be, involved in the setting-up and supervision of all NFE centres;

(iii) The NFE instructors will be identified with the help of the community. Special efforts will be made to appoint women instructors wherever possible;

(iv) Training of NFE personnel, especially instructors, will be given top priority. Adequate training and re-orientation will be provided;

(v) Training responsibility will be shared by the project, district level institutions like DIETs, DRUs, State level institutions like SCERT, and National institutes like NCERT and NIEPA;

(vi) Project administration will be strengthened for effective decentralisation of management. Necessary administrative and management inputs will be provided at the State and district levels;

(vii) Arrangement will be made for testing of children in the NFE stream with reference to an equivalent stage in the formal system and specific instructions issued to facilitate lateral entry into the formal system for students of the NFE stream;

(viii) Efforts will be made to link non-formal courses with the Open Schools;

(ix) The NFE programme will be linked with the scheme of public libraries, Jana Shiksha Nilayams, etc.;

(x) In total literacy campaign districts follow-up programmes will be taken up for children in the age-group 9-14 to go beyond NLM literacy norms. This will form a part of the post literacy and continuing education programme of the district;

(xi) Vocational and technical courses of wide variety will be provided for children and youth who pass out of the Non-formal stream. Shramik Vidyapeeths and Voluntary agencies will be involved in this process; and

(xii) Voluntary agencies will be encouraged to undertake projects of NFE, especially in areas where the formal school system is not able to meet the demands of UEE.

The Cultural Perspective

Action Plan

I. *Pre-Primary Stage*

(a) Provision of minimum facility for playing space or park for children at this stage.

(b) Training of pre-school teachers in integrating cultural activities with pre-school learning programmes.

(c) Preparation of educational toys and games for pre-school students which are indigenous and aesthetic in quality and safe for use by small children.

Primary School Stage

The main objectives at the primary school stage would be:

(a) To impart the child with a basic core of facts about India's cultural heritage by encouraging rural teachers and students to collect folk songs, local history, local folk tribal community and archaeological artifacts;

(b) To integrate and develop students' physical and cognitive skills; and

(c) To create through awareness a feeling of love for India's natural and cultural heritage.

The major activities envisaged for achieving these objectives are the following:

(a) Children School Theatre Movement would be launched with the teacher and children reading/enacting stories, plays and poems in the textbooks in the classroom. Learning of the local folk/tribal community theatre conventions will also be promoted.

(b) Students will be encouraged to participate in creatively meaningful activities. Schools will be advised to invite local craftsmen, artisans etc. for demonstrations of their skills before the impressionable minds of the children.

(c) It shall be ensured that textual materials incorporate a strong and vitalising presence of our heritage, folklore, myths and symbols etc. without making texts either burdensome or obscurantist.

(d) Efforts will be made to incorporate suitable words, idioms, proverbs etc. from local dialects in the textbooks.

(e) Too much cultural indoctrination by covering the classroom walls with drawings, stickers, slogans, moral sayings, etc. would be discouraged. Right from childhood a sense of design, aesthetics of vacant space and a sense of space would be inculcated.

(f) Teachers' training programmes will be re-oriented to give the teachers capability of imparting instruction in theoretical and demonstrative methodologies in cultural instruction.

(g) Extensive training programmes for in-service teachers in each district will be organised.

(h) School museum corners largely with collections of students themselves in the form of stones, feathers, leaves, etc. will be set up.

(i) Tours will be organised particularly to monuments and places of historical and cultural significance.

Subsequently the above-mentioned activities would be systematised further and the emphasis would be on provision of more developed facilities and specialisation of training for teachers by way of:

(a) preparation of special books, educational material and audio-visual facilities for primary schools;

(b) institutionalising community interaction in terms of seeking help of local artisans and craftsmen including performing artists like dancers, singers on an organised basis of association, through honorarium, fees, incentives, etc.

NATIONAL ADVISORY COMMITTEE ON LEARNING WITHOUT BURDEN, 1992-93

To have a fresh look on the problem of academic burden on students, Government of India, set up a National Advisory Committee on March 1, 1992 under the Chairmanship of Professor Yash Pal. The committee submitted its report on July 15, 1993.

The Problem

Preamble

Our Committee was concerned with one major flaw of our system of education. This flaw can be identified briefly by saying that 'a lot is taught but little is learnt or understood'. The problem manifests itself in a variety of ways. The most common and striking manifestation is the size of the school bag that children can be seen carrying from home to school and back to home everyday. A survey conducted in Delhi revealed that the weight of school bag, on an average, in primary classes in public schools is more than 4 kgs. while it is around one kg in MCD schools. Nevertheless the load we want to discuss is not only the physical load but the load of learning which is there for all children irrespective of the category or type of schools where they study. Eminent writer R.K. Narayan had drawn the country's attention to this daily sight by making a moving speech in the Rajya Sabha a few years ago. The situation has become worse over these years, with even pre-school children carrying a bag of books and notebooks. And the sight is not confined to metropolitan cities alone; it can be seen in small towns and the bigger villages too.

The weight of the school bag represents one dimension of the problem. Another dimension can be seen in the child's daily routine. Right from early childhood, many children specially those belonging to middle classes, are made to slog through home work, tuitions and coaching classes of different kinds. Leisure has become a highly scarce commodity in the child's especially the urban child's life. The child's innate nature and capacities have no opportunity to find expression in a daily routine which permits no time to play, to enjoy simple measures and to explore the world.

Learning Without Burden: Report of the National Advisory Committee appointed by the Ministry of Human Resource Development, to Suggest Ways and Means to Reduce the Academic Burden on School Students, Ministry of Human Resource Development, Department of Education, New Delhi, 1993.

Joyless Learning

It is hard to reconcile the rigorous 'academic' regime that is imposed on children from an early age with the widespread complaint made about the declining norms and performance of the formal system of education. Teachers routinely complain that they do not have enough time to explain anything in detail, or to organize activities in the classroom. 'Covering' the syllabus seems to have become an end in itself, unrelated to the philosophical and social aims of education. The manner in which the syllabus is 'covered' in the average classroom is by means of reading the prescribed textbook aloud, with occasional noting of salient points on the blackboard. Opportunities for children to carry out experiments, excursions, or any kind of observations are scarce even in the best of schools. In the average school, especially the school located in a rural area, even routine teaching of the kind described above does not take place in many cases. In several states, school teachers encourage children to attend after school tuition given for a fee while regular classroom teaching has become a tenuous ritual.

One message of this situation is that both the teacher and the child have lost the sense of joy in being involved in an educational process. Teaching and learning have both become a chore for a great number of teachers and children. Barring those studying in reputed or exceptional institutions, the majority of our school-going children are made to view learning at school as a boring, even unpleasant and bitter experience. They are daily socialised to look upon education as mainly a process of preparing for examinations. No other motivation seems to have any legitimacy.

The contribution that teachers make towards this kind of socialisation is especially worrisome. Trained teachers are expected to be aware of the wider aims of education; indeed; aims like 'development of the child's total personality' are the shibboleths of teacher training institutions everywhere in the country. It appears that teachers feel they can do little to pursue such lofty aims in any realistic sense under the harsh circumstances created by factors like excessively large classes, a heavy syllabus, difficult textbooks and so on. Moreover, majority of them neither know nor have the necessary skills to realise the goals of education. The recommended pupil-teacher ratio of forty to one is now more an exception that a norm and in many parts of the country it is customary to have sixty to eighty students in one class. The committee learnt that in many states senior secondary classes often have one hundred or more students, many of them spilling into the corridor. In the national capital, many ' model' secondary schools, Central schools and several elite 'public' schools have classes, including primary classes, with more than sixty students.

This kind of class-size understandably generates a feeling of helplessness among teachers, but why must teachers feel helpless in the face of curriculum-related problems such as heavy syllabi, poorly produced textbooks, etc.? Why don't they act in more vocal ways and involve themselves in curriculum reform? Apart from the fact that there are very few forums encouraging curriculum inquiry and reform in any systematic manner, it seems to be an entrenched attitude among teachers to regard all decisions about curriculum and textbooks as the responsibility of 'authorities'. The fact is that while the teachers' involvement in the preparation of syllabi and textbooks is verbalised as a matter of principle, in practice it takes the shape of token involvement of a handful of teachers. Most teachers have reason, therefore, to think that they have little to say about the changes made from time to time in syllabi and textbooks. Even in such extreme cases where a textbook has a factual mistake, no complaints are made by teachers asking for correction of error. There is no established procedure or official forum to mobilise teacher vigilance and participation in curriculum improvement. On the contrary, there are cases where an individual teacher complained about an error in a state-published textbook, was taken to task. Even if such cases can be described as rare or exceptionally unfortunate, they explain why the majority of teachers intuitively feel that it is not their business to critically examine the syllabus and texts they teach.

Examination System

Much has been written by various official committees on the ills of our examination system. The major, well understood defect of the examination system is that it focusses on children's ability to reproduce information to the exclusion of the ability to apply concepts and information on unfamiliar, new problems, or, simply to think... The awe they generate, the responses they trigger, and the kind of preparation they demand have all got so entrenched into the social lore that minor improvements in the style of question papers do not make difference to the dominant influence that the examination system has on the processes of learning and teaching. The influence is so strong that schools start holding a formal written examination several years prior to class X indeed, in the primary classes in many parts of the country. And children receive the message almost as soon as they start attending that the only thing which matters here is one's performance in the examination...

Textbook as the 'Truth'

The pervasive effects of the examination system can be seen in the style and content of textbooks and not just guidebooks which are specifically manufactured to help children pass an examination. If 'facts' or 'information' constitute the main burden of an examination, the same is true of textbooks. Barring exceptions, our textbooks appear to have been written primarily to convey information or 'facts', rather than to make children think and explore. Over the years some attempts have been made to incorporate a certain amount of reflective writing in textbooks. Such writing is so exceptional that its examples can be spotted and named without difficulty. 'How leaves are designed' in a class VIII textbook is one such piece of writing.* It stands out from among the thousands of pages of textbooks in different subjects that our teachers and children have to go through painstakingly so that they can retain the information recorded in those pages in a highly compressed, usually abstruse manner. The more common style used in the textbooks is exemplified by passages of the following kind.**

The term pH is defined as the negative logarithm to the base 10 of the hydrogen ion concentration expressed in gramions per litre or moles per litre. (Class X)

Fatty acids are slowly hydrolysed during digestion in the small intestine to form glycerol and fatty acids through the enzyme action of lipase which is secreted by the pancreas. (Class X)

We find that while dividing a decimal by a multiple of 10,000 or 1,000 we first move the decimal point to the left as many places as there are zeros in the number and then divide the resulting decimal by the second factor of the divisor. (Class V)

The problem of readability in textbooks becomes grim in the context of a system which often leaves the child with no resource other than the prescribed textbook. The extent to which the child can rely on a teacher to elucidate tersely written text material is dependent on the quality of teachers, their training and their accountability. From what impression the Committee could form about these aspects of the system, it seems valid to say that the child is very often helpless in the face of a style of teaching that is far from being interactive, let alone the absence or irregular presence of teachers (And we are not saying that the teachers alone are responsible for the kind of teaching that takes place daily in lakhs of classrooms that have hardly any equipment and often even a proper means of ventilation or lighting). Under the circumstances that are widely prevalent in our country, a child is more likely than not to mug up the definition of 'pH' quoted above without grasping it. And mugging does get the child through the examination!

Textbooks and guidebooks form a tight nexus. In some parts of the country children are compelled to buy the guidebook (or 'key') alongwith

---

* Class VIII Science textbook prepared by the NCERT.

** We have decided to cite such examples without giving a reference in order to avoid the impression that we are criticising certain specific titles, authors, publishers or organisations.

the textbook. The economic of the textbook has become quite dubious indeed. It is not perceived as one of the resources for learning about a subject, but as the *only authoritative* resource. This kind of sanctity distorts what useful purpose the textbook could serve. Teachers see it as a body of 'truths' which children must learn by heart. This perception and the urge to 'cover' the chapters of the prescribed textbook, turn all knowledge into a load to be borne by the child's memory.

The distance between the child's everyday life and the content of the textbook further accentuates the transformation of knowledge into a load. We are not talking here about advanced science or mathematics, but about elementary science, social studies, language and arithmetic. Textbooks treat these subjects in a manner that leads to alienation of knowledge from the child's world. This tragic phenomenon takes different forms in different subjects. In the natural sciences, it takes the form of eroticisation of the subject. In the social sciences it becomes manifest in the coating of every inquiry in didacticism, suggestive of one preferred answer to every question. A common source of alienation of subject matter from the children's perspective and life is the presentation of the life-style and world-view of the urban well-off class. This life style is characterised by access to concrete housing, modern kitchens, electrical gadgets and so on. Of course there is nothing 'wrong' with this life-style; but the symbolisation of this life-style in every illustration and description that concerns a child's home life alienates millions of children who live in houses with traditional kitchens, or with no separate kitchens. Objects of daily use in common Indian homes, such as a broom or clay pitcher, are seldom seen in textbooks. One wonders whether the common Indian broom, which could be a versatile resource for learning about the social and physical environment, is perceived by our textbook writers and illustrators with a sense of stigma or as a symbol of backwardness. Or could it be that it is simply too common to be seen as being of any use in an educational material? Neither of the two guesses is totally irrelevant in view of the complete absence of common objects of ordinary Indian life in the world depicted in textbooks.

The most common message that children get from the textbooks is that the life ordinary people live is 'wrong' or irrational. And this kind of didactic rejection does not apply to non-middle class life alone. All simple joys of childhood are also criticised. No better example of this can be given than the message conveyed in a Class V exercise which asks children to decide whether the statement 'Road is also a playground' is correct or wrong. The right response is that this statement is 'wrong', the message of the lesson being that playing on the street can be dangerous. This message is of course true in a normative sense, but it ignores the reality of the overwhelming majority of urban children who have no other space except the street to play. The moot point is not the scarcity of space, but rather the need to accept the universally valid fact that children enjoy playing on the street. This joy must be respected in a text written from a child-centred point of view. To argue that a respectful acknowledgement of this joy will amount to sanctioning carelessness, or to say that children must be warned about the risks of playing on the street is to trivialise the issue. Every child who plays on the street fully knows the dangers involved in it. Science textbooks need not waste valuable pages on such trivial preaching which is precisely what they do throughout the elementary classes in place of using these golden years of childhood to arouse curiosity about things and ideas.

Language Textbooks

We hardly need to assert that our textbooks are not written from the child's viewpoint. Neither the mode of communication, nor the selection of objects depicted, nor the language conveys the centrality of the child in the world constructed by the text. This last dimension of language deserves some elaboration. The vocabulary and syntax used in the textbooks in the Hindi region were critically referred to by a number of individuals and groups whom the committee met during the course of its deliberations. Not just the textbooks used for the teaching of the natural and the social sciences, but even the textbook used for the teaching of the mother tongue are written in such stylised diction and sentence-structure, that children cannot be expected to see the language used in them as their own. Words, expressions and nuances commonly used by children and others in their milieu are all absent from textbooks. So is humour. An artificial, sophisticated style dominates textbook lessons, reinforcing the tradition of distancing knowledge from life. The language used in textbooks, thus, deepens the sense of 'burden' attached to all school-related knowledge.

Observation Discouraged

A highly disturbing tendency we discovered in text writing, which exacerbates the problem we are discussing, is that of treating pictures as substitutes for experience. We found textbooks asking children to observe a picture of the object under study rather than asking children and the teacher to go out and observe the object itself in nature. For example, a class V science text says: 'Look at the picture of a cactus plant'. Observe the thick green structure... 'Such an instruction preempts what motivation there may be in a teacher or child to bring an actual cactus plant to the class or to grow one. The most painful example of this phenomenon brought to our attention was one in which a private publisher claimed that he had made the teacher's task 'easier' by turning an official 'Teacher's Guide', which suggests that the teacher should take children outside the school and identify some common birds, into a text where the pictures of all the common birds with their names were provided for ready use. This case is especially painful as it shows how even a specific instruction is given in a Teacher's Guide. (Teacher's Guides are themselves rare; and in subjects in which they have been prepared in certain states, circulation has not been satisfactorily looked after) to encourage teachers to extend the lesson beyond the four walls of the classroom is co-opted within the dominant, traditional approach of teaching everything verbally from a textbook. Over the recent years, some textbooks have adopted the vocabulary of observation and exploration or discovery as a necessary part of science teaching, but even here virtually all commands for observation conclude with statements about what will be seen in an observation is actually made, thereby making it unnecessary for the teacher and children to find an object and actually observe it.

Structure of Syllabus

The absence of the child's viewpoint is also reflected in the organisation of syllabi in different subjects. We received a large number of complaints from parents as well as teachers that the content of syllabi lacks an overall organization or coherence. Gaps in the syllabi between the lower and the higher secondary stages are as common as repetitions of the same content. These weaknesses of organisation apparently lead to memorisation and poor comprehension, both exacerbating the sense of curriculum load... .

Repetitions of concepts and information also lead to boredom and a sense of load. The need to repeat is rooted in the flawed structure of syllabi. In the primary classes, ideas and information are presented in a synoptic manner, making the text look deceptively simple. In the later classes, the same ideas are repeated, with some elaboration which does not prevent the child from viewing the ideas as trivialised by repetition. In the study of nutrition and health, for example, virtually the same ideas and information are given in the syllabi and texts of classes III, IV, V, VII and X. Even the questions given at the end of the lessons in the texts are almost of the same kind. Apparently, the structure of syllabi is not carefully thought out...

History is the most clear case in point. Although it forms one part of the subject called social sciences, it offers a prime example of curriculum load. Despite many changes that have come about in the style of history texts, the history syllabus continues to be frustrating and meaningless experience for children. The aim of teaching history is defeated because children are not enabled to relate to their own heritage. Traditionally, it requires children to form an overall picture of the 'whole' of India's known history, from ancient to modern times, during the three years from classes VI to VIII. Since the texts for these classes are required to cover such a vast span, the density of these texts becomes extremely high which means that historical time is greatly compressed, i.e., a few sentences are deemed to 'cover' several decades. The synoptic style forces the child into 'accepting' whatever is narrated. There aren't enough details that a child could use to work out some kind of argument or interpretation, but the sheer volume of text (which is supposed to 'cover' 'all' of India's history in three years) forces the child (and the teacher) to 'take in' as much text as possible without 'wasting' time in studying or constructing an argument.

This common problem of the history syllabus apart, we found that the content of the history syllabus in certain states was conceived as a densely packed box of informations. The syllabus of history in West Bengal illustrates this tendency in tragically exaggerated proportions. For example in class VIII, children are required to learn seventeen topics in all which are:

1. Modern age; 2. Renaissance in Europe; 3. Europeans widen the world; 4. Reformation in Europe; 5. The English Revolution in the 17th century; 6. India; 7. Foundation and growth of the British power in India till 1857 in short narrative form; 8. World in the 18th century; 9. Europe since 1815; 10. (a) Developments in China till 1911; (b) Rise of Japan as a great power till 1914; 11. India under the crown 1858-1914; 12. The First World War; 13. The Bolsevik Revolution; 14. Europe 1919-1939; 15. The Second World War; 16. India 1919-1947; 17. (a) Revolution in China 1911-1949; (b) Revolution in South East Asia after 1945; (c) Spread of nationalism and unrest in subject countries during World War II.

The entire syllabus is to be covered in 135 pages of a text, according to the instruction given in the syllabus itself. Apparently, the syllabus makers believe that compression of information in terms of page-space does not affect the readability, let alone comprehensibility, of a text.

Teaching Everything

The problem of densely packed syllabi like this one cuts across disciplines. In geography, it takes the form of all the continents being 'covered' under regional geography between classes VI and VIII. In mathematics and the natural sciences, the packing of details makes any kind of learning with understanding, leave alone enjoyment, virtually impossible. Numerous examples could be given from these disciplines to illustrate the problem. In *one* page of a class VII science textbook we find all these items 'covered': definition of time period, how to find the number of oscillations per second, definition of frequency, 'Hertz' unit of frequency, the idea that vibrations have amplitude and frequency, definitions of these, the concept of sound as vibration, loudness and pitch and finally frequency/pitch and its relation to speed of rotation and tension. We are not citing this example as a specific case to be looked into, but as evidence of a deeply rooted tendency, rather an ideology, which impels syllabus and textbook planners to include 'everything' without any regard for children's ability at different ages to learn and the time available in an average school for teaching a subject...

In mathematics, the situation seems to be grim right from the start of the child's school career. Far too many abstractions are introduced all at once with scant attention paid to well-known facts about development of mathematical thinking in children. To begin with, children are expected to handle arithmetical operations on a very large numbers early. In class I, they are supposed to go upto 100 (compared to this a British child in this class spends the whole year working with numbers upto 20), in class II upto 1000, in class III, upto 10,000 in class IV upto a million and in class V upto a crore. Even tough the conservation of volume and weight are known to emerge in the child's mind after the conservation of length is fully established, all three are introduced simultaneously (usually in one unit of study) at the young age of seven or eight years, with the expectation that children will compute with standard units. Concrete operational thought, which is characteristic of elementary school children, demands manipulation of objects and activities using a variety of materials (to enable 'elaboration' of a concept i.e., its dissociation from any one material or object). Such activities become impossible to organise under a curriculum which 'progresses' so swiftly from concept to concept. Also, children of this stage find proportional reasoning difficult, yet percentage and ratio are introduced in classes IV and V. In the middle and higher classes the tendency to follow the logic of the discipline of mathematics rather than psychology of learning as the basis of the curriculum becomes even more dominant. Mathematics, thus, acquires the image of an esoteric discipline which has little application in the real life of the child.

Starting Early

The general problems of curriculum conceptualisation that we have discussed in this part of our report can all be seen reflected in the emerging pre-school sector of the education system. Despite official stipulations that no textbooks be used at this stage, pre-school teachers and parents in the urban centre are feeling 'compelled' to burden the young child with textbooks and the formal learning they represent. The sense of compulsion comes from a widespread feeling that unless academic training of a child starts early, he or she cannot cope with the fast-paced pedagogy and the competitive ethos of the later school years. The pernicious grip of this false argument manifests itself in absurd and of course deeply harmful, practices in pre-schools and primary schools, such as early emphasis on shapely drawing, writing and memorising information. Intrinsic motivation and the child's natural abilities are being smothered at a scale so vast that it cannot be correctly estimated. Our national commitment to the development of human resource is daily challenged in our nurseries and primary schools.

Not Just an Urban Problem

The problem we have tried to identify in this part of the report is not confined to urban areas as some people think. It is deeply relevant to children's education in rural India although there, more basic problems-such as abysmally poor condition of schools, absenteeism among teachers, etc., may cloud the problem of curriculum load. In our view, the problem of a high drop-out rate, which has rightly preoccupied our policy-makers for a long time, has one of its origins in the curriculum scenario we have portrayed. A curriculum policy that takes away the elements of joy and inquiry from learning obviously contributes to the rate at which children leave school in the early years, undoubtedly under the force of economic and social circumstances. As we have indicated earlier, symbolic tilt towards an urban, middle class way of life in textbooks can also be expected to make the rural child's association with his or her experience at school thin and brittle. Quality of teachers and the equipment available to them also make an impact on the tenuous and fragile link that the first-generation learner in many parts of rural India tries to establish with the system of education.

Roots of the Problem

Knowledge vs. Information

In our discussions with people directly involved in syllabi and textbook preparation all over the country, we found one argument repeated over and over again as the main justification for the phenomenon... The argument was that India has to catch up with the developed countries where an explosion of knowledge has occurred; therefore, our children must learn a lot more than they used to, which means that new topics, new concepts and information have to be added to the syllabi and textbooks. This argument seems to be so widespread and so tenacious that those who believe in it use it as an undebatable 'given'. When it is pointed out to them that children of the so-called developed countries learn certain concepts a lot later than our children do (for example, in chemistry, the concept of valiancy is not taught in our schools in class VII whereas European children do not hear about it till they are in class IX), supporters of the 'explosion of knowledge' argument simply say that the European societies are already way ahead of us, so they can afford to instruct their children at a relaxed pace. In geography, when it is pointed out that European and North American children do not have to study every continent (only selected countries are intensively studied instead), the answer given is that in Western societies children have access to many resources of learning outside the school whereas the majority of our children are dependent on the school for getting to know about the world. The idea entrenched in the 'explosion of knowledge' theory finds similar justifications for the present state of syllabi and texts in other school subjects.

The notion that there has been an explosion of knowledge apparently treats knowledge and information as synonymous. It is true that the twentieth century has been a period of massive expansion in human capacity to find new facts and to store them, but the concept and theories that assist in the generation and organisation of information can hardly be said to have multiplied at an 'explosive' rate. (It is another matter that in an ex-colonial society it often looks as if all new 'knowledge' is being produced by 'others' and our job is simply to 'learn' and consume this knowledge). Also, the important thing in children's education ought to be concept-formation and growth of capacity for theory-building, rather than possession of vast amounts of information. The 'explosion of knowledge' idea prevents us from appreciating that learning in childhood is not the same thing as storing information about different subjects. If we say that a child has knowledge of phenomenon 'x', we can anticipate three possible ways in which this statement will be interpreted:

(i) the child has been given information about phenomenon 'x';
(ii) the child can reproduce information about phenomenon 'x';
(iii) the child has understood phenomenon 'x' and s/he can apply this understanding on other phenomena.

It is mostly the first two meanings that hold in the context of formal education in our country, the first being used as a basis for the second. 'Understanding' is often confused with 'acquisition of facts'.

Such a confusion leads to the neglect of 'understanding' as an aim of education. It would be correct to say that this neglect of understanding has gone so far and deep in our education system that a child can pass almost any examination without any understanding of the phenomena she has been told about in books or in the classroom. To a great extent, this paradoxical situation can be attributed to the excessive emphasis placed in our syllabi and textbooks on information or 'names' of things. Children have no choice but to memorise all the 'names' in order to 'prove' at an examination that they have 'understood' a phenomenon. Despite all kinds of claims that examinations have been reformed, they continue to focus on testing the possession of 'correct' information (i.e., the names of things, definitions, examples, etc.). Recall type questions outnumber the questions that test the child's capacity to speculate, evaluate or judge and to apply an idea in an unfamiliar context...

Isolation of Experts from Classroom Realities

The new topics and information put into the syllabus and textbooks at the time of each successive revision are usually added at the behest of experts of different subjects. These experts are university-level teachers, sometimes including individuals of high stature in the research world. Their involvement in the writing or revision of textbooks is indeed appreciable but they have little exposure to children in classroom situations. Their exposure to school teachers is also confined to interaction with the few teachers who are selected as members of syllabus and textbook committees. Several factors, such as the difference of social and official status, make it difficult for school teachers serving on these committees to freely put across their feelings and experiences regarding the teachability of a syllabus or the style of a textbook.

Teachability can be defined as the quotient of content that an average teacher can put across at a comfortable pace in a thirty-five minute school period. If our textbooks were to be judged in the light of this criterion, most of them, especially in the sciences, mathematics and the social sciences, would appear as unteachable. The amount of information and concept load they present are far in excess of the amount that can be put across in any meaningful way in thirty-five minute periods allocated for a school subject in one academic session. It appears that no rigorous count, using the thirty-five minute period as a unit, of the total teaching time available for a subject in any year is used as a basis for determining syllabus and text content. Indeed, the syllabi and textbooks are evidence to say that the experts involved in preparing them have little knowledge of school and classroom realities. This limitation of the experts extends to their possible ignorance of childrèn and of the processes that children use for learning new ideas. Text books simply do not reflect the versatile search of the ordinary child for clues to make sense of natural or social phenomena. Typically, school texts proceed in a linear fashion adding bits of information in and concepts as they go along. The linear patterns they follow often spill across school years, i.e., something left off in class VII is picked up again in Class IX and so on. Very seldom is an effort made to construct knowledge-patterns in non-linear ways.

We feel that if experts involved in the preparation of syllabi and textbooks had the opportunity to work with children and their teachers, they would have a chance to develop some insight into children's learning strategies. This would have helped them to develop the ability to emulate such strategies in script-writing for textbooks. Interaction with children might enable experts to develop a certain amount of sensitivity towards the living and versatile approaches used by children. Also, in the course of such interaction, the experts might also perceive the need to equip themselves with knowledge of children's psychology, particularly the psychology of learning, before venturing out on the task of textbook preparation. This, of course, implies that the job of syllabus and textbook preparation be perceived as a serious professional activity, not as a part-time obligation.

Centralised Character

In the specific context of the curriculum planning and textbook production, we feel, the system invites a number of problems upon itself on account of being unnecessarily centralised. It seems there is a wide-spread misconception which justifies centralisation in these matters. This misconception treats the content of syllabus and textbooks as synonymous with learning and testing norms. On the basis of this confusion, it is argued that syllabi and textbooks should be the same all over a state, even all over the country, in order to ensure uniformity of standards. This kind of argument completely overlooks the lopsided manner in which standards are set under the present system by an examination system which focusses on information rather than on skills and capacity to apply skills. Indeed, there is a 'catch 22' situation: the examination system ignores skills, concentrating on memorised information, definitions and descriptions; therefore, syllabus and textbooks, which cannot do justice to diversified milieux, varying needs and facilities, become necessary to ensure that all children 'know' the same 'facts'.

This circular argument has created a situation in which curriculum and textbook preparation is confined to the state capitals and New Delhi. At regional and local levels, teachers do not perceive curriculum development and preparation of educational materials as part of their job. And indeed, the way these tasks have been defined and traditionally carried out in our country, they are not the teacher's job. The teacher sees his or her role as one of elucidating whatever content of knowledge is prescribed in the syllabus. At the primary and lower secondary stages, teachers come to know the syllabus through the textbook which acts as the *de facto* syllabus. 'Covering' the syllabus means 'covering' or finishing the textbook. This kind of perception results in the confinement of classroom life to a narrow orbit. Classroom knowledge assumes total independence from the child's own experience and knowledge of the world. As a consequence of this de-coupling, children begin to compartmentalise knowledge into two categories: that which has currency in the school and classroom and the other which has uses and relevance outside the school. Necessarily, the knowledge in the first category ceases to have any 'life' and becomes increasingly ritualistic and burdensome. Teachers also carry the same kind of categorisation in their mind; very few of them are able to help the child make bridges between what is learnt at school and what is required to face real-life situations. One teacher who tried to make such a bridge in a lesson about letter-writing was asked by a class VI child: 'Madam, shall we write it the way we write at home or in the school way?'

While several factors, including those related to the training of teachers, can be held responsible for this aspect of the situation, we feel that the centralised structures of syllabus and textbook preparation set the tone. Howsoever 'good' a textbook produced at central level may be on professional standards, it cannot reflect the subtler nuances of life in a village of Kashmir or Assam. Adaptation to local conditions is indeed officially carried out to match the content of textbooks with local conditions, but it does not change the basic character of a textbook. Adaptation of syllabi to local conditions is even less effectively possible.

Convention of 'Teaching the Text'

Lack of adequate opportunities for teachers to participate in the processes of syllabus and textbook preparation is a major factor indirectly responsible for the problem of unrealistic syllabi or curriculum load. Teachers perform a more direct role in the context of this problem by perceiving the content of the textbook as a rigid boundary or definer of their work in the classroom. Boredom is the inevitable outcome when a tersely written textbook is taught in a rigid, mechanical manner. Poor grasp among teachers of their role as translators of the curriculum into classroom activity is a widely prevalent characteristic of our system. We are citing this as a relevant aspect of the phenomenon of curriculum load without suggesting that there is a vicious cycle here, i.e., teaching cannot improve unless there are better textbooks, etc. We feel that strategies to improve textbook writing and production must work parallel to strategies for improvement in teacher training and for creating an ethos in which teachers would feel motivated to take an academic interest in their work. The perception that a teacher can do little in the classroom that is different from what the textbook says is part of a historical legacy. This legacy must be transcended and the self-perception rooted in it must be changed. Teacher training institutions and the mass media both can assist in making this change possible.

In the context of constructing a new self-image of the teacher, pre-service training is a key but elusive area of reform. Past attempts to improve teacher training programmes and institutions have met with rather limited success. By and large, teacher training continues to be isolated from mainstream academic areas related to education. In-service training too in most of the places, has assumed the character of a ritual devoid of academic substance or the capacity to stimulate. The current efforts to provide statutory status to the National Council of Teacher Education (as envisaged in the National Education Policy) may perhaps make some impact on the weak training that is generally available in the country to people who want to work with children, especially young children.

Administrative and legal concern needs to be applied to several training programmes running as commercial success-stories, such as those offering a degree by correspondence. Similarly, there is need to examine existing policies with regard to nursery teacher training courses and institutions.

Indeed, what is required is a review of the overall training policy which permits the traditional bifurcation of degree-programmes from non-degree programmes and their application to different stages of school education. We hope that after acquiring statutory status, the NCTE will work out a comprehensive training programme to cover all stages of schooling, ending the bifurcation we have mentioned above. Such a programme will have to be radically different from the present ones which are anchored in the culture of late-19th century Normal schools and are sadly lacking both in perspective and means to equip teachers with the capacity to understand children and their learning processes in a professional manner.

Competition based Social Ethos

Our social ethos, particularly in the urban areas, is now fully entrenched in the competitive spirit which is fast becoming our way of life. The desire to catch up with the industrially developed countries has given it further impetus. Rising aspirations of people in all sections of the society and the growing realisation that education is an important instrument to fulfill their aspirations have resulted in a craze for admission to English-medium schools which start imparting formal education too early in the child's life.

The educated sections of the society believe that command over English is the key to upward mobility in social life. This has led to unprecedented growth in the number of private schools where English is not only taught as a subject but is also used as medium of education in all subjects right from class I. It is a well known fact that young children studying in English medium schools mug up the content of science and social sciences without understanding. It is an accepted principle of pedagogy that whatever is memorised without understanding proves burdensome for children. Any language other than the mother tongue of the child, if used as medium of instruction, is a big source of academic burden on children. Most of the parents in urban and semi-urban areas do not realise it, in fact they try to promote the use of English as a medium of education. Unfortunately, instead of resisting the pressure of the competitive spirit prevalent in the society or directing it in appropriate channels, our educational system has succumbed to it. The most conspicuous manifestations of this phenomenon in education are upgradation of content of syllabus by advancing introduction of many topics and subjects in utter disregard of the process of maturation. The entrance tests for admission to professional courses like engineering and medicine have influenced the objectives, content and methodology of education in many ways. The 'Quiz culture' which has taken roots in education, can be attributed to these tests.

With a view to provide incentives to 'high achievers' and 'talented' in different fields, high profile competitions are organised by different departments and institutions in the name of 'talent search' which at the most provide moments of brief glory to the winners but damage the 'ego strength' of numerous others who participate in the contests at the cost of leisurely pursuit of knowledge at their own pace and in their own ways. The experience of the ignominy of failure on the part of millions of children have long term deleterious effect on the personality of the individual and the matrix of society. It would be better to reward group performance so as to convey the message to everyone that excellence in group work rather than individual effort should be the target.

Absence of Academic Ethos

Adequate time, staff accommodation and its maintenance funds, pedagogical equipment, playgrounds are essential pre-requisites for effective curriculum transaction but, unfortunately, an overwhelming majority of schools do not have even the minimum essential facilities. It is a matter of great concern that the number of teachers with a sense of commitment is gradually shrinking while cynicism, feelings of helplessness and hopelessness are on the rise. Lack of adequate infrastructural facilities, rigid administrative structures and growing cynicism are responsible for the absence of academic ethos in majority of schools.

The methods of teaching used by majority of teachers are devoid of any type of challenge for the students. Transmission of information rather than experimentation or exploration or observation characterises the teaching learning process in most of the classrooms. We have no reason to believe that there is something wrong with our children, rural or urban. Luckily they have not compartmentalised knowledge; they are interested in seeking understanding rather than mere information. As they are educated by us, while they grow older, freshness goes away, as does romance and curiosity. Before anything is learnt they want to find out why they need to know. Must we, in the name of so-called 'proper education' go on committing the murder of their innate desire to discover and to learn on their own?

Children are not allowed to observe and explore natural phenomena, but at the same time they are also not provided opportunity to explore the world of books. The concept of a library as a readily available resource for learning simply does not exist in most schools. Even those rare schools that do happen to have a library stock little more than copies of prescribed textbooks, often stored behind locked doors. If children are to be prepared for experiencing the beauty and richness of nature and the fascination of ideas without feeling the curricular load, priority has to be given to developing school libraries and their adequate and appropriate utilisation.

Similarly, science laboratories even in the few cases where they are adequately equipped are not used for experimentation and discovery. A laboratory is not perceived as a place where children can conduct even those experiments which are not prescribed in their syllabi and come out with novel observations that need exploratory frameworks. The main purpose of a laboratory programme is to visualise children's natural talents and develop their ability to learn through observation and exploration. Over regimentation of prescribed experiments with the entire emphasis on getting the final result, is contrary to this spirit. Laboratories should be conceived as exploratories and schools should have the freedom to structure experiments to suit the needs of their children.

Recommendations

We have come to the conclusion that the problem of the load on school children does not arise only from over-enthusiastic curriculum designers, or poorly equipped teachers, or school administrators, or book publishers, or District, State or Central education authorities. Yes, what all these groups, agencies and administrations can do is exacerbate or alleviate the problem. But, there is a deeper malaise in our society, which affects our young children. If we continue to value a few elite qualifications far more than real competence for doing useful things in life and if the economic distance, between those who can manage to cross some academic hurdles and those who can't, continues to widen, we will probably continue to spend our effort in designing hurdles, instead of opportunities for children to learn with joy. As the body of the report analyses, a major problem is connected with the notions of "knowledge explosion" and the "catching up" syndrome. We believe that these problems cannot be fully addressed through easily manageable administrative actions. They need wider discussions because they are centrally connected with images of our civilization, self-esteem and societal goals. Such a wide discussion can come about through publication of this report and through a set of seminars, meetings and media discussions. Academicians, thinkers, need to pour over this basic problem.

The question of medium of instruction, particularly in early life, will not be fully resolved till the time our dominant and externally connected sections of society continue to give more importance to elementary graces in a foreign language, than to intimate connections with the "vernacular" knowledge which our children gain during every week of their growing up before they go to school. It is because of this reason that we have restrained ourselves from repeating the recommendation that mother-tongue alone should be the medium of instruction at the primary stage.

1. A number of organisations and departments organise competitions at district, state and national level for students in various fields such as school subjects, exhibitions, essay writing, elocution etc. Perhaps the spirit behind these activities is to recognise and reward the talent in diverse fields. But, unfortunately this tends to produce somewhat unhealthy singling out of people for their brief moment of glory. Competitions where individual achievement is rewarded need to be discouraged since they deprive children

of joyful learning. However, group activities and group achievements must be encouraged and rewarded to give a boost to cooperative learning in schools.

2. (a) The process of curriculum framing and preparation of textbooks be decentralised so as to increase teachers' involvement in these tasks. Decentralisation should mean greater autonomy, within state-level apparatus, to district-level boards or other relevant authority and to heads of schools and classroom teachers to develop curricular materials on their own, best suited to the needs of local environment. All the schools be encouraged to innovate in all aspects of curriculum, including choice of textbooks and other materials.

(b) Voluntary organisations with a specific commitment to pedagogical innovations within the formal or non-formal system be provided greater freedom and support in development of curriculum, textbooks and teacher training. A suitable and adequate mechanism be evolved for wider dissemination of the experiences of such organisations.

(c) We endorse the idea of setting up education committees at village, block and district level to undertake planning and supervision of schools under their jurisdiction.

(d) Sufficient contingency amount (not less than 10% of the total salary bill of the school) be placed at the disposal of heads of schools for purchase, repair and replacement of pedagogical equipment.

3. The culture of writing textbooks be changed so as to involve a much large number of teachers in the preparation of textbooks. The scientists and experts in various disciplines may be associated with the preparation of textbooks as consultants and not as writers of the books. Initiative in this regard should rest with groups of enlightened and innovative teachers who should be provided training in book writing.

4. At least three parallel systems of school education (syllabus, textbooks and examination) are running concurrently in different states. In each state majority of schools are affiliated to the State Board of Education while a few are affiliated to either CBSE or ICSE. The schools affiliated to CBSE in the states other than Delhi enjoy the prestige of being elite schools. The CBSE curriculum becomes a trend setter for the State Boards leading to heavier curriculum for majority of children. Therefore, the committee recommends that jurisdiction of CBSE be restricted to Kendriya and Navodaya Vidyalayas and all other schools be affiliated to the respective State Boards.

5. (a) Appropriate legislative and administrative measures be adopted to regulate the opening and functioning of early childhood education institutions (pre schools). Norms regarding accommodation, staff, apparatuses, play materials be laid down for the recognition of these

schools. It should be ensured that these institutions do not perpetrate violence on young children by inflicting a heavy dose of 'over education' in the form of formal teaching of Reading, Writing and Numbers. The practice of holding tests and interviews for admission to nursery class be abolished.

(b) Norms for granting recognition to private schools be made more stringent. This will prove conducive for improving the quality of learning on the one hand and arrest growing commercialisation on the other. The norms, thus developed, be made uniformly applicable to all schools including the state run institutions.

6. There is no justification for torturing the young children by compelling them to carry very heavy bags of books every day to schools. Textbooks should be treated as school property and thus, there should be no need for children to purchase the books individually and carry them daily to homes. A separate time table for the assignment of home work and for the use of textbooks and notebooks be prepared by the school and be made known to the children in advance.

7. The nature and character of homework needs a radical change. In the primary classes, children should not be given any homework save for extension of explorations in the home environment. In the upper primary and secondary classes, homework, where necessary, should be non-textual and textbooks, when needed for work at home should be made available on a rotation basis.

8. The existing norm for teacher-pupil ratio (i.e. 1:40) should be enforced and an attempt should be made to reduce this to 1:30, at least in the primary classes, as a basis for future educational planning.

9. Greater use of the electronic media be made for the creation of a child-centred social ethos in the country. A regular television programme addressed to students, teachers and parents and possibly called 'Shiksha Darshan' be launched, along the lines of the 'Krishi Darshan' programme.

10. (a) Inadequate programme of teacher preparation leads to unsatisfactory quality of learning in schools. In B.Ed., programme should offer the possibility of specialisation in secondary or elementary or nursery education. The duration of the programme should either be one year after graduation or 3-4 years after higher secondary. The content of the programme should be restructured to ensure its relevance to the changing needs of school education and to make it more practice-centred. The emphasis in these programmes should be on enabling the trainees to acquire the ability for self learning and independent thinking. Preservice teacher education programme, being a professional course, has to be a rigorous, thorough and intensive programme. Therefore, B.Ed. degree courses by correspondence be derecognised.

(b) The continuing education of teachers must be institutionalised. The organisation of in-service education programmes and other activities aimed at professional growth of teachers be systematically designed and conducted imaginatively.

11. The public examinations taken at the end of class X and XII be reviewed with a view to ensure replacement of the prevailing text based and 'Quiz type' questioning by the concept-based questioning. This single reform is sufficient to improve the quality of learning and save the children from the tyranny of rote memorisation.

12. (a) A Project team with a number of sub-groups be set up in each state to examine the syllabi and textbooks for all school classes. The sub-groups be required to decide the following:

(i) the minimum number of topics required to be taught.

(ii) the minimum number of concepts to be introduced within each topic.

(iii) the total time needed for teaching this minimum number of concepts comfortably by a teacher in the total working days realistically available in a year.

(b) Mathematics curriculum for primary classes in all parts of the country be reviewed with a view to slowing down the pace at which children are required to learn basic mathematical concepts and broadening the scope of primary mathematics to include areas other than number worked (e.g., space and shape related concepts and problem solving). The tendency embedded in the syllabi and textbooks of primary mathematics to accelerate children's mathematical skills by teaching them mechanical rules at the expense of understanding and intelligent application ought to be discouraged in future syllabi and texts.

(c) Language textbooks should adequately reflect the spoken idiom. An attempt should be made in future textbooks to give adequate representation to children's life experiences, imaginary stories and poems and stories reflecting the lives of ordinary people in different parts of the country. Pedantic language and excessive didacticism ought to be avoided.

(d) Science syllabi and textbooks in the primary classes should provide greater room and necessity for experimentation than they do at present. In place of didacticism in areas like health and sanitation, the texts should emphasise analytical reflection on real-life situations. A great deal of trivial material included in primary-level science texts should be dropped.

(e) The syllabi of natural sciences throughout the secondary and senior secondary classes be revised in a manner so as to ensure that most of the topics included are actively linked to experiments or activities that can be performed by children and teachers.

(f) Besides imparting knowledge of history and geography, the social sciences curriculum for classes VI-VIII and IX-X should convey the philosophy and methodology of the functions of our socio-political and economic system and enable the students to analyse, understand and reflect on the problems and priorities of socio-economic development. The repetitious nature of history syllabus should be changed. The history of ancient times should be introduced for systematic study in secondary classes (IX and X). The history syllabus for classes VI-VIII should focus on the freedom struggle and post-independence developments. The civics, as it is taught today, puts a great load on children's capacities to memorise. Therefore, it may be dropped in its present form and be replaced by 'contemporary studies'. The study of geography be related to contemporary reality.

CABE COMMITTEE ON DECENTRALISED MANAGEMENT OF EDUCATION, 1993*

To suggest guidelines on decentralised management of education Central Advisory Board of Education, set up a Committee on February 2, 1993 under the chairmanship of M. Veerappa Moily.

Recommendations

Constitutional Provisions

4.1 The Committee in its deliberations has been guided by the provisions of the Seventy-third, and the Seventy-fourth Constitutional Amendment Acts, the National Policy on Education and Programme of Action (1992). The recommendations of the Committee are in the nature of guidelines, which may be considered as comprehensive though not exhaustive. The States may after due consultations and deliberations choose a pattern and system suited to their needs and keeping in view the spirit of the Constitutional amendments and need to foster people's participation if educational goals are to be achieved. While the States which are delegating powers to the institutions of local self-government for the first time may prefer to proceed cautiously, those States which have already gained experience in this sphere may decide to improve on these proposals and give higher levels of responsibilities to Panchayati Raj/Municipal bodies.

4.2 The Constitution makes a mandatory provision for establishment of Panchayats at the village, intermediate and district levels in each state. Keeping in view the three-tier structure (States and population below 20 lakhs need not have the intermediate tier) these proposals envisage delegation of responsibilities of educational management to the Panchayats, Panchayat Samities and Zila Parishads. A Summary of Committee's recommendations in this regard is presented in respect of Panchayat Level:

(a) Panchayats where jurisdiction is limited to one village,

---

* Ministry of Human Resource Development, Department of Education, Government of India, New Delhi, 1993.

(b) Panchayats where jurisdiction extends to a group of villages,
(c) Panchayat Samitis (intermediate level) and
(d) Zila Parishads (district level), in Statements IA, IB, II and III, respectively.

Panchayat Level

4.3 For the purpose of defining the jurisdiction of the Panchayat, the village is to be specified by the Governor by a public notification and may include a group of village so specified. A Panchayat area means a territorial area of a Panchayat. This implies that Panchayats at the Village level may comprise a village or a group of villages.

4.4 The Programme of Action approved by the CABE attaches considerable importance to Village Education Committees (VECs). The village normally represents a cohesive community and is ideally suited for promoting programmes, involving support of the community, such as; Early Childhood Care and Education, Primary Education, Non-formal Education and Adult Education. VEC may be considered the ideal organisation to mobilise and involve people in the educational efforts.

Panchayat Standing Committee on Education

4.5 The Education Committee at the Panchayat level where the panchayat comprises only one village can be named as the Panchayat Standing Committee on Education (PEC). It can be given statutory authority by bringing it under the Panchayati Raj legislation. The tenure of this Committee will be the same as the tenure of the Panchayat.

Composition

4.6 The Panchayat Standing Committee on Education may consist of not less than 7 and not more than 15 members. It may be headed by the Chairman of the Pnachayat. At least one third of its members should be women. one member each representing Scheduled Castes, Scheduled Tribes, Backward Classes and minorities should also be on the Committee. A parent representative of the Parent-Teacher Association, the Anganwadi worker and an educationist or a person interested in education from the village may also be members of the Committee. Those members of the committee who are not elected members of the Panchayat may be nominated by the Panchayat. The Member-Secretary of the Committee will be the Headmaster of a Panchayati Raj Primary or Upper Primary School in the village and will be nominated by the Panchayat.

Role

4.7 The role of the Panchayat Standing Committee on Education may include generation and sustenance of awareness among village community ensuring participation of all segments of population, developing teacher and community partnership to oversee and manage the effective and regular functioning of the schools and centres. It should be the endeavour of this Committee that every child in every family participates in primary education.

4.8 The Committee will exercise supervision over early childhood care and education, non-formal education, primary education and adult education programmes in its jurisdiction. It will also exercise supervision over composite upper primary schools under delegation of powers from the Panchayat Samiti.

Functions

4.9 The Panchayat Standing Committee on Education will be required to visit institutions and centres periodically and promote enrolment drives. Persuading parents of non-attending children to send their wards to schools and enthusing adults for literacy programmes may form a significant agenda for its activities.

4.10 Steps to promote attendance and prevent drop-outs in the various educational programmes may also be one of the responsibilities of this Committee. It may also undertake supportive measures and services for retention of students and will assist in the smooth functioning of the primary schools, composite upper primary schools and other institutions. It should be the Committee's endeavour to encourage and support the teachers in their tasks. It may provide essential facilities like drinking water, urinals, play-ground, etc., in the schools. The Committee will present periodical reports and proposals to Panchayat Samiti on development of education and will assess progress of the programmes in their territorial jurisdiction. It may meet as many times as required but not less than once in a quarter.

Powers

4.11 The Panchayat Standing Committee on Education will have the authority to visit educational institutions and centres providing early childhood care and education, non-formal education, primary education and adult education and will check attendance and other registers. It would also have the authority to enquire and report to the concerned authorities on education deficiencies and requirements of the village. The Committee would recommend the annual budget of the Panchayati Raj schools to the concerned authorities. It may report on irregularities of the attendance of students and teacher and functioning of the schools. It will prepare the school calendar indicating working days, holidays and vacation under the guidance of the Zila Parishad.

Funds

4.12 The Committee will depend largely upon funds provided by the Zila Parishad and Panchayat Samiti for various programmes to be undertaken in the village. It may also receive earmarked funds for specific programmes provided by concerned agencies of the State Government. The Committee may also raise funds locally from the parents and public.

Coordination

4.13 It will be desirable for VECs to hold meetings with similar bodies in the field of health and other subjects to seek their support in pursuance of its activities.

Administrative Support

4.14 The Village Education Committee (VEC) will function largely on the basis of the staff support provided by the Headmaster, staff and teachers in the Panchayati Raj schools and other educational programmes.

Training

4.15 The members of Village Education Committee would require orientation and training for discharging their functions effectively. The Headmasters may have to be given a special orientation to enable them to assist the Village Education Committees in their activities.

Village Education Committee as Sub-Committee of Panchayat

4.16 Where the Panchayat comprises more than one village, it may establish Village Education Committee (VEC) as the sub-Committee of the Panchayat for each village. It will have statutory authority as they will be established by the Panchayats under the powers conferred upon them by the State Panchayati Raj legislation. The Panchayat may be empowered statutory to delegate powers to these committees.

Composition

4.17 The Village Education Committee may be presided over by the President of the Panchayat where he is elected from the village. In other villages a member of the Panchayat representing the village concerned may preside over the VEC. The number of members of the VEC may be the same as provided for the Panchayat Standing Committee on Education. The composition of the Committee may also be the same, except that all the members must be drawn from the village.

4.18 The rest of the features of the Panchayat Standing Committee will also apply to VECs (Sub-committees).

Panchayat Samiti

4.19 The Panchayat Samiti will be the Panchayati Raj body at the intermediate level in terms of the Constitutional amendment.

Panchayat Samiti Standing Committee on Education

4.20 The Panchayat Samiti may set up a Panchayat Samiti Standing Committee on Education (PSEC) for management of education programmes in their territorial jurisdiction. This Committee will have the statutory recognition under the Panchayati Raj legislation and will have the same tenure as the Panchayat Samiti.

Composition

4.21 The Panchayat Samiti Standing Committee on Education may be headed by the Chairman of the Panchayat Samiti. The Committee may consist of not less than 11 and not more than 17 members with at least one-third of the members being women. One member each representing the Scheduled Castes, Scheduled Tribes, backward classes and minority communities should be on the Committee.

4.22 A parent from the Parent-Teacher Association may also be on the Committee. At least two representatives of the Panchayat Standing Committee on Education/Village Education Committees may be nominated by rotation. A Principal of a degree/pre-degree college, Headmaster of a school complex/secondary school and a representative of teachers may also be on the Committee. The Member-Secretary of the Committee will be the Block Level Education Officer. The non-elected members of the Committee may be nominated by the Panchayat Samiti.

Role

4.23 The Panchayat Samiti Standing Committee on Education will be responsible for management of adult education, non-formal education, early childhood care and education and schools of the Panchayati Raj bodies upto primary level, under the overall supervision of the Zila Parishad.

4.24 All existing government schools upto upper primary level with their staff will come under the control of Panchayat Samitis and schools in the state sector will in future be established only by the Panchayat Samitis. The Committee will also have supervisory power over aided upper primary schools and will channel grant to them under the guidance of Zila Parishad. In this regard, the Committee will function in the same manner as the present departmental set-up at this level.

4.25 The Panchayat Samiti Standing Committee on Education will undertake academic supervision of all the educational institutions upto upper primary level including the private schools in its jurisdiction.

4.26 The Education Committee at this level will endeavour to promote school complexes in its jurisdiction. The Committee will periodically review progress of education in its area and actively pursue the programmes of total adult literacy and universalisation of elementary education.

Functions

4.27 The Committee will exercise control over all Panchayati Raj educational institutions upto upper primary level. Academic supervision of all the schools upto upper primary levels, including private schools, will be one of its important functions. The Committee will be responsible for preparation of plans for development of education upto upper primary level in its jurisdiction and for their implementation. It will also prepare educational budget of the Panchayat Samiti and approve expenditure to be incurred. The Committee will coordinate with other bodies for social service programmes for mutual support.

Powers

4.28 The Panchayat Samiti Standing Committee on Education will exercise control over the staff in the government schools transferred to Panchayat Samiti including payment of salaries. It will appoint staff to schools under its control from the panel of names given by the appropriate body and transfer them within its jurisdiction subject to guidelines provided by the Zila Parishad/Government. The Committee will be responsible for channelising grants to aided schools under the supervision of Zila Parishad. It will have powers of academic supervision of all educational programmes in its jurisdiction upto upper primary level. The Committee will prepare the educational budget and plans of the Panchayat Samiti and sanction expenditure from the approved budget. It may raise its resources by levying development fees and other fees as well as by public contributions and donations. The Committee may propose measures to Panchayat Samiti and Zila Parishad for mobilisation of additional resources. It may delegate its power of supervision over composite upper primary schools to the Panchayat Standing Committee on Education/Village Education Committee.

Funds

4.29 The Committee will receive grants from the Zila Parishad and under various schemes for implementing different educational programmes in its jurisdiction. It may also receive earmarked funds from different agencies, voluntary donations and endowments and may raise funds on its own through the powers of taxation.

Organisational Support

4.30 The services of the staff of the education department at this level will be placed with the Panchayat Samiti. However, its control over the staff will be subject to guidelines laid down by the State Government and the academic norms adopted by the Panchayat Samiti Standing Committee on Education will be subject to over-all instructions issued by the department of education of the state.

4.31 The members of the Panchayat Samiti Standing Committee on Education will require orientation to prepare themselves for the effective discharge of the assigned tasks. They would also require to establish close rapport with officials at different levels and the state-level leadership for guidance in their work. The non-elected members of the Committee also will require orientation to enable them to work in harmony with others. Training for the officials and volunteers for effective implementation of various programmes may also be necessary.

Zila Parishad Level

4.32 According to the Act, the Zila Parishad will cover an entire district excluding municipal areas.

Zila Parishad Standing Committee on Education

4.33 The Zila Parishad may set up its Standing Committee on Education as a statutory body under the Panchayati Raj legislation for the management of educational institutions in its jurisdiction. The tenure of the Standing Committee will correspond with the tenure of the Zila Parishad.

Composition

4.34 The Standing Committee may be headed by the Chairman of the Zila Parishad. The Committee may consist of not less than 15 and not more than 21 members with at least one-third members being women. These should include representatives of Scheduled Castes, Scheduled Tribes, Backward Classes and Minorities. A parent from the Parent- Teacher Associations and one representative each of NGOs and teachers may also be on the Committee. At least two representatives of the Education Committees at Panchayat/Village level and Panchayat Samiti level may also be nominated to the Committee by rotation. A Principal of a College, a Professor of Education of a University, Principal of DIET and Headmaster of a School Complex or Secondary School may also be on the Committee. The Chief Education Officer of the Zila Parishad may be the Member-Secretary of the Committee. The power of nomination of non-elected members will rest with Zila Parishad.

Role

4.35 The role of the Zila Parishad Standing Committee on Education will be the overall management and supervision of all education programmes in the district upto secondary level in the entire district. It will review the progress of education upto secondary level in the district and will also have the specific responsibility for formulation and operationalisation of programmes to achieve total literacy and universal elementary education.

Functions

4.36 The Zila Parishad may establish and manage schools upto secondary level. It will supervise and provide grant to aided schools upto secondary level and will exercise academic supervision of all institutions upto secondary level in the district. Preparation and coordination of plans for development of education upto secondary level may also be the responsibility of this Committee. It will review the progress of education upto secondary level in the district with particular reference to universalisation of elementary education and adult literacy.

4.37 One of the important functions of the Committee will be to oversee and guide Panchayat Samiti Standing Committees on Education and Education Committees at Panchayat/Village level in their tasks. The Committee will undertake implementation of academic programmes.

Powers

4.38 The powers of the Committee will include establishment and maintenance of schools upto secondary level including recruitment and appointment of staff and payment of salaries, subject to government guidelines. All existing schools upto secondary level will be transferred to the control of Zila Parishad. In future all secondary schools in the state sector will be established only by the Zila Parishad. The Committee will also channelise grants to aided schools subject to government rules. It will also exercise academic supervision of all schools including private schools upto secondary level. Laying down academic and administrative norms and procedures under the overall departmental and government supervision may also fall under the purview of the Committee. The Committee will guide the work of Panchayat Samitis and Panchayat/Village Education Committees. It may recruit and appoint teachers in schools under its control subject to government guidelines. The Committee will also be responsible for preparation of education budget and plans for approval of the Zila Parishad. The administration of the district education funds will be its responsibility. Preparation of perspective plans for educational development of the district will be responsibility of the Committee.

Funds

4.39 The resources of the Zila Parishad will include grants from the State Government, the centrally assisted and sponsored schemes channelled through the State Government and funds provided by the other agencies. The Zila Parishad may also raise resources through appropriate taxation measures as well as raise funds through voluntary donations and contributions.

Organisational Support

4.40 The services of the staff of the education department at the district level will be placed with the Zila Parishad. The State Government, particularly the department of education, will provide necessary administrative and academic guidance to the Zila Parishad for undertaking its educational responsibilities.

4.41 The Panchayati Raj bodies must take full benefit of the District Institute of Education and Training (DIET) in their efforts to improve the quality of education. The DIET must be fully involved in the functioning of the academic wings of the Panchayati Raj bodies through organisation of orientation and training programmes for the academic staff and by undertaking surveys, evaluation studies and innovative projects. Its support may also be enlisted for improved methods of learning and assessment procedures for attaining the minimum levels of learning.

Training Needs

4.42 The non-officials of the Zila Parishads would require orientation to introduce them to the tasks of the Zila Parishad. They may also receive adequate orientation in respect of various schemes in operation as well as programmes, such as, universalisation of elementary education, adult education and non-formal education. The officials working under the Zila Parishads may also require training to enable them to establish effective working relationship with the members of the Committee and Zila Parishad.

4.43 It is now well-organised that both the non-officials involved in the Panchayati Raj programmes relating to education require orientation, training and preparation for discharging their responsibilities effectively in the new set-up. They need advice, guidance and support to develop sound and efficient methods of functioning in the Panchayati Raj set-up. The State would consider setting up appropriate arrangements both at the State and district levels to ensure required training and orientation. The establishment of State Institutes of Educational Planning and Administration offers one such possibility.

Personnel Management

4.44 Democratic decentralisation implies placing the services of employees with the Panchayati Raj bodies. Therefore, it is necessary to ensure that this is done in a manner and with such safeguards which enable these employees to work in a congenial and cordial atmosphere.

4.45 Following this approach, services of the teaching staff working in government primary, middle and secondary schools at the time of transfer to Panchayati Raj Institutions may be placed with the Panchayati Raj bodies. It is necessary to protect their service conditions while doing so. In future all teaching staff in schools under the Panchayati Raj bodies, selected and allotted by an appropriate organisation will be appointed by the Panchayati Raj bodies and will be under their exclusive control.

4.46 All the staff under the Panchayati Raj bodies, whether appointed by them or otherwise, should enjoy the same service conditions and benefits.

4.47 The non-teaching staff of the government schools and departmental officers whose services are placed with the Panchayati Raj bodies may be treated on par with similar staff of other departments whose responsibilities and services would stand transferred to the Panchayati Raj bodies.

4.48 Educational officers, such as, District Inspectors of Schools, Headmasters of Secondary Schools, District Education Officers and Deputy Directors, who may come under the control of the Panchayati Raj bodies, may be treated as on deputation or on loan of services to these bodies. The Panchayati Raj bodies would have full control over them including discipline, subject to such guidelines as the State government may lay down.

Recruitment of Teachers

4.49 Recruitment of teachers is a sensitive and responsible task. The State government may develop appropriate recruitment system including involvement of the State Public Service Commission wherever necessary. The objective must be to decentralise recruitment of teachers at district level through appropriate bodies with suitable representation of the Zila Parishad. The procedure must ensure impartial selection through well laid out procedures, with provision for reservation of posts for the prescribed categories. While allocating the candidates to various Panchayat Samitis, it may be ensured that local candidates are preferred. This may minimise the problem of subsequent transfers.

Disbursement of Salaries

4.50 The prompt and regular payment of salaries to staff is a matter of importance. The State government must stipulate that the Panchayati Raj bodies introduce mechanisms in their budgetary control to ensure that salary and service benefits flow to the teaching and non-teaching staff in schools in a regular and prompt manner.

4.51 The State governments may suitably adapt these recommendations to suit the local conditions.

Role of the State Government

4.52 While the Panchayat Raj bodies may perform the functions outlined above, the State government or an appropriate State level body would exercise overall supervision and retain residuary powers, particularly in regard to the following issues.

1. Laying down academic standards and norms, including academic calendar, teacher-pupil ratio, etc.
2. Formulation of syllabi and curricula.
3. Preparation and prescription of text-books, supplementary reading materials.
4. Conduct of public, scholarship and other examinations.
5. Teachers' training and retraining.
6. Academic innovations, over-all supervision and assessment.
7. Administrative norms, scale of fees, fee concessions.
8. Norms for transfer of teachers and disciplinary control, etc.
9. Periodic monitoring of the educational activities of the Panchayati Raj bodies and preparation of guidelines for their efficient functioning.
10. Establishment and management of organisations and institutions intended to improve the academic standards and staff development, such as SCERT, SIE, DIETs, etc.

The State and these bodies may consider delegating authority in stages to the Panchayat Raj bodies at different levels for preparation of academic calendar, conduct of examinations, of academic supervision under the over-all guidance of the Department.

Financial Support

Non-Plan Grant

4.53 Pending constitution of the State Finance Commission, the grant to Panchayati Raj bodies may include the following Non-Plan grants:

1. Grant for salary and other benefits to teaching and non-teaching staff- This will include two components:
   (a) The component for the government schools transferred to Zila Parishad.
   (b) The component for aided schools in the jurisdiction of Zila Parishad.
2. Maintenance Grant—This may include financial assistance to meet the cost of maintenance of building, equipment, library, contingencies, etc. This may again have two components pertaining to:
   (a) Government schools transferred to Zila Parishads, and
   (b) Aided schools, as per the norms laid down.

Development Grant (Plan)

4.54 This may include:

(i) Provision for opening of new schools including salary component for staff.

(ii) Provision for construction of building for existing and new schools.

(iii) Provision for purchase of equipment and teacher-learning aids for existing and new schools.

(iv) Assistance under the centrally sponsored schemes such as Operation Blackboard, etc.

(v) Provision for scholarships, fellowships, etc.

4.55 The ultimate objective is to transfer all funds which are now operated at district level to the Zila Parishads with authority to raise additional resources to support their efforts.

Special Grants

4.56 Provision for special grants to Zila Parishads which are educationally backward will have to be made for reducing disparities.

Incentive Grants

4.57 Provision for matching grants for those Zila Parishads, which perform well, according to norms to be laid down, may also need to be made.

Budget

4.58 The State budget should be suitably redesigned to reflect the allocation of funds to Panchayati Raj bodies. The education budget should depict the allocations preferably district-wise under each appropriate head and, if feasible, in accordance with different educational functions assigned to the Panchayati Raj bodies.

Mobilization of Additional Resources

4.59 The Zila Parishad and Panchayat Samiti may suitably be empowered to raise additional resources for educational activities through:

1. Levy of cess on land revenues, sales tax, quarrying, etc.
2. Levy of surcharge on building tax, professional tax, etc.
3. Local contributions towards different schemes for extending benefits to students.
4. Voluntary contributions by parents and community towards supporting development of educational institutions.

4.60 The objective must be to encourage the local bodies to generate local resources and supplement the support provided by the State government for undertaking development programmes. The Panchayati Raj bodies should be encouraged to develop cost effective programmes.

Financial Implications

4.61 It is an acknowledged fact that resource position of the local bodies is not too happy. Most of them depend upon grants from the state government and other sources. Very few of them have been able to identify and develop sources of income within their own jurisdiction. it is also a fact that by tradition and practice they have not made efforts to generate their resources. Over a period of time they have developed an attitude and approach which essentially implies dependence on outside support. It would, therefore, be necessary that the Panchayati Raj bodies inculcate a new approach which will favour generation of their own resources and gradual reduction in the dependence on external funding and support. There is also a need for building efficiency and cost effectiveness in their functioning.

4.62 These changes, however, can take place only over a period of time. Meanwhile, the transfer of management of education to Panchayati Raj bodies without providing adequate resources to them will be a harmful step. The State governments have to ensure sufficient financial support to the Panchayati Raj bodies for ensuring successful management of the educational programmes. Alongwith the transfer of responsibilities, the funds with which the State governments used to discharge such responsibilities, must be made available to the Panchayati Raj bodies.

4.63 Special measures are necessary to overcome the acute deficiencies of school infrastructure. The government may, therefore, consider setting up a financial institution for the development and maintenance of the schools managed by Panchayati Raj and Municipal bodies. This would provide a much needed financial incentive for devolution of powers to these bodies.

Management of Education in Municipal Areas

The Seventy-fourth Amendment Act to the Constitution of India provides for the establishment of the Municipalities in the urban area. It envisages to give the responsibility of "promotion of cultural, educational and aesthetic aspects" to Municipal bodies. The proposals of the Committee in this regard are described in the following paragraphs.

Jurisdiction

4.64 The area, population and resources of Municipalities vary significantly from State to State as well as within the State. The responsibilities of educational management to be assigned to the Municipalities will have to vary depending upon the specific circumstances of each Municipal body. It is difficult to lay down a broad pattern for this purpose as it has been done in the case of the Panchayati Raj bodies for rural areas. Broadly speaking, the States may categories the Municipalities according to their jurisdiction, resources and capabilities into three categories. The first category may include Municipalities which may be given the responsibilities of managing education upto primary level, the second category may be those Municipalities which may be given the control of education upto secondary level.

Structure

4.65 The Municipalities may constitute standing committees on education for managing the educational institutions and other responsbilities entrusted to them. These committees may provide for representation of Scheduled Castes, Scheduled Tribes, Backward classes and Minorities besides elected members of the Municipalities. The parent-teacher association may also be represented on the Committee. Educationists such as a Principal of a college, Headmaster of a secondary school or senior secondary school may also be members of the committee. Atleast one-third of the members of the committee must be women. The Member-Secretary of the Committee may be the Chief Education Officer of the Municipality or an officer nominated by it. These committees will be responsible for administering the educational programmes in their jurisdiction.

Functions

4.66 The government primary, upper primary and secondary schools in the municipal areas along with their staff may be transferred to different Municipalities. They will have control over the staff except in matters of recruitment which will be done by an organisation designated for this purpose by the State Government.

4.67 The channelisation of grant to aided schools in the municipal areas may be done through the Municipalities having adequate capabilities to undertake this task.

4.68 It is possible that some Municipalities have built up viable management structures which include academic wings. In such cases they may be entrusted with academic supervision of the institutions in the municipal areas subject to guidelines laid down by the Department of Education.

4.69 While the Municipalities may prepare plans and programmes for development of education in their jurisdiction, their plans will be coordinated by the District Planning Committee for the district as a whole. The Municipalities will be responsible for promoting universal elementary education and total literacy in their jurisdiction.

4.70 The State Government may periodically review the working of the Municipalities in the sphere of education and enlarge their areas of responsibilities with appropriate financial and staff support as they gradually gain experience.

Administrative Support

4.71 The staff of the schools transferred to the Municipalities and the headquarter staff provided by the Municipality would provide the administrative support.

Training

4.72 Orientation/training may be provided to the members of the Municipal Education Committee and the staff working with them to enable them to discharge their responsibilities successfully. The Municipalities may draw upon the resources of DIET to improve the quality of education. The State Government may also organise training programmes in various spheres of educational development for non-official and official members of the Municipalities who are assigned responsibility for education.

Funds

4.73 The State Government may provide adequate grants to these bodies for managing the institutions transferred to them. They may also provide development grants for plan programmes in municipal areas. Besides these grants, Municipalities may generate their own resources through appropriate taxation measures.

GROUP TO EXAMINE THE RECOMMENDATIONS OF THE NATIONAL ADVISORY COMMITTEE ON LEARNING WITHOUT BURDEN, 1993

Text of the Report

General Observations

The Group has observed with considerable appreciation the participative nature of the Yash Pal Committee Report about the load of curriculum on school students. While discussion on curriculum load has been extensive over the years in the mass media, it has been largely confined to the physical load of the school bag which a student has to carry. Many have felt that there has been a lot of generalisation in such discussions on the basis of the size of the school bag seen in metropolitan cities and particularly in regard to students studying in public schools even at the pre-school stage. The Report has taken note in the beginning itself that "a survey conducted in Delhi revealed that the weight of school bag, on an average, in primary classes in public schools is more than 4 kg, while it is around 1 kg in MCD schools". This finding of the Yash Pal Committee is in tune with the information with the educational managers that firstly, the load of the school bag is not a forbidding one in schools in villages and in small towns and secondly, even in big towns, the problem is in its most aggravated form in regard to students of public schools and children of pre-school classes. Luckily, there are signs recently of the more enlightened public schools de-emphasising subject-matter learning at pre-school stage as also de-emphasising the need to prescribe a lot of books and exercise books at pre-school stage. Since such schools are pace-setters, it is hoped that this example will soon influence other pre-primary schools. This Group is recommending subsequently some specific measures in pursuance of one of the recommendations of the Yash Pal Committee to accelerate this process.

The Yash Pal Committee has instead taken the problem at a more elevated plane by observing that in the present schools "a lot is taught but little is learnt or understood". It has, therefore, inferred that the load of non-learning or non-comprehension is the real load one should be concerned about. This approach of looking at the problem of academic burden has imparted to the Report of the Yash Pal Committee a great deal of significance.

Simultaneously, the Group noted that there are a few things to which the Yash Pal Committee could have given specific attention. The National Policy on Education (NPE) and the Programme of Action (PoA) enunciate the need to have a national core curriculum and have spelt out some of the features of this. The Policy also strongly enunciates a child-centred approach to education. It is in pursuance of this that the NCERT framed a curriculum framework for the school stage which has been accepted by all the states. The NCERT has also developed the levels of competencies to be attained at the end of primary stage. These exercises with a lot of validity in them have been the basis for developing syllabi and textbooks for different stages of school education. While there may be some flaws in the syllabi and the textbooks prepared by the NCERT, it does not seem that they can be accused of being grossly unsuitable or overloaded. In regard to curriculum load, the NCERT had carried out a study in mid-eighties which identified the physical overload of curriculum at some stages of school education and also pointed out that inadequate teacher competency, insufficient teaching days and inadequate classroom facilities, transfer the curriculum load to the students as well as indirectly to parents. The Yash Pal Committee has not referred to this work and the facts stated in the preceding statements. While the main argument forming the basis of the Yash Pal Committee Report is eminently sound, with regard to the main thrust of its recommendations, some of the statements in the Report do not indicate the data or basis on which the Committee has relied. Similarly, some of the recommendations like the one concerning affiliation of schools to the Central Board of Secondary Education (CBSE) are not accompanied by corresponding consideration in the main body of the Report. In a few cases like the one in regard to medium of instruction in schools, the Committee has noted in the main body of its Report: "the educated sections of the society believe that command over English is key to upward mobility in social life... It is a well-known fact that young children studying in English medium schools mug the content of science and social sciences without understanding. It is an accepted principle of pedagogy that whatever is memorised without understanding proves burdensome on children. Any language other than the mother tongue of the child, if used as medium of instruction, is a big source of academic burden on children". However, such strong statements do not have a corresponding recommendation. The Report also ignores the fact that for most of our students, medium of instruction is the mother tongue or regional language at all stages of school education. Overall it is an important Report which has brought to the fore an understanding about curriculum load which one does not frequently come across. For this it is bound to raise the level of debate about the curriculum load to a qualitatively higher level. It is expected that this report would lead to meaningful and adequate reform in curriculum formulation, textbook preparation, teacher training, etc. The Group feels that the nature of the problem is different for each stage of school education but the Committee has not specifically referred to the distinct problems of each stage and ways of dealing with them. The views of the Group in regard to individual recommendations made by the Yash Pal Committee are given below:

Recommendation No. 1 — Comments

The Group is of the view that group activity and individual effort are not mutually exclusive or antagonistic. Rewarding individual achievement does not take away the joy of learning and is also a means to motivate towards higher achievement. In the view of the Group, the educational system should promote performance of the students both as an individual and as a member of the group.

Recommendation No. 2 (a) — Comments

The Group noted that the curriculum and syllabi are designed by the NCERT/CBSE at national level and by the State Boards of Secondary Education/SCERTs at state level by involving teachers and through teachers. However, the number of teachers associated with this exercise is limited to the number of members of the Committee or the Board. The Yash Pal Committee has rightly underlined the need to increase teachers' participation in curriculum development. The Group feels that while the size of committees at national or state level cannot be increased beyond a limit, a meaningful way of improving teachers' participation would be for either the NCERT/CBSE/State Boards/SCERTs to prepare the draft syllabus and finalise it after subjecting it to regional or district level consideration by a large body of teachers or, in the alternative, to get multiple syllabi developed at regional and district levels on the basis of which the final syllabi could be prepared at the state/national level. The Group, however, does not recommend decentralisation in the preparation of syllabus or textbooks at the district or school level because it will be difficult to ensure adequate projection of national identity and of composite culture of India. Also, in such a situation, the adherence to even minimum standards in all parts of the country may become difficult.

In regard to textbooks, the Group agrees with the Yash Pal Committee that the primary responsibility for preparing textbooks, particularly for the lower classes should be that of teachers. It may, however, be remembered that the involvement of experts since the early 1960s led to qualitative improvement in school textbooks. They helped in weeding out dead wood, brought in new perspectives in tune with contemporary knowledge. The Group, however, shares the concern of the Yash Pal Committee that many textbooks presently tend to project predominantly the urban middle class life style. Therefore, the Group recommends that:

(a) The writing of textooks, as far as possible, should be assigned to school teachers and to those who have developed professional expertise in the area. Subject-matter specialists should be engaged as consultants or advisers to vet the content and presentation of the subject-matter to ensure its accuracy.

(b) In states which have distinct socio-cultural geographical zones, different and parallel sets of textbooks with the same learning objectives should be prepared and used in schools for each such distinct socio-cultural geographical region.

(c) A conscious effort should be made by the textbook preparation agencies to take examples from rural areas for illustrating various points because a large majority of students are in rural areas.

(d) The textbook preparation agencies should undertake systematic review of all textbooks in a time-bound manner to ensure that any trivial matter which may have got included in the textbooks is weeded out. Similarly, such a review should also try to eliminate elements of repetitions of the topic covered in previous classes.

(e) The Group noted that, in some cases, the textbooks for subjects other than languages in some classes are written in a language which is considerably more complex and difficult than the language used in textbooks for that class. It, therefore, recommends that the group which writes a textbook should include one language teacher who should vet the manuscript to ensure that the degree of difficulty of the language used in the subject-matter is not more than the degree of difficulty designed for language competency for that class. In regard to curriculum transaction and teaching materials, the Group noted that there are no restrictions on schools and teachers to innovate. Indeed, the teacher training courses have consistently advocated this and many organisations have introduced special programmes to promote this. Needless to say that schools and teachers should be motivated to innovate to the fullest extent in regard to teaching methods and use of teaching materials.

Recommendation No. 2 (b) — Comments

The Group fully agrees that voluntary organisations with a commitment to education should be encouraged in all possible manners. The Group also noted that the government, both at the national and the state levels have, in recent past, made a substantial move to expand such cooperation. The process needs to be continued. However, for reasons mentioned in 2 (a), the Group does not favour decentralisation in curriculum development and textbooks preparation to the extent of entrusting it to voluntary organisations because of the sensitivity of the matter.

Recommendation No. 2(c) — Comments

This is acceptable in principle. This has been strongly advocated in para 10.8 of the NPE, 1986. Following the Constitutional Amendment for decentralisation at Panchayat level, the Central Advisory Board of Education (CABE) has already constituted a Committee on Decentralised Management of Education to examine and recommended measures for effectively carrying out the desired involvement of the local committees. Therefore, this recommendation should be implemented in the light of the recommendations of the CABE Committee.

Recommendation No. 2(d) — Comments

This is acceptable. The State/UT Governments and autonomous bodies of the Central Government controlling their respective chain of schools (Kendriya Vidyalayas, Navodaya Vidyalayas, Central Tibetan Schools, Railway Schools and Sainik Schools and other schools run by the Defence establishments) should be urged to give this authority to the Principals/Headmasters of the schools to make repairs to school buildings, purchase, repair and replace pedagogical equipment and books and also to carry out innovative projects, subject to the control of the local education committees. The organisations controlling the schools and the State Governments should categorically specify that the Head of the school does not require approval of any higher educational authority and the School Management/Advisory Committee for using the available money for these purposes.

Recommendation No. 3 — Comments

The Group agrees with the purport of this recommendation—greater involvement of teachers—and the views of the Group on this recommendation is included in the comments on 2(a).

Recommendation No. 4 — Comments

The Group has been unable to appreciate the arguments put forth by the Yash Pal Committee in this recommendation. The choice of educational boards that the schools have is already very limited—there is no free choice-and it can be exercised only with the approval of the State Government. Therefore, if a school in any part of the country has the choice of affiliating with one Board or the other, it should be generally good for education. As for CBSE, it relies heavily on the NCERT for developing syllabi and preparing textbooks. The NCERT, in turn, operates within the national policy framework and on the basis of guidelines contained in the National Curriculum Framework. Rightly the NCERT keeps in view the existing standards in the country, the capability of students and standards in developed countries because the syllabus and textbook must take note of all these. If there is unnecessary material in some of the NCERT books, it should be eliminated as the Group has suggested in the preceding recommendations. However, there is not adequate material on record to substantiate that CBSE syllabi or NCERT books *per se* are overloaded. Also, the Yash Pal Committee has recommended that affiliation to CBSE should be restricted to Kendriya and Navodaya Vidyalayas with all other schools being affiliated to respective State Boards. If affiliation to the CBSE is good for Kendriya and Navodaya Vidyalayas it cannot be bad for other schools.

Recommendation No. 5(a) and 5(b) — Comments

The Group is in agreement with the recommendations. While the NCERT has prepared some norms for the staff, nature of curriculum and educational material for pre-primary stage, this sector of education in the country is largely unsupervised and unregulated. It is also a known fact that most of these schools are loading the students with the burden of formal teaching of various subjects. The Group advised that an appropriate regulatory mechanism should be urgently set up in the country to ensure that learning at this stage is by play way method and formal teaching of subjects is scrupulously prevented. Similarly, the Group agrees that recognition and affiliation of both private and government schools should be made more stringent so that schools lacking in minimum essential facilities are not allowed to function because it really means punishment to the students. Although there is a well set arrangement for recognition and affiliation of schools but due to extraneous pressures the standards sometimes are not observed. The Group would like to suggest that the possibility of having a legislation to specify norms of facilities in schools and providing for powers to prevent opening of schools which do not have facilities should be seriously considered.

Recommendation No. 6 and 7 — Comments

The Group has already agreed that there should be no formal teaching of subjects in the pre-school stage. The Group also feels that there should be no homework and project work at the primary stage (Classes I-V). However, it is an extreme point of observation that textbooks should be treated as school property. Besides the financial implications arising out of the burden on schools to purchase the textbooks and the concomitant responsibility on the schools to store the books when most of the schools of the country do not have either the financial resources or storage capacities, the children would be devoid of the opportunity to refer to the textbooks in their homes. For an overwhelming majority of school students of the country, the textbooks remain as the only source of reading material. The Group recommends that the class routine for the upper primary, secondary and higher secondary stages should be drawn up in such a way that every subject is not required to be taught everyday. This should be included in the norms for compliance by every school which the Group has suggested in para 5 (a) and 5 (b) above.

Recommendation No. 8 — Comments

The Group agrees with a higher teacher-pupil ratio with improved teaching and standards of education. It understands that in reality the existing teacher-pupil ratio is around 1:40 in most parts of the country. Attempts should be made to bring it to 1:30 over a period of time. Such change in ratio would have a very large financial implication because of the need to induct a large number of extra teachers and therefore, this can be done only over a period of time. Efforts should be made to ensure that the class size does not exceed 40.

Recommendation No. 9 — Comments

Greater use of electronic media for education is an essential part of modernising the educational system. A regular programme on TV addressed to students, teachers and parents would be very welcome. The Group took note of the fact that the Ministry of Human Resource Development, Department of Education, has already made a request for allocating one channel for education out of 15 or 16 channels which have recently become available with the commissioning of INSAT 2-A. The Group strongly suggests that an educational channel should be operationalised at the earliest and this channel should include a programme of the nature suggested by the Yash Pal Committee.

Recommendation No. 10(a) — Comments

There is a lot of merit in the argument advanced by the Yash Pal Committee for having a programme of B.Ed., aimed at elementary or secondary education. In metropolitan cities, a large number of teachers are actually getting recruited for pre-school and elementary schools with B.Ed., qualifications. Recruitment in KVS and NVS is also, in practice, based on B.Ed., qualifications. Therefore, this reality needs to be taken cognizance of and the present practice of focussing on secondary education in B.Ed., needs to be given up by enabling B.Ed., to be pursued with either specialisation in secondary or in elementary or in pre-school education. In any case the existing arrangements, including the District Institutes of Education and Training (DIETs) for preparing primary school teachers need to be continued and strengthened.

The recommendation of the Yash Pal Committee for derecognising B.Ed., degree by correspondence course is more problematic, while the National Council for Teacher Education (NCTE) has earlier made recommendations on these lines and the UGC has been interacting with the concerned universities during the last ten years on that basis, such courses are continuing. A recent expert committee of the UGC has expressed that for women candidates and for people from rural areas. B.Ed., correspondence course opens up valuable career opportunities. Also, in a large number of countries, B.Ed., through correspondence course is one of the prominent courses in distance mode. These arguments cannot be totally ignored. The Group understands that the matter is at an advanced stage of consideration in the UGC. Also the NCTE as a statutory body is expected to become operational in the near future. The Group recommends that this matter should be referred to the UGC and the NCTE for appropriate decision.

Recommendation No. 10(b) — Comments

The emphasis given by the Yash Pal Committee to continuing education of teachers is totally unexceptionable. Thus, DIETs are being set up in the country primarily to meet this need. Distance education system also is coming up in the country which can be used to meet the needs of in-service education. However, the progress in this regard has been slow. The Group fully endorses the need to set up arrangements for regular and periodic in-service training of teachers and recommends that the DIETs should be operationalised as early as possible and the distance mode of education should be used extensively to strengthen in-service training of teachers.

Recommendation No. 11 — Comments

The Group feels that the Yash Pal Committee's reference to the concept-based questioning perhaps advocates greater importance to questions of higher ability. The Group agrees with this but it should be remembered that assessment should test various kinds of abilities and not just of one kind. The Group also feels that the Boards of School Education should emphasise

Continuous and Comprehensive Evaluation (CCE) that incorporates both scholastic and non-scholastic aspects of education, spread over the total span of instructional time as stipulated in para 8.24 (iii) of the NPE, 1986.

Recommendation No. 12(a) — Comments

The Minimum Levels of Learning (MLLs) for language (mother tongue), mathematics and environmental studies for Classes I-V have already been prepared at the national level in 1990 and the NCERT, the Boards of School Education and the SCERTs have developed their resources to introduce the MLLs at the primary stage. Therefore, setting up another Project Team for the same purpose would amount to avoidable duplication. The Group feels that though in para 5.4.5 (vii) and para 21.3.1 (a), the POA, 1992 has called for laying down MLLs at the upper primary stage and in para 21.3.1 (b), the POA, 1992 has urged the Boards to lay down expected levels of attainment at Classes IX-XII, the reasonableness of laying down MLLs at the upper primary stage and above deserves a careful reconsideration since knowledge base is supposed to grow at a fast pace after the primary stage. Moreover, with emphasis shifting to subject-matter learning at the upper primary stage and above, the idea of laying down uniform MLLs after primary stage does not seem to be a viable proposition. However, at the time of curriculum renewal and preparation of textbooks, the curriculum/textbook designers should systematically check that those can be covered within the instructional time available to teachers. The NCERT at the national level and the State Boards/SCERTs/SIEs at the state level may consider the desirability of reviewing the school curricula/textbooks to ensure that non-essential matter and repetitive treatment of concepts in subjects in different classes is minimised as far as possible without sacrificing the requirements of cognitive development.

Recommendation No. 12(b) — Comments

The Group endorses the recommendation that mathematics and syllabi for other subjects should be reviewed to assess whether they are overloaded. But it would not like to state at this stage that they indeed are overloaded. The MLLs adopted by the MHRD are now being tried out and the question of review should be considered only on the basis of the feedback. As has been referred to in the preceding recommendations, syllabi have to be designed keeping in view the existing standards, and capacity of students and standards in developed countries. However, the Group endorses the statement of the Yash Pal Committee that the syllabus should emphasise understanding and intelligent application rather than memorising without understanding.

Recommendation No. 12(c) — Comments

These recommendations are acceptable. The NCERT and the Boards including CBSE and Council for the Indian School Certificate Examination (CISCE) should review their respective language textbooks from these angles.

Recommendation No. 12(d) — Comments

The Group has already given its views that all the existing textbooks should be screened in a time-bound manner for eliminating trivial matter and repetition. The Group endorses the recommendation that there should be greater scope for experimentation at the primary stage. This should be systematically promoted through a large programme of in-service education of teachers.

Recommendation No. 12(e) — Comments

The Group is of the view that while experiments and activities at all levels are important, the selection of topics in science curriculum at higher stages cannot be determined by the criterion that they are linked to experiment, etc. Every effort should, however, be made to see that experiments and activities, as much as possible, depending on the nature of the topic, are made a part of science teaching even at higher levels.

Recommendation No. 12(f) — Comments

As regards the Committee's suggestion that history syllabus for Classes VI-VIII should focus on freedom struggle and post-independence developments, the Group holds the view that a large majority of children drop out at the end of Class VIII, which is also the last year of compulsory education and therefore, it would not be educationally sound to allow such a big section of our children to remain oblivious of the entire heritage of India before the freedom struggle. The Committee seems to have linked spiral approach (which is based on a well-established principle of curriculum construction) with repetition which 'leads to boredom and load and trivialisation of ideas'. The Group feels that in geography greater importance should be given to study of contemporary problems. The context or implications of the Committee's recommendation for replacing 'Civics' by 'Contemporary Studies' are not clear.

5.2 Additional Suggestions of the Group

The Yash Pal Committee has made many thought-provoking recommendations which the Group has tried to recommend for implementation in a more specific manner. If these are implemented efficiently, the standards of school education will undoubtedly improve and as the Yash Pal Committee has envisaged alienation of students from education and the burden of 'non-understanding' on them would effectively diminish. However, in addition to the recommendations made by the Yash

Pal Committee, there are a few more issues which immediately present themselves for consideration while considering any exercises for reducing the load of curriculum. The Group would like to suggest these also for implementation.

1. *Age of Entry*: It is a known fact that in India children join school at a rather early age than their counterparts do in most of the developed countries. At the age of 4 and 5, a difference of one year in age makes a lot of difference in the mental capability of a child. A more mature child can easily cope with the learning requirements. The effect of early admissions of children in schools, particularly at the pre-primary stage, is that she/he is unable to cope with the demands that the syllabus makes and consequently she/he starts in a situation of personal inadequacy. This contributed significantly to the load of non-learning. It is, therefore, desirable that the minimum age of admission to pre-primary classes and in primary classes should be reconsidered for being raised by one year.

2. *Teaching Days*: Kothari Commission recommended 210 teaching days but the actual number of school days are 125-150. Since the syllabi are framed on the basis that 210 days will be available, this only means that either a part of syllabus is not covered by the teacher or that she/he covers the syllabus in a hurried manner which creates difficulty for students for being able to cope with a lot of content in a limited time. Effective action to increase the number of teaching days to 210 in a year would undoubtedly very substantially reduce the daily learning load and would also improve standards.

3. *Classroom Facilities*: In large number of schools in the country not only the facilities in the classroom but the classroom themselves are grossly deficient. This inevitably affects the quality of teaching and therefore, of learning. The Yash Pal Committee has recommended and we have endorsed that recommendation earlier in this Report that norms for school facilities should be effectively and strictly enforced for recognition/affiliation. However, since government is the major funding agency for most schools, there should be a positive movement for improving availability of classrooms and improving availability of educational aids in schools. For primary schools, the Government of India is implementing a large programme of Operation Blackboard and in the Eighth Plan it is being extended to cover upper primary classes also. At secondary level, the Government of India is implementing a scheme for assisting schools for improving science equipment. However, a much large effort needs to be made. It would be imperative that the effort of the government is supplemented by individuals and philanthropic bodies because the requirement is large. It would be appropriate that the governments and the school systems consider how best they can encourage such individuals and philanthropic bodies to help schools to develop.

4. *Strengthening of the Professional Support System*: An area which needs to be looked into is the qualitative improvement of professional bodies like the SCERTs, Textbook Bureaus and Boards of School Education who are primarily responsible for curriculum, textbooks and examinations. It is these bodies which will ultimately have to reckon with the problem of load. Under the centrally sponsored scheme of teacher education, there is a component of strengthening of SCERTs which should be taken up on a priority basis.

5. *Impact of Examinations, Admission to Higher Education Institutions, including Professional Courses*: This was one of the terms of reference of the Committee which has not been dealt with in the Report. The CABE may consider to refer this matter to a committee drawn from school and higher education. Another term of reference of the Committee related to "the measures such as formal recognition and weightage to sports and games and co-curricular and extra-curricular activities...". A CABE Committee is looking into this matter and its report is expected to be presented to the CABE shortly.

SIXTH ALL INDIA EDUCATIONAL SURVEY, 1995*

Objectives

(i) To create a database on different variables of Sixth AIES that can be shared by different agencies.

(ii) To develop Computerised Management Information System (CMIS) and update it on annual basis at various levels of administration.

(iii) To assess the present position of educational facilities at various school stages and the distance at which available, enrolment in general, and of Scheduled Castes (SC) and Scheduled Tribes (ST) and girls in particular, with special reference to UEE.

(iv) To assess the availability of physical facilities, like school building, playground, furniture, etc.

(v) To assess the availability of basic amenities, like medical check-up, drinking water, urinals, etc.

(vi) To identify incentive schemes and the number of beneficiaries.

(vii) To assess the position of educational inputs, like blackboard and chalk, library, textbook, bank, etc.

(viii) To know about the academic and professional qualifications of working teachers with special reference to teaching of science and

* *Sixth All India Educational Survey: Provisional Statistics*, National Council of Educational Research and Training, New Delhi, 1995.

mathematics and to determine attrition rate in the teaching profession.

(ix) To assess availability of other educational facilities like non-formal education, education for disabled children and pre-primary education.

National Summary

A. Educational Facilities within Rural Habitation
B. Schools
C. Enrolment
D. Teachers
E. Percentage of Female Teachers
F. Percentage of Girls Enrolment
G. Gross Enrolment Ratio.

SYNERGY SUB-GROUP CN PRIMARY EDUCATION AND LITERACY, 1995

Synergy Sub-Group was set up in May 1995 with a view to making an assessment of the existing status and making recommendations for achieving the objectives of primary education as envisaged in the revised NPE.

Recommendations

Minimum Levels of Learning (MLL)

While considerable progress is recorded in the last few years, much remains to be done in terms of improving real access, ensuring retention and achievement of MLLs. The focus in the coming years will be to accelerate and strengthen the processes which have already been set in motion and have demonstrated their success. New strategies will have to be evolved for the unresolved issues particularly those related to the quality improvement programmes and the education of the needy children in difficult circumstances.

That the private schools are intrinsically and uniformly better is a myth that deserves to be laid to rest. Some are among the best in the country, others are mediocre and sub-standard. The distance between the best and the average, be the Government or private schools, is too big for one's comfort. The State should or would continue to play a predominant role but the Government's role would be a departure from the past tradition of regulation and control. Government should be more open and receptive to the participation of other actors in civil society like NGOs and industry in the opening of schools, management of existing schools and teacher training institutions and in experimenting with a variety of alternatives in the teaching-learning process. We would recommend a review of the existing regulations in the country.

Educational discourse in the country has too often been exclusively devoted to pedagogic issues; while these are vital, the focus of discussions should shift to the logic of how to ensure the management of change.

Community Awareness and Mobilisation

We cannot have islands of school excellence in a sea of community indifference. Parents, teachers and students constitute what may be called the Golden Triangle, the civic foundations of education reform. Students should learn, teachers should teach and parents take on the responsibilities of sending children to school and facilitating the teaching-learning process in the school. While we do not favour a legalistic approach to compulsory primary education we would strongly urge societal and peer pressure being exerted by the community so that all children go to school.

The three R's. while perhaps outdated elsewhere, are still accepted by a vast majority as accepted learning goals.

We only add that while three R's are for a teacher, the fourth R is for parents. It is to emphasise their responsibility. Though family life is hectic and harassing, diminishing guidance from parents to children, yet it has to be emphasised that solution to students' unsatisfactory motivation and performance lies at home. Structuring of extra help at school would not suffice. A co-ordination between home and school is required. We need a forum and process for this. Caring and knowledgeable adults/parents are indispensable.

The shared vision of educational responsibility must emphasise not only goals for learning but also the responsibility that parents must accept for developing children's future. Community must start talking of "our children", instead of talking about "those children" and "my children."

There is a need to adopt a more flexible approach for involvement of community leaders and should not be limited to merely PR bodies. The model could vary from one state to another. The VECs must have representation of parents of children attending primary schools alongwith other representatives.

The enthusiasm and awareness generated by the total literacy campaigns need to be sustained through systematic environmental building efforts and effective management of the demand which is largely emerging from the hitherto uncovered segments of the society. The role of NGOs in this context needs to be further encouraged.

An analysis of the reasons for the large number of children being out-of-school needs to be made and its correlation with the economic development studied in the village specific situation. The evidence should be used for micro-planning.

Women empowerment programmes should be accorded high priority and implemented through an integrated rather than compartmentalized approach. Lessons learnt from successful programmes like *Mahila Samakhya* should be disseminated widely.

Comprehensive and need based programmes for the development of community leadership should be undertaken by the resource institutions like DIETs/SCERTs/SRCs. etc.

Role of Industry

The industry should be willing to share the social responsibility for educating their workers and children in the school going age-group. The industry should arrange classes for illiterate workers and open and fund primary schools in the large residential colonies/complexes used for residential purposes for their workers. Other possibilities to share this responsibility should be explored.

The industrial houses should be encouraged to financially support the strengthening of primary schools, DIETs and other resource institutions particularly those located in educationally backward areas.

The financial contributions made by the industrial houses and individuals to the cause of primary education should be eligible for tax relief.

Education of the Girl Child and Special Groups

The education of the girl child must be given high priority and concerted efforts must be made to ensure that the enrolment, retention and achievement of girls in primary education are improved. Incentive schemes like free textbooks, free uniforms, mid-day meals should be pursued and implemented more vigorously.

Necessary support in terms of basic facilities and security arrangements needs to be provided to encourage women teachers to work in rural and backward areas.

Extensive use of the media should be made to educate the community, create necessary awareness and provide appropriate role models to encourage the girls to join the mainstream of education.

As progress towards Education for All is attained, it will be necessary to reach marginal groups of population through local specific approach. Specific disadvantaged groups like pavement dwellers and communities in violence prone areas, should be given special attention through identification of their educational needs. Research should be initiated and action plans drawn accordingly.

ICDS scheme should be expanded to include creches for younger children to prevent drop-out of older children, particularly girls.

Curriculum Development

To develop a child into a creative and contributing member of society, the school should link the quest for knowledge through instruction with a quest for improving life around the child through well thought out activities. How tedious and time consuming tasks done in dull surroundings could be easily done in much more delightful surroundings should be the dictum of the new approach. This would equip her/him with an inner confidence to be creative and useful in later life. Skills are liberating and can only be acquired by learning through work. Similarly, the effort to familiarise students with their past should not be at the expense of dwelling on elements of modern scientific life located in time and place familiar to the child.

The learning process should also instill in the child an inquisitive mind, a joy and zest for discovery, a love and respect for nature. The school calendar should adequately provide for extra-curricular and after school activities including games and sports.

To encourage fuller participation and utilisation of primary education facilities at the field level, the school programme should be adapted to a more flexible mode which can attract children and is convenient in terms of timings, curriculum, school climate, etc.

The school climate must be made joyful and interesting for children through an attractive school environment, activity based child centred pedagogy and a nurturing rather than intimidating school ethos for which the basic resources and appropriate staff preparation are critical inputs.

The curriculum for Grades I and II should be reviewed to ensure that it matches with the developmental status of the children and is able to provide a proper foundation for later learning.

The relationship between higher education and primary education should not become so close as to let the primary school lose its identity and its purpose. In the name of good relationship and partnership there is a temptation to lose the critical place of primary education and reduce the latter to a preparatory stage of higher stages of education.

While the national statement of MLLs provides the necessary framework, the content of the curriculum should be adapted to suit district/state specific context. Children should be emancipated from the back breaking load of books; the curricular and textual overload should be realistically assessed.

We will have to drive out fear of education from the children, instead put confidence in them to achieve a drive towards meeting further learning challenges. The present system of examination, wherever it exists, derails the process. As a tool of assessment it measures neither the breadth of understanding nor the sharpness of skills of small kids and should therefore go. Assessment is not an end in itself but a means of enhancing student achievement. "Assessment is an advocacy process". Teachers should find less fearsome, more reliable and loving ways of diagnosing impediments to learning. We must not threaten (burden) the child with assessments that frustrate rather than facilitate learning.

The system of continuous and comprehensive evaluation must be implemented in schools to ensure reasonable learning outcomes in the primary grades with greater accountability.

The issue of mother tongue being different from the medium of instruction for a large percentage of children has serious implications for learning and achievement. Bridge materials should be developed to facilitate transition to the standard language for the initial grades.

Classroom is not an oasis but part of the world, closely intertwined and intimately interdependent on surrounding socio-economic conditions that do not offer a means of escape from the spiral of despair. Our students inhibit a world that extends beyond classroom. They will perform better when we will perform better as architects of a just and compassionate social order. We will have to rediscover some aspects of erstwhile schools which prided in imparting moral (religious) teaching. Education has a role in developing well adjusted and creative adults with right moral values.

Teacher Preparedness and Motivation

We must empower teachers to evolve ways of working appropriately, with State continuing to provide "Scaffolds" of support. Standardised teaching tasks and greater routinisation of teaching work with less reliance on innovative methods of communication reduce teaching to the status of semi-skilled' labour. Changing educational demands would require more flexible teaching forms and problem solving responses more contextual to the needs of the students and realities of local situation/surroundings, more freedom than what current educational bureaucracies allow.

For years to come we have no option but to live with schools of sub-optimal size; a teacher in a typical rural primary school would have to simultaneously teach more than one class. The issue of multi-grade teaching has not been adequately addressed. The achievement of satisfactory levels of learning in disadvantaged schools depends on ability to master the challenge of multi-grade teaching.

Recruitment of women teachers for primary schools is necessary to facilitate the girls enrolment and retention. Teachers are overwhelmingly male. Major efforts to recruit and train women teachers ought to be initiated. Teaching will be substantially transformed by infusion of women teachers. A leaf can be taken from the new Tamil Nadu policy of appointing only women as primary school teachers.

There is a continuing under-investment in teacher training. We will never have better schools until we have better teachers. Teachers training, accountability and reward system is critical for improving the quality of education. This should be accompanied by confidence building and motivation enhancement.

Schools require support and pressure. Both are needed in ample proportion. Without close supervision, education could become peripheral. There must be rigorous appraisal of school and teachers' performance. Failing schools and incompetent teachers should be weeded out. Indeed there should be zero tolerance of half baked and ineffective teaching. Simultaneously there should be a battery of measures to encourage more effective schooling. Local authorities should also have the authority of supervision and providing local support. Dual control by local authority and school inspectorate should not be an exercise in teacher bashing. In fact community must give them esteem and respect.

Teachers' guilds, forums and associations have a role since they exercise a mix of support and pressure which should be listened to. While teachers and parents are targeted, "Teachers' trade unions" are sometimes shunned.

Machinery for the redressal of teachers' grievances should be created in a manner that quick decisions in matters of pensions, allowances and service conditions are taken.

Local teachers should be involved in the development of school curriculum and teachers training materials so that the content of the educational programme emanates from the living conditions of the target group and make it relevant and need based. This will also enhance motivation of teachers.

Special problems like large class sizes, multi-grade teaching, inadequate facilities, etc., being faced by teachers in the school situation should be examined and solutions provided to facilitate the classroom teaching and learning.

Teachers competency in use of materials and equipment supplied under various schemes like Operation Blackboard, should be fully developed through in-service training programmes.

Primary school teachers have little chances of promotion and vertical mobility. New avenues for their professional advancement for horizontal and vertical mobility should be explored through distance education. Professionally qualified and competent primary school teachers could be recruited/inducted as DIET faculty.

Training institutions should be adequately strengthened and they should be able to adopt a group of schools and develop them into model institutions in their area of operation. The NGOs which have established themselves should be involved as resource institutions.

Planning and Management of Primary Education

Block should become the unit of educational planning. All programmes like teacher training, curriculum development and evaluation should be attempted at the block instead of at the district level.

The SCERTs and DIETs should provide necessary support for block level planning.

The DIETs and SCERTs should be strengthened as resource institutions so that these become outward looking and should work in close co-operation with NGOs and the community.

A long term development plan based on micro-planning should be evolved for each block/district. The plans should be such that these take into account the social, economic and other considerations while suggesting strategies to achieve the national goals.

The quality of educational statistics, particularly on enrolment needs is to be improved and if necessary should be revalidated by independent surveys.

The States should ensure that devolution of powers to VECs takes place as recommended by the CABE committee.

Particular emphasis should be given to those efforts which develop methodologies of micro-level planning and aim at capacity building at the district and lower levels for undertaking micro-planning experiments.

The inter-linkages between ECE, NFE and primary school programmes need to be viewed and strengthened in a holistic perspective in terms of mid-day meals, timings, location, infrastructural facilities, etc.

While there is no optimum size of a school, we should advance towards the ideal of having at least one separate section for each class with a headmaster who can provide the much needed administrative and academic leadership. Small schools tend to be children-friendly and particularly in urban areas, large schools may need to be reorganised as a cluster of children-friendly and viable schools.

Since most of the primary schools have now two teachers, the staff provision in primary schools must, therefore, include a head teacher for whom necessary training in institution building could be organised by the resource institutions.

The officers of the education department require a comprehensive training in educational planning, monitoring, evaluation, supervision and developing linkages with the community.

Minimum specification for primary education in terms of staffing, resources, infrastructure must be worked out and provision for primary education made in conformity with these.

Resources for Education

The Prime Minister has made a commitment to raise the resource allocation to 6 per cent of GNP during the Ninth Five Year Plan. A greater share of GNP is welcome but usually additional funds lead to proliferation of bureaucracy and expansion of administrative and supervisory cadres. It should be ensured that the additional resources flow for improvement of the teaching-learning process; it should also be ensured that disparities among states of per capita education expenditure are reduced.

While there is a need to have increased allocations for education as a whole, the intra-sectorial allocations could be re-examined and pre-primary and primary education should be accorded highest priority.

The early childhood years are crucial as foundation for human development and as feeder programmes for primary education. We must develop a national children policy. A connection has to be built between provision of minimal base of support for health care, nutrition and support for development of cognitive skills through primary education. It is time that we invest in the future of our children. We have the examples of a few states where such investments have paid rich dividends.

A trust fund be set-up at the block level to extend support to the extra-curricular activities of the school-going children.

COMMITTEE OF EDUCATION MINISTERS ON MAKING ELEMENTARY EDUCATION A FUNDAMENTAL RIGHT, 1997

A Committee of Education Ministers of 13 States and headed by Minister of State for Human Resource Development Muhi Ram Saika was constituted to examine and consider the legal, academic, administrative and financial implications of the proposal to amend the constitution to make the right to free and compulsory elementary education a fundamental right. The Committee submitted report to the Government on January 24, 1997.

Summary of Recommendations

State Governments should consider levying an education cess so as to raise revenues and augment their resources for education and improving facilities in schools.

This recommendation comes in the light of the Committee's estimate that an additional Rs. 40,000 crores will be required to implement the proposal to amend the Constitution as to make free and compulsory elementary education a fundamental right.

The Committee also suggests that an explicit provision should be made in the Constitution to make it a fundamental duty of every citizen who is a parent to provide opportunities for education of all children upto 14 years.

Since the education is a State subject, the report said there is no need to enact a Central legislation making elementary education compulsory. Instead states should either amend their existing legislation or else the Centre should issue guidelines providing a broad framework for enactment of fresh legislation on compulsory elementary education.

As regards the additional funding, the report suggests the Finance Ministry and the Planning Commission evolve an appropriate formula with the State Governments to share the additional resources needed to implement the proposal. It also said that the Centre and the State Governments allocate 50 per cent of budgetary allocations for education to elementary education and ensure that the funds so allocated are not reappropriated or diverted to any other sector.

While suggesting that each state formulate its own approach on education in keeping with the local situation, the report says to ensure uniformity, free elementary education may include exemption from tuition fee, provision of free textbooks for all primary school children and girls upto upper primary level and provision of essential stationery to all children in primary classes.

According to the Committee, the legislation to be enacted by the States provide for "permissive compulsion to enable state governments and local governments to enforce the law selectively in a phased manner." (*The Times of India*, 27-1-1997).

EDUCATION COMMISSION, 1964-66 (KOTHARI COMMISSION), GOVERNMENT OF INDIA, 1966

COMPOSITION OF THE COMMISSION

Chairman

Prof. D.S. Kothari, Chairman, University Grants Commission, New Delhi.

Members

1. Shri A.R. Dawood, formerly Officiating Director, Directorate of Extension Programmes for Secondary Education, New Delhi.
2. Mr. H.L. Elvin, Director, Institute of Education, University of London, London.
3. Shri R.A. Gopalaswami, Director, Institute of Applied Manpower Research, New Delhi.
4. Prof. Sadatoshi Ihara, School of Science and Engineering, Waseda University, Tokyo.
5. Dr. V.S. Jha, formerly Director of the Commonwealth Education Liaison Unit, London.
6. Shri P.N. Kirpal, Educational Adviser and Secretary to the Government of India, Ministry of Education, New Delhi.

7. Prof. M.V. Mathur, Professor of Economics and Public Administration, University of Rajasthan, Jaipur (later Vice-Chancellor, Rajasthan University).
8. Dr. B.P. Pal, Director, Indian Agricultural Research Institute, New Delhi (later on Director-General, and Vice President, Indian Council of Agricultural Research and Additional Secretary to the Government of India, Ministry of Food and Agriculture).
9. Kumari S. Panandikar, Head of the Department of Education, Karnataka University, Dharwar.
10. Prof. Roger Revelle, Director, Centre for Population Studies, Harvard School of Public Health, Harvard University, Cambridge, USA.
11. Dr. K.G.S. Saiyidain, former Educational Adviser to the Government of India, Director, Asian Institute of Educational Planning and Administration, New Delhi).
12. Dr. T. Sen, Vice Chancellor, Jadavpur University, Calcutta.
13. Prof. S.A. Shumovsky, Director, Methodological Division, Ministry of Higher and Special Secondary Education, RSFSR, and Professor of Physics, Moscow University, Moscow.
14. M. Jean Thomas, Inspector-General of Education, France and formerly Assistant Director-General of UNESCO, Paris.

Member Secretary

Shri J.P. Naik, Head of the Department of Educational Planning, Administration and Finance, Gokhale Institute of Politics and Economics, Poona.

Associate Secretary

Mr. J.F. McDougall, Assistant Director, Department of School and Higher Education, UNESO, Paris.

TERMS OF REFERENCE

The Commission will advise Government on the national pattern of education and on the general principles and policies for the development of education at all stages and in all its aspects. It need not, however, examine the problems of medical or legal education, but such aspects at these problems as are necessary for its comprehensive enquiry may be looked into.

PRIMARY EDUCATION: FULFILMENT OF THE CONSTITUTIONAL DIRECTIVE

7.08 *Targets*: We shall now proceed to discuss the another highly significant programme of educational reconstruction, namely the fulfilment of the Directive Principle contained in Article 45 of the Constitution that the State should strive to provide free and compulsory education for all children up to the age of 14 years. This was to have been achieved by 1960. But in view of the immense difficulties involved such as lack of adequate resources, tremendous increase in population, resistance to the education of girls, large numbers of children of the backward classes, general poverty of the people and the illiteracy and apathy of parents, it was not possible to make adequate progress in primary education, and the constitutional Directive has remained unfulfilled. There has, therefore, been an insistent demand that Government should fix an early deadline for its fulfilment and prepare a concrete programme of action for the purpose. We are in sympathy with this demand and we believe that the provision of free and universal education for every child is an educational objective of the highest priority not only on grounds of social justice and democracy but also for raising the competence of the average worker and for increasing national productivity. In view, however, of the magnitude of the problem the uneven development of primary education in the different parts of the country and the large financial resources needed for the programme, we th7ink that the best strategy for fulfilling the Constitutional Directive would be as follows:

1. Each State, and even each district should prepare a perspective plan for the development of primary education taking into account the stage of development already reached and the local conditions and problems. The objective of the plan should be to fulfil the Constitutional Directive as early as possible;
2. Each State and district should be assisted to go ahead at the best pace it can, and the progress in no area should be allowed to be held up merely for want of essential facilities or financial allocations; and
3. While the Constitutional Directive will be fulfilled in some places such as urban areas or advanced States as early as in 1975-76, all the areas in the country should be able to provide five years of good and effective education to all the children by 1975-76 and seven years of such education by 1985-86.

7.09 The targets proposed above may appear to be rather modest. But a closer examination will show that they are really formidable, and that the nation will have to strive its utmost to realise them.

7.10 But we would like to emphasise not the increase in enrolment, but two other more significant and difficult aspects of these proposals. The first is the reduction of wastage and stagnation. At present out of every 100 children who enter Class I, only about half complete Class IV and only 34 complete Class VII. The extent of stagnation is extremely large, particularly in Class I. We shall have to rectify this position and ensure that every child who enters Class I will progress regularly from year to year and reach Class V, and that not less than 80 per cent reach Class VII. Secondly, we must emphasise quality. It is generally agreed that the standard of education given in the primary schools is unsatisfactory and that it imparts little beyond literacy and some elementary knowledge in a few academic subjects. What is expected is that primary education should lay the foundation for a child to grow into a responsible and useful citizen of the country. The magnitude of the targets proposed above would be realised in its proper perspective if due weight is given to both these considerations.

7.11 A further point needs clarification. Our proposal for making a seven-year course of primary education compulsory does not conflict with the Constitutional Directive of providing education to all children till they reach the age of 14 years. For various reasons, a large number of children reach the age of 14 even before they come to the end of Class VII. There is also no problem about those children who will complete Class VII earlier but proceed to secondary education. This leaves only those children (estimated to be about 10 per cent of the age group) who are not yet 14 at the end of Class VII and who wish to enter working life as early as possible. We consider that the needs of these children will b better served not by lengthening the primary course by one year, but by the provision of short vocational courses of their choice. Such provision has been included in our estimates.

7.12 *The Programmes*: We have now to consider certain practical measures for the implementation of this programme of providing good general education of seven years' duration to every child. A careful study of the development of compulsory primary education in the advanced countries of the world shows that this programme is divided into three stages requiring:

- the provision of a school within easy distance from the home of every child;
- the enrolment of every child of the prescribed age into Class I of a school through propaganda, persuasion and even penal action, if necessary; and
- the retention of every enrolled child in school till he reaches the prescribed age or completes the prescribed course.

These are the three stages of universal provision, universal enrolment, and universal retention. They are not mutually exclusive and generally overlap and run into one another. Moreover, they presume the simultaneous implementation of a programme of qualitative improvement of education, because universal enrolment or retention depends very largely on the attracting and holding power of the schools. The progress of universal education in India can also be expected to follow this broad general pattern.

7.15 *Universal Enrolment of Pupils*: A programme of increasing enrolment should be organised side by side with attempts to provide primary schools in the remotest parts of the country. Obviously, there are two main points at which fresh enrolments are made at this stage—Class I and Class V. The problems that arise at each of these points are very different and have to be examined separately.

7.16 *Enrolment in Class I*: The problem of enrolment in Class I (which may be called the initial cohort of the educational system) is of great significance. In all progressive countries, this initial cohort is homogeneous and consists mostly of children of the prescribed age for admission. In India, on the other hand, the initial cohort in Class I has always been extremely heterogeneous and its heterogeneity is being reduced only slowly.

In a good system the children of the age 7, the prescribed age for admission, who are enrolled in school, should form the bulk of the total enrolment in Class I and should be about 95 to 97 per cent of the total population of children in the age group.

7.17 A large number of parents, especially in rural areas, cannot even give the ages of their children correctly, and in many cases the teachers are required to guess them. Moreover, when enrolment drives are organised, the general trend is to enrol children of all drives are organised, the general trend is to enrol children of all ages into Class I. This heterogeneous character of the enrolment creates difficult pedagogic probiems in the class besides increasing stagnation and wastage. We, therefore, recommend as follows:

1. A system of pre-registration should be developed for all fresh admissions. The school teachers should take an annual census of all the children whose age is less than the prescribed admission age by one year and who would be seeking admission to the schools in the following year. Except in some big cities where the migratory population may be large, such census taking and pre-registration will be very useful and will not present any insuperable administrative problems. During the pre-registration year, an attempt should be made to provide children's play centres.
2. Fresh enrolments to Class I should, as far as possible, be restricted to children within the single year prescribed for admission. In the beginning, older children who have not yet been to school will have to be admitted to the class; but if intensive efforts are made every year to enrol all the children of the prescribed admission age, the number of over-age children seeking entry into Class I will diminish year by year and will disappear almost completely in a period of about 5-10 years.

7.18 *Enrolment in Class V*: At present, the rate of transfer of pupils from Class IV, which is the end of the lower primary stage, to Class V is about 85 per cent. This transfer rate should be raised to 90 per cent by the end of the Fourth Plan and to 100 per cent by the end of the Fifth Plan.

7.19 *Universal Retention of Pupils*: Having enrolled every child in a school it is essential to see that he progresses regularly from year to year (i.e., there is no stagnation) and that he does not leave the school till he completes the prescribed age or class (i.e., there is no wastage). As is well known, the extent of wastage and stagnation in our system is very large. The evil was first highlighted about forty years ago by the Hartog Committee; and although the issue has been discussed almost continuously since, very little effective action has been taken to reduce it. Precise studies of the problem spread over a time series are not available.

In a good system of school education, the distribution of pupils over the different classes should be fairly uniform, but it is not so in our country.

7.20 *Stagnation*: In order to have some idea of the extent of stagnation at the primary stage, from class to class, the Commission collected data regarding enrolments in Classes I-VIII in 29 districts out of 312. For each class, information was gathered on two points: total enrolment and number of repeaters, classified according to the total pre-period they had spent in the class. From this information, the average period spent by the pupils in the class was calculated and its excess over one year—which is the normal period—was described as the 'stagnation index' for the class in that year.

7.23 The foregoing discussion shows that the most important programme to be implemented at the primary stage during the next ten years is to improve the quality of education and to reduce stagnation and wastage to the minimum. In fact, the task of universal education begins when children are enrolled in Class I. It is completed only when they are successfully retained till they complete Class VII. In this overall programme, the reduction of wastage and stagnation in Class I is obviously the most important element.

7.25 The remedy for some of these defects is self-evident; and most of them could be eliminated through the development of qualitative programmes which are being discussed separately. In this connection, however, we would like to emphasise the following programmes:

1. The examination at the end of Class I should be abolished and the first two classes (and wherever possible, even the first three or four) should be regarded as one teaching unit, within which each child can progress according to his own pace.
2. The introduction, as recommended earlier, of a year of pre-school education of an economical type.
3. The adoption of play-way techniques in Class I for introducing the child to school life in a pleasant way. For this purpose, methods of instruction in Class I should be patterned in the light of the techniques utilised at the pre-primary stage and the teachers in-charge of this class should be trained or oriented accordingly.

7.26 *Stagnation and Wastage in other Classes*: The extent of stagnation and wastage in other classes of the primary stage is comparatively small. Its causes may be broadly divided into three categories—economic, educational and social education. A closer analysis of these causes will also show the remedies.

7.32 *Part-time Education at the Higher Primary Stage*: 1. The second programme to offset wastage is to provide part time education to children who have completed the lower primary stage, and who desire to study further but cannot for economic reasons afford to do so on a full-time basis. The number of such children is large even at present; and it will increase as education reaches the still proper sections of society. The only way in which these children can receive education is by getting it on a part-time basis; and it should be a deliberate object of policy to provide such education on as large a scale as possible.

2. The content of this part-time education would have to be elastic and should be determined according to the needs and aptitudes of the children receiving it. For some children who desire to complete this stage of education and prepare themselves for the next, it should be patterned on the lines of the full-time courses. But for those who do not wish to do so and these would be the large majority—the content of education should have a large vocational element and should be so developed as to serve their immediate needs.

7.35 It has to be remembered that wastage and stagnation, like headache and fever, are not diseases in themselves, they are really symptoms of other diseases in the educational systems, the chief among which are the lack of proper articulation between education and life and the poor capacity of the schools to attract and hold students. To these may be added a third ailment-poverty, which falls outside the system. Urgent action is needed to remove the first two educational weaknesses; the effect of the third can be offset only as the economy of the country improves. The goal of universal retention of pupils, therefore, is the most difficult of all and can be reached only over a period of time. This makes it all the more necessary to organise immediately an intensive programme for the reduction of wastage and to pursue it till the goal is reached. A beginning should be made with Class I, where the target should be to reduce the wastage by half before the end of the Fourth Plan and to reduce it to the minimum by the end of the Fifth Plan. In the lower primary stage, all wastage should be reduced to the absolute minimum by the end of the first decade (1966-76) and at the higher primary stage, by the end of the second decade (1976-87).

5

Elementary Education: 1997 Onwards

NINTH FIVE YEAR PLAN, 1997-2001

Primary/Elementary Education

The Indian Constitution attaches high priority to education. Article 45 declares, "The State shall endeavour to provide, within a period of 10 years from the commencement of the Constitution, for free and compulsory education of all children until they complete the age of 14 years". The Constitution also guarantees educational rights for minorities and calls for the educational development of weaker sections of society. Through the 42nd Amendment of the Constitution, the subject of education has been brought to the Concurrent List in the Constitution for fulfilment of nationally accepted goals. The 73rd and 74th Constitutional Amendments further empowered the Panchayati Raj Institutions (PRIs) to render their contribution to the development of education at the grass-root level. The Judgement of the Supreme Court in Unnikrishnan J.P. vs. Andhra Pradesh (1993) states: "The citizens of the country have a fundamental right to education. The said right flows from Article 21 of the Constitution. This right is, however, not an absolute right. Its contents and parameters have to be determined in the light of Articles 45 and 41. In other words, every child/citizen of this country has a right to free education until he completes the age of 14 years. Thereafter his right to education is subject to the limits of economic capacity and development of the State".

Critical Issues at Primary/Elementary Stage

(i) *Backlog of Un-enrolled Children*

In order to achieve Universalisation of Primary Education (UPE), it had been estimated for the year 1993-94 that approximately 142 million children in the age-group 6-11 years would have to be provided primary schooling, out of which 69 million would be girls.

(ii) *Drop-outs*

The problem is further accentuated by high drop-out rates. Among those who are enrolled, it is estimated that large number of children in Classes I-V drop-out in between, before completing their class V. The latest available data on drop-out rates for Classes I-V for the year 1996-97 reveal that the drop-out rate for the country as a whole was 38.95 per cent. It was 39.37 per cent among boys and 38.35 per cent among girls. Further, there were wide inter-State disparities. The major problem of drop-outs as well as access to schooling is in the educationally backward States of Andhra Pradesh, Arunachal Pradesh, Assam, Bihar, J&K, Madhya Pradesh, Orissa, Rajasthan, U.P. and West Bengal.

(iii) *Unserved Habitations with Primary/Upper Primary Schools/Sections*

According to the Sixth All India Educational Survey (Excluding J&K where the survey was not done), out of 10.60 lakh rural habitations, 8.84 lakh (83.4%) were served within the national norm of one-km distance. Thus about 16.6 per cent of habitations were not served by primary schools within a distance of 1 km. The survey results also revealed that about 41,198 primary schools were being run in thatched huts, tents and open space. In case of upper primary schools, about 23.85% habitations were not served within the official distance norm of 3 km. 5,638 upper primary schools were being run in thatched huts, tents and open space.

(iv) *Lack of other Physical Infrastructure*

Apart from availability of access to primary school within a walking distance of habitations, there are other problems which have to be addressed on an urgent basis. These relate to lack of physical infrastructure like toilet facilities for girls, drinking water facilities in schools, teaching-learning equipment etc.

(v) *Availability of Teachers*

With regard to availability of teachers, the Survey further pointed out that about 4000 schools were without teachers and 1.15 lakh primary schools were being run by single teachers. However, the position has improved since then, as additional teachers have been provided under Operation Blackboard (OB).

(vi) *Low Levels of Achievement*

It is not only physical infrastructure that is inadequate to achieve UPE, there is equally important dimension of quality which needs attention. For instance, evaluation studies on children's achievement show low levels in language and mathematics.

(vii) *Equity and Regional Disparities*

Then, there are regional disparities. Some States (like Kerala, Maharashtra, Gujarat, Tamil Nadu) have done well in providing physical access to schooling facilities as well as in improving quality of education. Some others (like Uttar Pradesh, Bihar, Madhya Pradesh, Orissa and Rajasthan) have still a long way to go. There are equity concerns like low enrolment o girls, educational requirements of special need groups, like SCs/STs, OBCs, minorities, disabled children, working children, children from disadvantaged locations like deserts, hilly, coastal and deep forest areas, children from migratory families, etc.

Action Plan

(i) *Broad Approach*

The action plan needed to address the critical issues and achieve the desired objectives will be based upon ground realities. It will resort to a multi-pronged strategy which is both imaginative and innovative and also carries with it the attributes of flexibility, decentralisation, improvement of quality, cost-effectiveness, result-oriented and time-bound commitment. This can be achieved through micro-planning with a focus on 'area approach' and 'target population'. It will also mean community involvement, monitoring, supervision and academic support at all levels. The existing schemes will be examined with respect to these parameters and those found suitable will be promoted.

(ii) *Phasing*

Under the Constitutional obligation, Government is to provide free and compulsory education up to Class VIII. Greater emphasis will naturally have to be laid on achieving UPE at the lower primary stage, in the first phase.

(iii) *Mobilisation of Community Support for School Improvement Programme*

The 73rd and 74th Constitutional amendments have further empowered the Panchayati Raj Institutions (PRIs) to make a positive contribution for development of education at the grass-root level. Village Education Committees (VECs) will be actively involved in School Improvement Programme (SIP).

Training will be imparted to VEC members wherever such committees have been constituted. Arrangements for this will be made through District Institutes of Education and Training (DIETs), Block and Cluster Resource Centres and through the Distance Mode. Area of concern of VECs in the development of SIP will be:

(a) door-to-door survey of children of school-going age and help in enrolment, particularly of girls;
(b) planning and execution of civil works of school buildings;
(c) mobilisation of physical and financial resources;
(d) provision of free accommodation to teachers, wherever possible;
(e) improvement in children's attendance;
(f) institutional capacity building for sustainability of schools;
(g) community ownership of the School Improvement Programme;
(h) to help in implementation of the Scheme of National Nutritional Support to Primary School Children;
(i) other functions delegated by the State Governments.

(iv) *Strengthening Teacher Education Programme*

(a) Curriculum Development: The draft curriculum framework developed by the National Council for Teacher Education (NCTE) will be finalised and made the basis for curriculum change in institutions for teacher education. This will help to improve the quality of Teacher Education Programme.
(b) Initiative for North-Eastern States: The North-Eastern States, which have a larger percentage of untrained teachers in elementary schools will launch programmes to cover this gap by adopting the following measures:
   — A Diploma Programme for Primary Education developed by Indira Gandhi National Open University (IGNOU) will be launched in collaboration with the State Governments.
   — NCTE will establish a Regional Committee for North-Eastern States to provide the necessary fillip to the teacher training institutions.
   — Induction programmes of four to six weeks' duration of DIETs will enrich the capabilities of freshly appointed teachers.
(c) Upgradation of Infrastructure: The process of strengthening Teacher Education Programme will be given a further impetus by upgrading the physical and academic infrastructure of:
   — State Councils of Educational Research & Training (SCERTs)
   — Colleges of Teacher Education (CTEs)
   — Institutes of Advanced Studies in Education (IASEs), District Institutes of Education and Training (DIETs), Block Resource Centres/Cluster Resource Centres (on a pilot basis).
   — National Council for Teacher Education (NCTE)
   — Departments of Education in Universities
(d) Reaching out to Primary School Teachers in Remote Areas: To supplement the efforts to improve school effectiveness, an institutional mechanism will be put in place to provide on-the-spot

counselling and guidance to teachers located in remote areas. This will be in the form of Mobile Teams of Resource Persons (MTRPs). Logistic arrangements will be location-specific, based upon felt needs and environment.

(v) *Alternative Education*

In order to provide access to drop-outs, working children, girls, migratory population and other similar categories, alternative education will be provided through institutional arrangements.

Non-formal Education centres for such categories of children as are unable to avail themselves of the formal system of schooling in hilly, desert and forest areas, or due to the migratory nature of the population will be expanded. The expansion will be based upon a 'cluster approach', so as to make the scheme cost-effective.

It has been found by experience that NFE centres achieve more meaningful results when these are run by NGOs. Accordingly, the number of centres run by NGOs will be enhanced significantly.

Where NGO participation is not forthcoming, State-run NFE centres will be established.

The scope of the National and State Open Schools will be expanded by bringing elementary education within their fold for the purpose of providing a lateral entry to NFE children as well as to neo-literates for certification.

Private initiative will be tapped in industrial project sites to run "project schools". Incentives like allotment of land on a subsidised basis and other concessions under the Companies Act or the Income Tax Act will be provided.

(vi) *Education of Working Children*

According to the 1991 census, there were 11.28 million working children in the country. More than 90 per cent of them were engaged in agricultural labour, rearing of livestock, forestry and fisheries.

Ministry of Labour has a direct responsibility at the Centre for the following:

(a) to lay down policies and programmes for elimination of child labour, particularly in hazardous trades,
(b) to monitor the progress of implementation of programmes, projects and schemes for elimination of child labour; and
(c) to coordinate implementation of child labour-related projects of the various sister Ministries of the Government of India in order to ensure convergence of services for the benefit of the families which have child labour. Ministry of HRD will extend all support to the Ministry of Labour in the setting up of 'education-related projects'. These will be 'area-specific' and focussed particularly in States of

Andhra Pradesh, Madhya Pradesh, Maharashtra and Uttar Pradesh, where there is a large concentration of child labour.

TENTH FIVE YEAR PLAN, 2002-2007

Source: Planning Commission, New Delhi

Elementary Education (Chapter 2.2)

2.2.1 Education is a critical input in human resource development and is essential for the country's economic growth. Though the major indicators of socio-economic development viz., the growth rate of the economy, birth rate, death rate, infant mortality rate (IMR) and literacy rate, are all interconnected, the literacy rate has been the major determinant of the rise or fall in the other indicators. There is enough evidence even in India to show that a high literacy rate, especially in the case of women, correlates with low birth rate, low IMR and increase in the rate of life expectancy. The recognition of this fact has created awareness on the need to focus upon literacy and elementary education programmes, not simply as a matter of social justice but more to foster economic growth, social well-being and social stability.

At the state level, the programme is implemented through existing structures of educational administration. Janshala has started a large number of alternative schools in small and remote habitations in the programme areas, besides evolving strategies and setting up schools with community participation in the urban slums of Jaipur, Hyderabad, Ajmer, Bharatpur, Puri and Lucknow. Other major areas of achievement are in teacher training, multi-grade teaching, intervention for education of the disabled, setting up of block and cluster resources centres and strengthening capacities at the state, district and block level.

Sarva Shiksha Abhiyan

2.2.31 The Sarva Shiksha Abhiyan was launched towards the end of the Ninth Plan to achieve the goal of UEE through a time-bound integrated approach, in partnership with states. The medium-term goals for the scheme are given in Box. The programme, which aims to provide elementary education to all children in the 6-14 age group by 2010, is an effort to improve the performance of the school system and provide community-owned quality elementary education in the mission mode. It also envisages bridging of gender and social disparities at the elementary level. The Sarva Shiksha Abhiyan has a special focus on the educational needs of girls, SCs and STs and other children in difficult circumstances.

Box II.2: Objectives of Sarva Shiksha Abhiyan

- all children to be in schools, Education Guarantee Scheme centres, alternate schools, back-to-school camps by 2003;
- all children to complete five years of primary schooling by 2007;
- all children to complete eight years of schooling by 2010;
- focus on elementary education of satisfactory quality with emphasis on education for life;
- bridge all gender and social disparities at the primary stage by 2007 and at the upper primary level by 2010; and
- universal retention by 2010.

2.2.32 Under the programme, habitation plans, prepared after micro-planning, household surveys, school mapping and diagnostic studies, form the basis for the District Elementary Education Plans (DEEP). Funds released to states would be channelised to registered societies at the State level. The Sarva Shiksha Abhiyan is expected to accord the highest priority to community monitoring, transparency in programme planning and implementation of capacity building at all levels as also to the adoption of a mission approach by the mainstream Education Department functionaries. A National Mission for Sarva Shiksha Abhiyan was constituted in November 2000 with the Prime Minister as the Chairman and the Minister for Human Resource Development as Vice-Chairman.

2.2.33 The scheme is expected to absorb most of the existing programmes, including externally-aided programmes, within its overall framework with the district as the unit of programme implementation. To make the approach totally holistic and convergent, efforts would be made to dovetail programme implementation at the district level with all other departments. This would include programmes for children in the 0-6 age group under the Department of Women and Child Development, sports-related interventions of the Ministry of Sports and Youth Affairs, establishment of public libraries under the Department of Culture and nutrition and health programmes of the Ministry of Health.

Goals, Targets and Strategies for the Tenth Plan

Goals and Targets

2.2.35 In the elementary education sector, the Sarva Shiksha Abhiyan is in place with clear focus and medium-term goals as specified in Box II.3. The Tenth Plan targets in respect to elementary education are:

Universal Access

- All children in the 6-14 age group should have access to primary schools, upper primary schools or their alternatives within a walking distance of one km. and three km. respectively.

- All children in the 3-6 age group must have universal access to early childhood care and education centres.
- Need-based expansion of upper primary education facilities, particularly for the disadvantaged sections. There should be one upper primary school for every two primary schools.
- All schools should have buildings, toilets, drinking water, electricity, playgrounds, blackboards and other basic facilities. There must be provision of one classroom for every teacher at the elementary stage.

Universal Enrolment

- Enrolment of all children in schools or alternative arrangements by 2003.
- All children to complete five years of primary schooling by 2007.

Universal Retention

- Universal retention in the primary stage by 2007.
- Drop-out rate to be reduced to less than 10 per cent for grades VI-VIII by 2007.

Universal Achievement

- Improvement in the quality of education in all respects (content and process) to ensure reasonable learning outcomes at the elementary level, especially in literacy, numerics and in life skills.

Box II.3: Innovative Programmes in Education in Different States

- Bridge all gender and social gaps in enrolment, retention and learning achievement in the primary stage by 2007 and reduce the gap to 5 per cent in the upper primary stage by 2007.
- Special interventions and strategies to include girls, SC/ST children, working children, children with special needs, urban deprived children, children from minority groups, children below the poverty line, migratory children and children in the hardest-to-reach groups.

Strategies for Universalisation of Elementary Education

2.2.36 The strategies and interventions during the Tenth Plan will mainly be guided by three major considerations: (a) magnitude of the task; (b) present challenges; and (c) the existing administrative and policy framework and the one that will be in place during the Plan period.

2.2.37 *Magnitude of the Task*: The Working Group on Elementary and Adult Education for the Tenth Five Year Plan has estimated that in order to achieve the goal of UEE by 2010, enrolment at the primary level needs to grow at an average annual growth rate of 1.12 per cent for boys and 4.16 per cent for girls during the Plan period. At the upper primary level, the growth rate must be 4.62 per cent for boys and 8.03 per cent for girls. The average growth rate for boys and girls taken together should be 2.51 per cent at the primary and 6.08 per cent at the upper primary levels. The year-wise estimated additional enrolment during the Plan period are given in Table II.5.

2.2.38 *Present Challenges*: Achieving the goal of UEE poses three main challenges: (i) access to basic education for the unreached segments and social groups; (ii) qualitative improvement in content and processes so as to raise learning achievements; and (iii) tackling high drop-out and low retention rates in primary and upper primary schools.

2.2.39 *Administrative and Policy Framework*: The administrative and policy framework needs to be guided by the following concerns:

- The national resolve to provide free and compulsory education of satisfactory quality to all children up to the age of 14 years, as stipulated in the National Policy on Education;
- The 93rd Constitutional amendment making the right to elementary education a fundamental right and enforcing it through necessary statutory measures; and
- The spirit of the 73rd and 74th Constitutional amendments setting the stage for greater decentralisation of power and a significantly enhanced role for local bodies, community organisations as well as voluntary agencies in the efforts towards UEE.

Salient Features of the Tenth Plan Strategy for Achieving UEE.

2.2.40 Given this backdrop, the Tenth Plan strategy for achieving UEE must have the following salient features:

2.2.41 *Holistic and Convergent Approach*: As the existing policies and programmes are either for specific target groups/regions, there is need for an all-comprehensive programme covering the entire country. The Sarva Shiksha Abhiyan is such a programme and will be the main vehicle for achieving the goals of UEE.

Table II.5: Year-wise Estimated Additional Enrolment

(*in million*)

Year	*Additional Enrolment*					
	Primary (Grade I-V)			*Upper Primary (Grades VI-VIII)*		
	Boys	*Girls*	*Total*	*Boys*	*Girls*	*Total*
2002-03	0.57	2.01	2.68	1.14	1.44	2.58
2003-04	0.67	2.10	2.77	1.19	1.54	2.73
2004-05	0.67	2.18	2.85	1.25	1.67	2.92
2005-06	0.69	2.27	2.96	1.31	1.81	3.12
2006-07	0.69	2.37	3.06	1.37	1.95	3.32
Total	3.39	10.93	14.32	6.26	8.41	14.67

2.2.42 *Community Participation in UEE Programmes*: The involvement of the community will be made more systematic by involving the Panchayati Raj Institutions (PRIs) and urban local bodies. Further down the hierarchy, VECs, Mother-Teacher Associations (MTA) and Parent-Teacher Associations (PTA) would have a formal role in the management of schools in the village.

2.2.43 *Target-Groups Oriented Strategy*: The Tenth Plan will lay emphasis on identifying the problem areas and formulating a separate strategy for each area, under the overall umbrella of the Sarva Shiksha Abhiyan. There will be special focus on children who have never enrolled or those who have dropped out without completing eight years of elementary schooling. Specific strategies would be devised for the difficult-to-reach groups in order to ascertain the reasons for their staying away from school system and to take steps to provide them quality elementary education.

Schemes for Achieving UEE

2.2.44 The following schemes would be the instruments by which these strategies would be translated into action during the Tenth Plan. Scheme-wise break-up of the Tenth Plan outlay is given in the Appendix.

2.2.45 Sarva Shiksha Abhiyan. Out of the approximately 207.76 million children in the 6-14 age group in 2000, the number of children not attending the schools is 40 million. Those outside the school system are mostly girls, SCs/STs children, working children, urban deprived children, disabled children and children in difficult circumstances. Providing access and motivation to these difficult to reach groups, without compromising on the quality of education, would be the challenge that the Sarva Shiksha Abhiyan would tackle in the Tenth Plan.

2.2.46 The Sarva Shiksha Abhiyan will totally subsume all existing programmes, barring the Mid-day Meals scheme, and the scheme of Restructuring and Reorganisation of Teachers' Education. All legal agreements regarding externally-aided projects such as Mahila Samakhya, DPEP, Lok Jumbish, Shiksha Karmi, etc, will continue to apply unless specific modifications have been made in consultation with the funding agencies. In order to achieve a holistic and convergent approach, efforts would be made to dovetail programme implementation at the district level with all other programmes. This would include programmes for children in the 0-6 age group under the Department of Women and Child Development, sports-related interventions of the Department of Sports and Youth Affairs, establishment of public libraries under the Department of Culture, nutrition and school health programmes of the Ministry of Health and the employment generation/poverty alleviation programmes of Ministry of Rural Development. This dovetailing exercise would be undertaken while formulating the DEEPs.

2.2.47 *Gender-Specific Programmes*: The Tenth Plan would also rely on some women-centric programmes such as the existing Mahila Samakhya, and two new schemes, the Kasturba Gandhi Swantantra Vidyalaya (KGSV) and the National Programme for the Education of Girls at the Elementary Level (NPEGEL). Mahila Samakhya will be expanded both in terms of geographical reach and activities like the Mahila Shikshan Kendras. However, it will retain its objectives, identity and non-negotiable principles.

2.2.48 The KGSV and the NPEGEL are proposed to be taken up during the Tenth Plan, with the following features:

- focus on educationally backward areas in girls' education;
- focus on girls from the disadvantaged sections like those belonging to SC/ST, minorities, etc;
- tackling gender-specific issues that prevent girls and women from having access to education;
- providing women and adolescent girls with the necessary support structure, and an informal learning environment to create opportunities for education;
- creating circumstances for larger participation of women and girls in formal and non-formal education programmes; and
- helping girls to overcome socio-cultural and economic factors inhibiting their access to elementary education.

2.2.49 *Mid-day Meal Scheme*: A Supreme Court order in 2001 makes it obligatory for states to provide cooked meals instead of dry rations within the stipulated timeframe, under the Mid-day Meals scheme. Further, in order to achieve the goals set in the Sarva Shiksha Abhiyan programme, modifications would be made in the scheme in the light of feedback received from evaluation studies, the experience gained from the working of the scheme, and the opinions of experts. The modifications would include the following:

- Expanding the programme to cover the children of the EGS & AIE scheme.
- Ending the present practice of distributing food grains and providing hot cooked meals or ready-to-eat food based on sound nutritional principles.
- Allowing adequate flexibility in the management of the programme by the local bodies/community through VECs, School Management Committees (SMCs), PTAs etc. Also, fostering stronger community participation in the implementation of the programme and encouraging the participation of credible NGOs, wherever possible.
- Decentralising the management of the programme to enable reduction in leakages and mismanagement etc.
- Providing funds in advance to the implementing agencies through their state nodal officer for the transportation of food grains.

- Limiting teachers' involvement in the programme to supervision activities.
- Extensive use of the computerised MIS (CMIS) net for monitoring purposes. External agencies are to be involved in monitoring and supervision to ensure greater accountability. Elected representatives will also be involved in supervision.
- Linkage with poverty alleviation programmes in rural and urban areas, adequate support of the Union Ministry of Health and the state Health Departments for a school health programme and support from the Department of Women and Child Development for nutrition education.
- A memorandum of understanding be entered into with the key stakeholders (state governments, local bodies, etc.) on the key parameters of the programme.

Strategies for Quality Improvement

2.2.50 While the goals of universal literacy and enrolment are laudable in themselves, the achievements in these areas would remain hollow without ensuring quality education. A qualitative improvement in the content and processes of basic education, in order to make them more responsive to the learning needs of individuals and the development needs of different socio-economic sectors, continues to be a major challenge. The challenge for providing quality education at the elementary level involves improvements in the preparation, motivation and deployment of teachers, the quality of textbooks and of infrastructural facilities. It also involves making education relevant to society's needs and strengthening the management and institutional capacity of educational institutions especially at the state, district and local levels.

2.2.51 Improving the quality of textbooks is crucial as they are the main instructional aids in elementary schools, and are the only reading material for most students.

2.2.52 The quality of infrastructural facilities (particularly toilets for girls), equipment and support services, also has a significant impact on enrolment and retention. In this context, the main challenge is to provide a classroom for every teacher in the primary and upper primary schools and a separate room for the headmaster in upper primary schools along with playground facilities and clean toilets. Although one-third of the expenditure approved under DEEP is earmarked for the construction of buildings etc., there are still a substantial number of primary schools without these facilities. The main thrust in the Tenth Plan should be to ascertain that all the primary schools have pucca buildings with all supporting infrastructural facilities.

Systematic Learner Evaluation

2.2.59 A mechanism for regular learner assessment will be designed and put in place to evaluate the impact and efficacy of measures taken for improvement in school quality.

Strategy for Drop-outs

2.2.60 A large number of children drop-out of school because of reasons relating to the school environment. These include attitude of teachers, irrelevant curriculum, sub-standard and uninteresting teaching, teacher absenteeism, corporal punishment, poor school infrastructure, inability to cope with the pace of learning, lack of parental support in the case of first generation learners, maladjustment, etc. Girls form the majority of the drop-outs in all categories. The National Family Health Survey-II (NFHS-II), conducted in 1998-99, also observed that the main reasons for students dropping out include their not being interested in studies, the high private cost of education and the need for them to work, whether in their own farms, business/households or outside. These reasons held true for 75 per cent of drop-outs.

2.2.61 The main challenge for education authorities at the central, state and district levels is to (a) improve the supply, quality and retention power of education, particularly in rural primary schools and in the unreached segments; and (b) introduce innovative methods of providing education to identified disadvantaged and difficult groups to suit their timing and interests. The focus in the Tenth Plan would, therefore, be on pedagogic improvement and adoption of child-centered methods, which have been developed in programmes like DPEP; and building a positive environment that would include more attractive classroom designs, local contextual curriculum and more friendly evaluation techniques. Apart from a number of steps undertaken under the Sarva Shiksha Abhiyan to reduce the private cost of education, an incentive scheme linked to attendance has been suggested for girls, SCs/STs and poor children.

2.2.62 Where the children are dropping out because of the need to work, the emphasis would be on involving the community in motivating the parents to bring their children back to school so that they are in a position to complete eight years of elementary education. For those children who have already dropped out, suitable alternative education systems such as bridge courses, remedial teaching, back to school camps, etc., would be provided so that they can be mainstreamed into the formal system.

NATIONAL CURRICULUM FRAMEWORK FOR SCHOOL EDUCATION (2000), NCERT

1.4.8 Universalisation of Elementary Education

As per the Indian Constitution, the country is committed to providing free and compulsory education to all children up to the age of 14. This commitment has been reiterated in all the official documents during the past five decades. Efforts have been made to provide universal access to education including emphasis on universal enrolment and universal retention to arrest the drop-out of children from schools. The initiative of Sarva Shiksha Abhiyan is an important step in this direction. All this would require the allocation of a higher portion of GDP to the education sector. The developed countries have already reached the stage where they normally allocate 9-10% of their GDP as Government's spending for education.

Equality of the opportunity of access to education is necessary if more women are to become the agents of change. Therefore, education of women is an important key to improving health, nutrition and education in the family, and also empowering them to participate in decision-making. Investment, both in formal and non-formal education of young children in general, and of the girl child in particular is expected to yield exceptionally high social and developmental returns.

In order to achieve the mission of universal elementary education, alternative systems, besides the formal school structure, may be promoted, because the education system needs to adapt itself to the requirements of the young learner. Reaching the still unreached, therefore, emerges as a major concern. It will require designing and developing new modules and delivery systems that would suit the needs of specific groups so as to ensure relevant and high quality basic education for every learner. Initial education meant for all, will comprise essential life skills and the potential for meeting the basic learning needs of all. This itself becomes an important concern of Universalisation of Elementary Education (UEE). It will have implications for curriculum in terms of the identification of basic learning needs, making provision for the minimum essential facilities, and providing for competent and qualified teachers who can ensure proper transaction of the curriculum to help children grow in a multi-dimensional manner. While there would be some identified competencies of universal nature to be acquired by all children, there would always remain scope for some competencies identified separately for varying contexts to meet the local specific challenges of life.

Parental education and community involvement towards achieving the goals of UEE would be a matter of concern for curriculum makers, planners and administrators and for all those concerned with the quality of education at the elementary stage. Since the involvement of the Panchayati Raj Institutions in elementary education has been ensured through a constitutional amendment, it would be desirable to get it streamlined and properly operationalised.

Thus, proper planning and its effective implementation is the soul of achieving quality education for all - the most cherished goal of UEE. Children at the elementary stage need to be equipped with proper attitudes and values along with necessary skills to help them emerge as social human beings, capable of contributing for themselves and the society at large and learning throughout life. While concerted efforts for this would need to be made in all the academic areas, the issue of UEE will require a solid and unshakable politico-administration will to achieve this goal.

ORGANISATION OF CURRICULUM AT ELEMENTARY AND SECONDARY STAGES (CHAPTER 2)

Context

The main thrust areas of Indian school education, as mentioned in the National Curriculum for Elementary and Secondary Education: A Framework, 1988, demand a fresh look. Some of these merit reformulation in the light of the country's experience in the field of school education and the others have to be re-affirmed. Some new thrust areas may also need to be added in the light of the changes all around. School education in the present scenario has to have the main thrust on the following:

- Inculcation and sustenance of personal, social, national and spiritual values like cleanliness and punctuality, good conduct, tolerance and justice, a sense of national identity and respect for law and order and truthfulness.
- Elimination of poverty, ignorance, ill-health. casteism, dowry, untouchability, and violence, and ensuring equity, health, peace and prosperity.
- Thinking, experiences and innovations which are rooted in the Indian tradition and ethos and relating these with global thinking.
- Establishing uniformity of structure of school education, i.e., 10+2+3 throughout the country.
- Broad based general education to all learners up to the end of the secondary stage to help them become life long learners and acquire basic life skills and high standards of Intelligence Quotient (IQ), Emotional Quotient (EQ), and Spiritual Quotient (SQ).
- A common scheme of studies for the elementary and secondary stages with emphasis on the skill of 'learning how to learn' with flexibility of content and mode of learning to suit all learners including those with special needs.

- Inclusion of Fundamental Duties and the core curricular areas at all the stages of school education.
- Human Rights including the rights of the child, especially those of the girl child.
- Ensuring the minimum essential level of the acquisition of knowledge, understanding and skill at all, stages, commensurate with the learners' abilities and the societal context.
- Freedom, flexibility, relevance and transparency in the selection of content, transaction and procedures at different stages of school education.
- Nurturance and sustenance of multiple talents and creativity among all learners in various domains of knowledge.
- Shift of emphasis from information-based and teacher centred education to process centred and learner friendly education.
- Development of a responsive and supportive system of evaluation.

2.7.2 Elementary Education (8 Years)

Primary Stage (5 Years)

Primary stage of education has been visualised in two segments with inherent internal continuity. The first segment comprises Classes I and II, where children are just introduced to formal teaching and are at a stage of development which requires a smooth transition from informal and non-formal environment to a formal one. The second segment consists of Classes III-V wherein the children get prepared to understand the environment and learn in a systematic way. The scheme of studies for these two segments is given below:

A. Classes I and II

(a) One Language — the mother-tongue/the regional language
(b) Mathematics
(c) Art of Healthy and Productive Living

Experiences to be provided in areas (a) and (b) will constitute an integrated whole taking into its fold, the natural and the man-made environment. Teaching and learning of language and mathematics would be woven around the environment of the learners and integrate environmental concerns as well.

Experiences to be provided for art of healthy and productive living will further contribute toward all-round development of the personality of the child. These will be organised keeping child in central focus involving students in activities commensurate with their developmental stage. Activities related to health will get a prominent place so that children acquire necessary skills, attitudes and habits to keep themselves healthy and participate in games and sports suitable for their age. Children will be initiated into preliminary yogic exercises and will be exposed to various soothing experiences in the field of music, drama, drawing and painting and clay modelling. In organising these activities local factors may be given due importance. They will be encouraged to participate in creative activities such as free hand drawing and painting. Besides this, children will be involved in the activities related to work education so as to enable them to be free from Inhibitions and like to work. For value Inculcation stories and anecdotes would play an effective role. These will also generate and strengthen the element of curiosity, imagination and a sense of wonder. All the experiences will need to be presented in an integrated manner for which themes will be identified and teachers will make use of locally available resources and harness community support wherever necessary.

B. Classes III to V

(a) One language — the mother-tongue/the regional language
(b) Mathematics
(c) Environmental Studies
(d) Art of Healthy and Productive Living

Children will be provided with experiences to help their socio-emotional and cultural development with a realistic awareness and perception of the phenomena occurring in the environment. This may be accomplished by emphasising, observation, classification, comparison and drawing of inferences through activities conducted within and outside the classroom. The integrated approach would be most suitable to achieve the desired objectives.

The experiences gained earlier will be further strengthened by ensuring participation of all children in the activities related to music, dance, drama, drawing and painting, puppetry, health and physical education, games and sports, yoga and productive work. Integrated approach will be used. Autonomy and flexibility incorporating the locally developed curriculum and materials will be encouraged. Concerted efforts will be made to ensure proper value orientation among children.

Upper Primary Stage (3 Years)

(a) Three Languages — the mother-tongue/the regional language, modern Indian language and English
(b) Mathematics
(c) Science and Technology
(d) Social Sciences

(e) Work Education
(f) Art Education (fine arts: Visual and Performing)
(g) Health and Physical Education (including games and sports, yoga, NCC and scouting and guiding)

THE CONSTITUTION (EIGHTY-SIXTH AMENDMENT) ACT, 2002

[12th December, 2002]

'THE CONSTITUTION OF INDIA'

[Supplement to the Fourth Edition, Manager,
Government of India, Press, Faridabad (2004)]

An Act further to amend the Constitution of India

Be it enacted by Parliament in the Fifty-third year of the Republic of India as follows:

1. *Short title and commencement.*—(1) This Act may be called the Constitution (Eighty-sixth Amendment) Act, 2002.

(2) It shall come into force on such date as the Central Government may, by notification in the Official Gazette, appoint.

2. *Insertion of new article 21A.*—After article 21 of the Constitution, the following article shall be inserted, namely:—

"*21A. Right to Education.*—The State shall provide free and compulsory education to all children of the age of six to fourteen years in such manner as the State may, by law, determine".

3. *Substitution of new article for article 45.*—For article 45 of the Constitution, the following article shall be substituted, namely:—

"45. Provision for early childhood care and education to children below the age of six years.—The State shall endeavour to provide early childhood care and education for all children until they complete the age of six years".

4. *Amendment of article 51A.*—In article 51A of the Constitution, after clause (j), the following clause shall be added, namely:—

"(k) who is a parent or guardian to provide opportunities for education to his child or, as the case may be, ward between the age of six and fourteen years".

"NATIONAL CURRICULUM FRAMEWORK 2005"
NCERT (2005)

Chapter 3: Curricular Areas, School Stages and Assessment

group has been excluded from the purview of Article 21. In addition, ECCE is also seen to have critical linkages with enrolment of children in schools and learning outcomes. To provide ECCE of equitable quality to all children, it is not only necessary to vastly enhance the funds committed for this purpose, but also to address through different strategies the five basic

dimensions of quality, namely, developmentally appropriate curriculum, trained and adequately rewarded teachers, appropriate teacher-child ratio and group size, infrastructure supportive of children's needs, and an encouraging style of supervision. While there is need for decentralisation, flexibility and contextuality in these programmes, there is also an urgent need to evolve appropriate norms and guidelines and set in place a regulatory framework so that children's development is not compromised. Capacity building at all levels in relation to the plurality of roles that different functionaries play, as well as fair wages, must also be ensured.

3.10.2 Elementary School

The period of elementary school (from Class I to Class VIII) is now also recognised as the period of compulsory schooling vide the constitutional amendment making education a fundamental right. The beginning of this period marks the formal introduction of the child to reading, writing and arithmetic, culminating in the introduction of the formal disciplines such as the sciences and the social sciences towards the end of elementary school. This period of eight years is one of tremendous cognitive development, shaping reason, intellect and social skills, as well as the skills and attitudes necessary for entering the work place

As the effort to achieve UEE is stepped up, the elementary school classes now cater to many children of school-going age coming from diverse backgrounds. Plurality and flexibility without compromising on standards need to become the hallmark of education for this period. Education during this period must be of an integrated character, enabling children to acquire facility in language and expression and to grow in self-confidence as learners, both within and outside school.

The first concern of the school is on the development of the child's language competence: issues related to articulation and literacy, and the ability to use language to create, to think and to communicate with others. Special stress is needed to ensure that there are maximum opportunities for those who wish to study in their mother-tongue, including tribal languages and linguistic pockets, even if the number of students is small. The ability of the system to promote and nurture these options, along with working out mechanisms to ensure that future options remain open, should become a marker of its ability to provide for quality education. To achieve this, there must be a creative and concerted effort to maintain the multilingual genius of Indians and implement the three-language formula. While English may be taught during this period, it must not be at the expense of learning Indian languages.

The development of mathematical thinking, beginning with learning numeracy and moving towards the enjoyment of and facility with more abstract ideas, needs to be supported with concrete experiences and work with manipulations. It is in the early years, up to Class IV, that efforts at diagnosing learning difficulties and addressing remedial work in language and mathematics must be directed.

Such concrete experiences are also essential in the introduction to the integrated study of the environment through which children's intuitive knowledge of the world is integrated into school knowledge. Over the years, this study should move towards a more disciplinary approach, but with integrative themes, within which there are located opportunities to develop concepts and learn the vocabulary and methods of the discipline.

The study of arts and crafts is essential for developing not only the aesthetic sensibility but also for learning how to manipulate materials and developing attitudes and skills essential for work. The curriculum must expose children to practical life skills and work experiences of varied kinds. Physical development through sports activities is also a must. A variety of activities at this stage of schooling should be made available, including participating in cultural programmes, organising events, travelling to places outside the school, providing experiences to develop socially and emotionally into creative and confident individuals sensitive to others, and capable of taking initiative and responsibility. Teachers with a background in guidance and counselling can design and lead activities to meet the developmental needs of children, thus laying the foundation for the necessary attitudes and perceptions towards the self and the world of work. They can also provide the needed support and guidance to children belonging to various strata of society for their sustenance through the elementary school years. The approach to the whole curriculum should be process oriented rather than outcome oriented. All these areas of development should be made available to all children. Care must be taken to ensure that the curriculum does not reinforce stereotypes about preferences, choices and capabilities of different groups. In this context, the gradual inclusion of vocationally oriented skills as a part of exposure to work would be an important aspect of an inclusive curriculum.

CABE COMMITTEE ON "FREE AND COMPULSORY EDUCATION BILL AND OTHER ISSUES RELATED TO ELEMENTARY EDUCATION (2004-05)"

Composition of the Committee

Sl No.	*Name & Address*	
1.	Shri Kapil Sibal Minister of State for Science & Technology	Chairman
2.	Minister (In-charge of Elementary Education), Government of Madhya Pradesh	Member
3.	Minister (In-charge of Elementary Education), Government of Meghalaya	Member

4.	Minister (In-charge of Elementary Education), Government of Bihar	Member
5.	Minister (In-charge of Elementary Education), Government of Andhra Pradesh	Member
6.	Minister (In-charge of Elementary Education), Government of Orissa	Member
7.	Prof. Anil Sadgopal	Member
8.	Shri Vinod Raina	Member
9.	Ms. Shanta Sinha	Member
10.	Smt. Kumud Bansal, Secy. EE&L	Member
11.	Shri A.K. Sharma, Former Director, NCERT	Member
12-16	Representatives of the Ministries of Tribal Affairs, Social Justice and Empowerment, Finance, Law and Planning Commission	Members
17.	Prof. Krishna Kumar, Director, NCERT	Member
18.	Prof. Govinda, Director, NIEPA	Member-Secretary

The terms of reference of the Committee are:

(a) To suggest a draft of Legislation envisaged in Article 21A of the Constitution.

(b) To examine other issues related to elementary education for achieving the objectives of free and compulsory basic education.

'REPORT OF THE CENTRAL ADVISORY BOARD OF EDUCATION (CABE) COMMITTEE ON Free and Compulsory Education Bill and Other Issues Related to Elementary Education', 2005

2. Financial Estimates for Implementation of the Bill: Alternative Scenarios

Based on the proposed Right to Education Bill 2005, four alternative scenarios have been developed, and accordingly financial estimations, including teacher salary, the cost of additional classrooms, toilets, drinking water, upgradation of school infrastructure and equipment, mainstreaming of out-of-school children, pre-school education, inclusive education, teacher development, incentives and school support materials, maintenance of school infrastructure and equipment, establishment of resource organisations such as DIETs, BRCs and CRCs, monitoring and evaluation, management and other related components, have been made. It is assumed that the Bill will commence from 2006-07. Accordingly, all financial estimations have been done from the year 2006-07. According to the Bill, all out-of-school children need to be mainstreamed in three years from the commencement of the Art. Therefore, while making enrolment projections in alternative scenarios, the number of out-of-school children has been brought down to zero from the year 2009-10. In all alternative scenarios, the financial estimates have been done for six years from 2006-07 to 2011-12, to correspond to the final year of the 11th Five Year Plan period. Component-wise financial estimates have been done separately for primary and upper primary levels of education.

Four alternative scenarios of financial requirements (from 2006-07 to 2011-12) for implementation of the Act have been considered. These alternative scenarios are based on mainly two parameters i.e., Pupil-Teacher Ratio (PTR) and average teacher salary. In the financial estimation, mainly the norms of the Bill and the unit costs of various components as specified in the Sarva Shiksha Abhiyan (SSA) have been applied. In case of some of the components like one-time grant for providing basic materials in the pre-school classes, provision of kitchen and utensils in primary schools, salary of part-time art, health, and work education instructors, and pre-school instructor, the estimates have been made based on allocations made under different schemes of the MHRD. The estimated additional financial requirements (from 2006-07 to 2011-12) for implementation of the proposed bill in different alternative scenarios are given in Table 2.

The basic differences between the four alternative scenarios are given in Table 1. The total estimated additional financial requirements (from 2006-07 to 2011-12) for implementation of the proposed Bill in different alternative scenarios are given in Table 2. Chart 1 gives the size of the estimated total cost in various scenarios to implement the Bill.

Table 1: Alternative scenarios for estimation of financial implications for implementation of the proposed Bill 2005

Alternative Scenario	*Pupil-Teacher Ratio*	*Average Teacher Salary*
1(A).	PTR = 35:1 both at Primary and Upper Primary Levels	Average Teacher Salary = Rs.7965/- per month (Basic pay of Rs. (4500/- + 50% DP + 18% DA) with an annual increase of Rs.800/- (KVS pay scale of non-graduate trained teacher).
1(B).	PTR = 35:1 both at Primary and Upper Primary Levels	Average Teacher Salary = Rs.6000/- per month (state level average teacher salary) with an increase of Rs.600/-.
1(C).	PTR = 40:1 both at Primary and Upper Primary Levels	Average Teacher Salary = Rs.7965/- per month (Basic pay of Rs. (4500/- + 50% DP + 18% DA) with an annual increase of Rs.800/- (KVS pay scale of non-graduate trained teacher).
1(D).	PTR = 40:1 both at Primary and Upper Primary Levels	Average Teacher Salary = Rs.6000/- per month (state level average teacher salary) with an increase of Rs.600/-.

Table 2: The Total Estimated Financial Requirements (from 2006-07 to 2011-12) in the alternative scenarios for achieving the goal of UEE by 2010

Scenario	*PTR and Average Teacher Salary*	*Total Estimated Cost (In Crores)*
1(A).	(i) PTR = 35:1 (ii) Average Teacher Salary = Rs.7965/- per month (Annual increase of Rs.800/-)	436459
1(B).	(i) PTR = 35:1 (ii) Average Teacher Salary = Rs.6000/- per month (Annual increase of Rs.600/-)	393307
2(A).	(i) PTR = 40:1 (ii) Average Teacher Salary = Rs.7965/- per month (Annual increase of Rs.800/-)	346299
2(B).	(i) PTR = 40:1 (ii) Average Teacher Salary = Rs.6000/- per month (Annual increase of Rs.600/-)	321196

Chart 1: Additional Financial Requirement for Free and Compulsory Education Bill, 2005 from 2006-07 to 2011-12

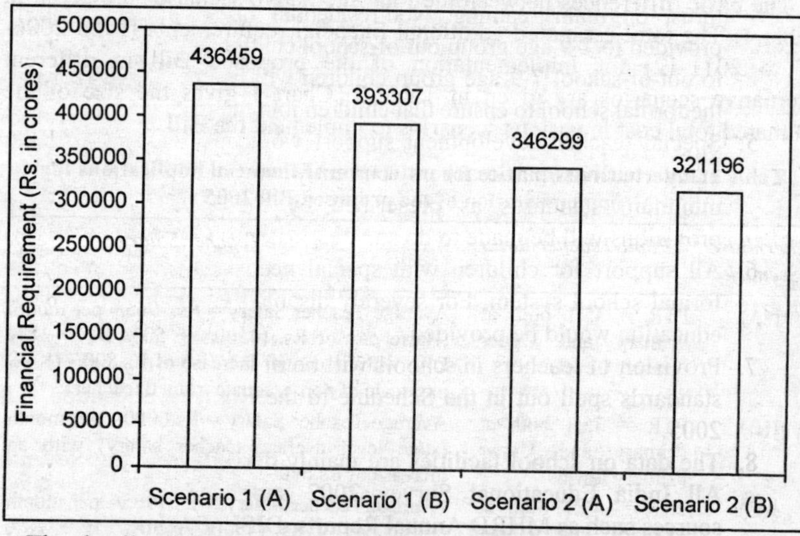

The details of the general assumptions and specific norms and unit costs of various components and technical notes on the methodology of estimation have been given in the following sections.

3. General Framework for Estimation of Financial Requirement to Implement the Bill

The estimation of additional financial requirements for implementing the Bill from 07 to 2011-12 are based on the following general assumptions and guidelines:

1. It is assumed that the child population in single ages from 6 to 3 years would grow during 2001 and 2011 at the same as it had grown during 1991 and 2001 censuses.
2. The additional schools required are estimated to ensure the provision of primary schools within one kilometer of every habitation and upper primary schools within three kilometers and at least one upper primary school for every two primary schools.
3. All children will attend regular schools of equivalent standards. All other forms of learning centres established over the last few years shall either come up to minimum standards prescribed in the Schedule 2005 or close down.
4. Residential bridge courses for the 10-14 age group out-of-school children will work in close cooperation of the formal school with a thrust on mainstreaming. Non-residential bridge courses will be provided to 7-9 age group out-of-school children. Additional support to out-of-school 7-9 age group children will be coordinated through the formal school to ensure that children join the formal school.
5. Special teacher development support would be required to bring many teachers/part-teachers currently teaching in schools to minimum standards as prescribed by the NCTE and special provisions will be made to do so.
6. All support for children with special needs shall be met by the formal school system. For severely disabled children, home-based education would be provided.
7. Provision of teachers in schools will be in line with the norms and standards spell out in the Schedule to the Right to Education Bill 2005.
8. The data on school facilities are mainly derived from the Seventh All India Educational Survey 2002 supplemented from other sources such as MHRD Annual Reports, DISE, PAB of SSA etc.
9. Submissions before the PAB of SSA and information from DISE would be used to work out the unmet need for CRCs, BRCs, DIETs/Pre-service Teacher Education in states.
10. Number of existing teachers (as on 30th September 2002) have been taken from the 7th All India Educational Survey, and updated with developments thereafter, as reported in the PAB of SSA and Annual Reports of the MHRD.

11. Norms and unit costs have been worked out as per the current practice in states and provisions of the Right to Education Bill, 2005 and as per the Sarva Shiksha Abhiyan.
12. The non-salary components have been increased by 5 per cent each year to account for the cost of inflation.

NATIONAL KNOWLEDGE COMMISSION, JUNE 8, 2005

National Knowledge Commission to the Prime Minister is constituted by Planning Commission, GoI, New Delhi on June 8, 2005 under the chairmanship of Shri Sam Pitroda.

Composition

Shri Sam Pitroda, Chairperson
Dr. Pushp Bhargav, Vice-Chairperson
Shri Nandan Nilekani, Member
Dr. Pratap Bhanu Mehta, Member-Convenor
Dr. Andre Beteille, Member
Dr. Jayoti Ghosh, Member
Shri Ashok Ganguly, Member
Dr. Deepak Nayyar, Member

One of the Terms of Reference is - Build excellence in the educational system to meet the knowledge challenges of the 21st century and increase India's competitive advantage in fields of knowledge. The method of operation is that the Commission will address its terms of reference through Working Groups to be constituted by the Ministry connected and for building excellence in educational system it is the Ministry of HRD.The Commission will wind itself up on October 2, 2008 with a report on tasks done.

SACHAR COMMITTEE REPORT, 2006

The Justice Rajinder Sachar Committee Report of 404 pages on the social, economic and educational status of Muslims in the country tabled in the Lok Sabha on 30 November, 2006 by Minority Affairs Minister A.R. Antulay has produced a compendium of information required by the Government for planning, formulating and implementing specific interventions, policies and programmes to address issues of backwardness of the community.

The right to education is a fundamental right; the Report establishes the extent of educational deprivation experienced by the Muslim community. Muslims are at a double disadvantage with low levels of education combined with low quality education. Their deprivation increases many-folds as the level of education rises. 25 per cent of Muslim children in the age group 6-14 have either never attended school or are dropped out.

Selected Excerpts

3.1 *Criticality of Education*

Access to education is critical for benefiting from emerging opportunities that are accompanied by economic growth. The report brings out clearly the educational deprivation experienced by the Muslim community. From lower levels of enrollment to a sharp decline in participation in higher levels of education, the situation of Indian Muslims is indeed very depressing as compared to most other SRCs; in fact their situation seems to have worsened in relative terms. And the problem is more acute for girls/women. Reasons for this are varied - ranging from poverty to perceived discrimination resulting in alienating school environment. While the overall situation remains bad, the enrolment rates of Muslims have picked up in recent years and the policies should help sustain the momentum that can get created through this change. Our analysis also shows that the major problems lie in school education; the likelihood of Muslim children completing school education is significantly lower than other SRCs, except SCs/STs, once factors like household expenditure, place of residence, gender etc. are controlled for. Once the "hurdle" of school education is crossed, the differences across most SRCs in the likelihood of completing graduate studies narrow down and are at times not very significant. Therefore, a sharper focus on school education is desirable.

Free and compulsory education up to the age of 14 is the responsibility of the State. And the fulfillment of this obligation is critical for the improvements in the educational conditions of Muslims, in fact, of all socio-economically deprived children. In addition, a sharper focus on a few areas listed below is desirable.

Adequate Reflection of Social Diversity in the Content of School Text Books

The school text book is one of the most enduring influences in the formative years of childhood. Along with the family, the school teaches the child not only the three Rs. but values and attitudes that shape the child's character and create a sense of values. Given the influence of the text book, the Committee feels that it can work as an important instrument of imparting social values. The text book should not only reflect reality but also help in creating appropriate values. Since the children tend to read their text books several times, their familiarity with the text is significant and acts to reinforce the values being suggested in the text. If the texts do not reflect diversity or are derogatory with respect to specific communities, they can alienate children of those communities from the wider society. Simple things in the text books can sow the seeds for religious intolerance, create caste bias and/or reduce sensitivity to gender differences, while the intent and purpose of texts should be to do just the opposite. The Committee recommends that a process of evaluating the content of the school text books needs to be initiated to purge them of explicit and implicit content that may impart inappropriate social values, especially religious intolerance.

Initiatives in School Education

Muslims have the largest percentage share of children in the age group of less than 10 years with 27 percent falling in this range as compared to the 23 per cent for the country as a whole. However, the current enrollment and continuation rates at elementary level (though picking up in recent years) are the lowest for the Muslims. These facts make primary education particularly important for the Community and the need to ensure that all children in the age group 0-14 have access to free and high quality education more urgent. In addition, the following initiatives are desirable:

Given the fact that a substantial proportion of households in urban settlements live in one- room accommodation it is absolutely necessary to create local community study centres for students so that they can spend a few hours to concentrate on their studies. This is an area in which the government, NGOs and the corporate sector can co-operate.

High quality Government schools should be set up in all areas of Muslim concentration.

Exclusive schools for girls should be set up, particularly for the 9-12 standards. This would facilitate higher participation of Muslim girls in school education. In co-education schools more women teachers need to be appointed. Availability of primary education in one's mother tongue is constitutionally provided for. There is an urgent need to undertake appropriate mapping of Urdu speaking population and provide primary education in Urdu in areas where Urdu speaking population is concentrated.

Once again utilization of JNNURM funds for this purposes should be explored

CONFERENCE OF STATE EDUCATION MINISTERS, APRIL 11, 2007

The Conference of State Education Ministers was organized at New Delhi on 10th and 11th April, 2007, by the Ministry of HRD. Shri Arjun Singh, Minister for HRD, presided over the Conference which was attended by Education Ministers of 19 of the 28 States. Senior officers of the Education Departments represented the other States and Union Territories. The two Ministers of State in the HRD Ministry, Shri M.A.A. Fatmi and Smt. D. Purandeswari, and Dr. Bhalchandra Mungekar, Member (Education), Planning Commission, also participated in the Conference. Constructive discussion took place in the sessions during the Conference on the major issues raised by the Central and various State Governments.

Select Excerpts

2. *Elementary Education*

- The conference endorsed the view that the issue of the Centre-State funding pattern in the SSA to be continued on a 90:10 ratio for the NE States and on a 75:25 ratio for other States be examined appropriately by the Government of India.
- A consensus emerged in the meeting to continue the implementation of the SSA programme with vigour and commitment, and with the fullest attention to equity issues; improvement of learning outcomes of students; implementing focused programmes for improving language and mathematics basic levels in early primary grades and tracking student as well as teacher attendance rates at elementary levels.
- State Ministers agreed on the need to consolidate the initiatives taken over the past 2-1/2 years on the Mid Day Meal programme and to streamline delivery systems to ensure better management and distribution of foodgrains and other commodities required for serving a hot cooked meal. States are required to put in place mechanisms that would ensure that schools are not deprived of timely financial assistance to meet the daily requirements of running the programme.
- State Ministers expressed apprehension that, in the expansion of the Mid Day Meal Programme to the upper primary stage in educationally backward blocks, the current parameters for identifying such blocks could exclude some of the poorer and backward blocks in the country. The Government of India will re-formulate the parameters such that the entire upper primary stage is covered by the end of the XI Plan.

Source: www.pib.nic.in

COMMITTEES AND COMMISSIONS ON ELEMENTARY EDUCATION

SHIPRA